BRITISH BANKING, 1960–85

BRITISH BANKING, 1960–85

John Grady

and

Martin Weale

St. Martin's Press New York

First published in the United States of America in 1986

Printed in Hong Kong

ISBN 0–312–10041–8

Library of Congress Cataloging-in-Publication Data
Grady, John
British banking, 1960–85.
Bibliography: p.
Includes index.
1. Banks and banking—Great Britain—History—20th century 2. Great Britain—Economic conditions—1948– I. Weale, Martin, 1955– . II. Title.
HG2988.G68 1986 332.1'0941 85–26238
ISBN 0–312–10041–8

Contents

List of Tables

NOTE The sources from which the data are drawn are indicated on each table. In some cases rounding errors mean totals differ slightly from the sum of component parts.

List of Figures

Preface

John Grady spent his career working firstly for the Post Office, where he established the National Giro, and then in the City, where he became a director of Samuel Montagu Ltd. After retiring he gained a history degree at the Cambridgeshire College of Arts and Technology. In 1979 he was admitted to Emmanuel College, Cambridge, to study for the degree of Doctor of Philosophy. Sadly he died after his thesis, 'The Growth of the British Non-clearing Banks: 1960–1974', was completed and he was awarded his degree posthumously. This book has evolved from that thesis – in particular, sections 2.4 to 2.6 of Chapter 2, sections 3.1 and 3.3 to 3.5 of Chapter 3, sections 4.3 and 4.8 of Chapter 4, sections 5.1, 5.2 and 5.3 of Chapter 5, sections 6.1 to 6.3, 6.7 and 6.8 of Chapter 6, sections 7.3 to 7.6 of Chapter 7 and section 8.1 of Chapter 8 follow it closely. However, I have endeavoured throughout to extend the statistical material where I thought this would help illustrate points made in the text.

As well as recognising debts to Edith Grady for making John's notes available, and to the Bank of England for very helpful discussion, I gratefully acknowledge the comments of Charles Goodhart, Linda Hesselman, Jane Humphries, James Meade, Cliff Pratten, Brian Reddaway, Jack Revell, Alan Scowcroft, David Vines and Chris Wright on earlier drafts. Thanks are also due to Bobbie Coe and Shirley Seal for typing the text. Extel Statistical Services kindly gave permission to publish the tables in section 7.5. This work was made possible by the financial support of the Economic and Social Research Council to the Cambridge Growth Project, of which I was a member while preparing this text.

Department of Applied Economics and Clare College, Cambridge MARTIN WEALE

NOTE Billion (bn) is now usually referred to as meaning 'thousand million'; this is the case in this book.

Abbreviations

ARIEL	Automated Real-time Investments Exchange
BACS	Banks Automated Clearing System
CBI	Confederation of British Industry
CD	Certificate of Deposit
CHAPS	Clearing House Automatic Payment System
FNFC	First National Finance Corporation
GDP	Gross Domestic Product
GEC	General Electric Co.
IMF	International Monetary Fund
LDC	Less Developed Countries
LIBOR	London Interbank offered rate
MEPC	Metropolitan Estates & Property Corporation
MLR	Minimum Lending Rate
NBER	National Bureau of Economic Research
OPEC	Organization of Petroleum Exporting Countries
PWLB	Public Works Loan Board
REIT	Real Estate Investment Trusts

Introduction

The period since 1960 has witnessed major changes in the structure and functioning of the United Kingdom banking sector which have created entirely new problems for the authorities in their attempts to control and supervise financial institutions. The reasonably stable banking system of the 1950s was transformed into an unstable system by the early 1970s leading to a crisis of confidence in the British banking sector. Only prompt action by the Bank of England and the clearing banks prevented the crisis from gravely damaging the functioning of the financial system. The repercussions of the crisis are still visible today as the Bank of England continues to grapple with the problems of the prudential supervision of financial institutions which it is prepared to recognise, or license, as bona fide banks under the Banking Act, 1979.

TABLE I.1 *Sterling deposits with banks in the United Kingdom, 1960–84*

£million	*Clearing banks*	*Accepting houses*	*Other British banks*	*Foreign banks*
1960	7 806*	424*	n.a.	1 467*
1962	8 261*	365	26	1 253
1966	9 890*	686	254	1 953
1970	11 423*	1 370	1 850	3 141
1974	25 201*	2 167	6 830	8 864
1975	25 629	2 263	8 867	7 183
1980	48 357	5 296	16 663	20 034
1984	96 574	9 800	29 066	44 680

*Figure includes foreign currency deposits.

NOTE A number of foreign banks were reclassified as, "other British" in 1975. Some small retail banks are included as "other Banks" until 1980 but with the clearing banks in 1984.

SOURCES *Bank of England Statistical Abstract,* nos 1 and 2; *Financial Statistics.*

TABLE I.2 *Foreign currency deposits with banks in the United Kingdom, 1960–84*

£million	*Clearing banks*	*Accepting houses*	*Other British banks*	*Foreign banks*
1962		298*	2*	1 063*
1966		449	104	3 361
1970		1 620	1 633	17 334
1974	3 726*	2 649	4 584	54 798
1975	4 408	2 802	9 238	68 707
1980	13 039	6 180	22 019	152 109
1984	34 218	13 663	52 258	433 994

*Figures before this date included in sterling deposits.

NOTE A number of foreign banks were reclassified as 'other British' in 1975. Some small retail banks are included as 'other British' until 1980, but with the clearers for 1984.

SOURCES *Bank of England Statistical Abstract,* nos 1 and 2; *Financial Statistics.*

The magnitude of these changes is summarised by Tables I.1 and I.2 which show deposits in sterling and foreign currency with the four banking groups identified in the United Kingdom.

This book describes the factors underlying the expansion of the first three categories of bank. In doing this it is intended to illustrate the institutional changes which took place affecting the manner in which, and the ability of, the authorities to pursue techniques of monetary and credit control. Such a topic is usually given little consideration in standard economics text-books.[1] But it is helpful to have some perception of the way in which the different types of bank have developed, both to illuminate the role of the financial institutions in the economy, and to facilitate an understanding of the aims and mechanisms of monetary regulation. It is inevitable that such an account devotes considerable attention to the monetary expansion of the early 1970s and the implications this has had for monetary management more recently.

The book does not consider in the same detail the development of foreign banking in Britain. There are now more than 200 foreign banks operating in Britain. The expansion of this sector, associated with the growth of the eurodollar market, is thus clearly a large topic to be considered in its own right. Here discussion is limited to the aggregate sector, which is considered briefly in Chapter 7 but, as the text makes clear, is also closely involved in the topics of Chapters 6 and 8. The important specific issue of whether banks in Britain provide adequate funds for industrial investment is also best considered on its own rather than as part of a book describing the evolution of the British banks.

The year 1960 forms a natural starting point for a study such as this. In 1959 the report of the Radcliffe Committee was published and the conclusions of that committee provided the basis for Bank of England monetary policy for at least the ensuing decade (*Report of the Committee on the Working of the Monetary System,* 1959). Secondly, by 1960 most European currencies had become, *de facto,* convertible for current transactions (to be formally ratified by the International Monetary Fund in 1961), opening the way for the development of the eurodollar and eurocurrency markets and, indirectly, of the inter-bank market.

Since the conclusions of the Radcliffe Committee formed the centrepiece of monetary policy for the first part of the period, it is worth looking at some of those conclusions which bear on the present study. The committee adopted a Tobinesque approach (as Gowland, 1978, describes it) to monetary policy by stressing that it was the liquidity of the economy as a whole that mattered rather than the control of the money supply, even if that were possible (Tobin, 1963). Liquidity in the economy was represented by a weighted average of all assets with the weights declining as liquidity declined[2] but with market sentiment also exercising an influence. So the committee argued:

> Though we do not regard the supply of money as an unimportant quantity, we view it as only part of the wider structure of liquidity in the economy. It is the whole liquidity position that is relevant to spending decisions . . . The authorities thus have to regard the structure of interest rates rather than the supply of money as the centrepiece of the monetary mechanism (para. 397).

The Radcliffe Committee firmly rejected the view of Dr Holtrop of the Netherlands Central Bank, that bank deposits which could be drawn on by cheque possessed a unique and 'virulent' liquidity. The committee believed that the authorities should seek to control bank lending (para. 395) through liquidity ratios since the effective base of bank credit has become the liquid assets (of the banks) . . . instead of the supply of cash (para. 376), supplemented by direct controls on lending in an emergency (para. 397). The committee's report was written at a time when the banking system was virtually synonymous with the clearing banks: in the committee's view, the non-clearing banks were of trivial importance in the domestic banking scene. Nevertheless, the committee warned against the danger of singling out the clearing banks for discriminatory action since although:

> regulation of the (clearing) banks is required . . . because they are the biggest lenders . . . at the most liquid end of credit markets . . . any severely restrictive control of their operations is certain, over a period of time, to be defeated by the development of rival institutions (para. 504).

As it happened, the committee's policy prescriptions were literally adopted by the Bank of England so far as the clearing banks were concerned but its prophetic warning was disregarded for far too long.

In 1960 the banking system was dominated by the clearing banks, which used the discount market as a home for their surplus funds. The major merchant banks, involved in financing trade, were members of the Accepting Houses' Committee. There was also a group of smaller merchant banks and some foreign-owned banks registered as companies in the UK, but these only held a small proportion of total bank deposits, and the Bank of England did not regard them as important.

1 An Overview of the Economy, 1960–85

Before discussing developments in British banking it is helpful to form an overview of the major movements in the British economy during the period. This chapter therefore begins by considering the path of output and fluctuations in inflation during the period. This is followed by a brief survey of movements in money and credit and a discussion of fluctuations in interest rates and asset prices. The purpose of this is to emphasise the factors which had important impact on the evolution of the banking sector, rather than to provide a complete analysis of the economy.

1.1 MOVEMENTS IN OUTPUT

The 1950s were a period of economic success. The decade started with rationing and high inflation, but also showed relatively rapid growth which continued into the 1960s; indeed it is usually suggested that the period of rapid economic growth continued with cyclical fluctuations but generally unabated until 1973. While the widely-held view of an economy which grew rapidly up to 1973 and then came to an abrupt halt is perhaps slightly mistaken, it is clear that growth was slower in the second half of the period than it had been in the first.

In 1959–60 the economy was booming, stimulated by tax cuts timed to fit the 1959 general election. But balance of payments problems and pressure on sterling emerged; a more restrictive stance was rapidly adopted. The level of unemployment rose again, aggravated by the severe weather of early 1963. With an election again imminent, 1964 saw the 'dash for growth'; but the attempt to reflate the economy led again to an increased balance of payments deficit and the incoming Labour government responded by restraining the economy. The balance of payments 'constraint' continued to be seen as a barrier to rapid growth for much of the period, until North Sea oil revenues started to appear in the late 1970s.

After 1964 the first straws in the wind, foretelling the depression of the 1970s, started to emerge. Steel output only passed its 1965 peak of 27.4m tonnes once, in 1970. Housebuilding, although not reaching the target level of 0.5 million, peaked at 411 700 completions in 1968. Motor-car output only briefly surpassed its 1964 peak in 1972. Unemployment rose from the post-war low of 232 000 in 1955, despite another trough in 1964.

But in the late 1960s activity remained at a fairly high level, boosted by the export boom which had followed the 1967 devaluation, into 1970.[1] The Conservative government, in 1970, was initially committed to restraint, but it became alarmed by the rapid growth in unemployment, which rose in 1971 to its highest level since 1940, and stimulated the economy to an extent which had not been seen before. The policies led to a major boom. Although the growth rate was only slightly higher than those of 1960 and 1964, the labour market showed signs of unparallelled tightness. Unemployment did not fall to the level of 1955, but it was well below the number of unfilled vacancies. The economy was less able to cope with rapid growth than it had been a decade earlier. That this was not always appreciated at the time is seen by the support that Ball and Matthews (1973) gave to the policies which had led to this boom.

In June 1972 sterling was allowed to float in the hope that this would allow the economy to grow rapidly without encountering the balance of payments constraint. But the balance of payments 'constraint' is only a symptom of an inability to produce goods which are demanded. This problem cannot be cured by treating the symptoms. In any case the floating rate did not balance the current account. Rapid growth led again to a worsened balance of payments position and the problem was aggravated by an upturn in commodity prices and the oil price rise at the end of 1973. It did not lead to any immediate depreciation of sterling because there was a tendency for the oil exporting countries to re-invest their surpluses in sterling. But the oil price increase had the effect of drawing purchasing power out of the industrial countries leading to the depression of 1975.

The inflation which accompanied this depression was particularly acute in the United Kingdom, and an incomes policy was introduced in 1975. But pressure gradually developed on the exchange rate leading to a series of falls; after a severe run in the summer of 1976 a credit was negotiated with the IMF in exchange for cuts in public spending spelt out in a letter of intent. Interest rates were also raised to levels not seen for a century.

The world gradually recovered from this depression and for a period seemed to have resumed its old growth path. Unemployment declined from a peak of 1.7m in early 1977 and in 1978 output grew by 4 per cent, a rate high by the standards of the earlier period, if not at quite the levels of 1964 and 1973. But a natural cyclical downturn coincided with the second oil price rise of 1979–80; throughout the world restrictive policies were adopted in order to prevent the oil price rise leading to general and sustained inflation.

In the UK this problem was aggravated by an unexpected appreciation of sterling and the direct deflationary impact of higher interest rates and higher taxation coupled with lower public investment. These policies were designed in the belief that they would remove inflation and this would allow more rapid growth to take place. The mechanism supposed to generate faster growth was never clear, and Brown (1982) finds little connection between productivity growth and inflation. The 'Thatcher experiment' is often seen as a major cause of the growth in unemployment in the UK, and certainly the economy suffered a depression in which output (excluding North Sea oil) fell further than it had between 1929 and 1931. Buiter and Miller (1981, 1983) offer an account of the period. Although a degree of economic stability had been restored by 1983, the situation, with high and at best stable unemployment, and output growing at 2.5 to 3 per cent in the mid 1980s, did not compare favourably with that of the 1960s.[2]

Thus for the real economy, although a neat break is usually considered to exist after 1973, the break is perhaps not quite as clean as might be hoped, especially for someone who sees the oil price inflation of 1973–4 as the cause of the reduction in the growth rate. With hindsight the argument of Matthews (1968), that the post-war years represented a long investment boom which could start to wind down, is supported.

1.2 INFLATION

In parallel with these variations of output growth there has been considerable variation in the rate of inflation over the period. During the 1950s inflation had declined from a rate of 9 per cent, reached at the time of the Korean War, and in the 1960s the rate remained, by more recent standards, low. Despite this it was a source of concern because it had proceeded at a higher rate than in many of the UK's trading partners, with the consequence that exports became decreasingly competitive. Thus in 1961, and again in 1966, incomes policies were introduced with the aim of restraining inflation and allowing some recovery in competitiveness. But the devaluation of 1967 was a recognition that the ground could not be adequately recovered in any other way and probably also a consequence of the fact that there had been losses in non-price competitiveness.

The pay policy broke down in 1968–9, and upward pressure on wages developed as workers attempted to make up lost ground. Inflation at a level of 5 per cent became an issue in the 1970 election, and continued to rise to a rate of 9 per cent in 1971. But unofficial incomes policies started to have an effect and the rate fell briefly to 5 per cent in 1972. The floating of sterling led to rises in import costs; these were compounded by the effects of a severe labour shortage and increasing raw materials prices producing a rate of 12 per cent by the end of 1973; this happened despite the incomes policy introduced in late 1972 which was intended to allow rapid growth to proceed without inflation.

Thus there was considerable inflationary pressure at the time of the oil-price rise of late 1973. The incomes policy had included indexation provisions and these became an engine of inflation in the last few months of the policy before its abolition by the new Labour government. Additionally, workers attempted to recoup the effects of higher oil prices and this generated increased inflation. The rate rose to a maximum of 27 per cent in 1975 when another incomes policy was introduced. This successfully reduced the rate to 8 per cent by 1978, albeit with a hiatus arising from sterling's depreciation in the summer of 1976.

In the winter of 1978–9 the incomes policy broke down and again there were attempts to make up lost ground. This was compounded by a second sharp rise in the price of oil and a budget in which an increase in value added tax added 4 per cent to the retail price index. Despite the deflationary stance of the government, and the rising exchange rate, inflation rose to a rate of 22 per cent in May 1980 before beginning an even more rapid descent to settle at a level of around 5 per cent in 1983–4. Many commentators would ascribe much of the fall in inflation to the level of unemployment in the first half of the 1980s. But it is not clear, in 1985, why the rate of inflation remains at about 5 per cent despite the continuance of mass unemployment.

There are a number of explanations of inflation. Some authors contend that most of the inflation over this period was driven by wages and import costs. Wages were determined by workers attempts to achieve some sort of target real wage (Sargan, 1964; Rowthorn, 1977). In this framework the higher inflation of the 1970s is explained by the reduction in national income arising from adverse movements in the terms of trade, or an increasing tax burden. Wages are pushed up as workers want to achieve their real target and prices respond to costs with a lag.

Such a model does not offer such a good explanation of the decline in inflation since 1980. It is probably necessary to argue that unemployment and slower real growth have finally (but perhaps temporarily) modified workers' aspirations and thus the inflationary pressures are reduced.

Models of this type can be modified to incorporate either unemployment or the change in unemployment as explanatory variables. An emphasis on these variables is satisfactory at explaining directly the recent decline in inflation, but this approach tends to perform less well in explaining the 'stagflation' of the 1970s against the low unemployment and low inflation of the 1960s.

The monetarist approach to inflation is demand based. Nominal demand is supposed to be related to the stock of money in the economy; in any economy which has a natural tendency to full employment, fluctuations in the money stock will be transmitted to fluctuations in prices. This may happen immediately; if everyone knows what the future price level will be, prices rather than output will adjust to the change in nominal demand. Or there may be fluctuations in output with the transmission to prices taking time.

While the relationship between money, nominal income, and inflation, is considered in section 1.3 it should be noted here that there are two different monetarist approaches to inflation. The simpler view is that the money stock is fixed by the government and is a direct consequence of policy. A rather different view is that the government can at least partially offset changes in the money stock arising from the behaviour of the private sector. The first view places the blame for price instability firmly with the government, while the second implies that positive action may be needed to maintain stability of the price level. This action may have costs which conflict with other policy objectives.

1.3 MONEY

There were historically two major monetary indicators used in the

United Kingdom, M1 and £M3. M1 includes notes and coin in the hands of the public and private sector non-bank sterling sight deposits with banks. £M3 also includes sterling time deposits by the non-bank private sector. Very recently emphasis has shifted from M1 to M0. M1 includes an increasing proportion of interest-bearing sight deposits, and it is hoped that M0, the wide monetary base, covering notes and coin in circulation together with bankers' deposits at the Bank of England, will provide a better indicator of the transactions' demand for money.

It is clear from the bank deposit identity[3] that all types of bank-lending have to be analysed in order to interpret movements in the money stock. It also follows that any desired change in holdings of money by the private sector can be met by the substitution of bank credit for non-bank loans; an active rather than passive policy will be needed by the government if it wishes to hold the stock of bank deposits to any particular level in the presence of such "shocks" to the demand for money.

During the period considered, both M1 and £M3 have tended to fall relative to GDP. This increasing velocity of circulation of each type of money (ratio of GDP/M1 or GDP/£M3) is shown in Figure 1.1. There are two major breaks to the increasing velocity of £M3. First, between 1971 and 1973, and secondly but more slowly, after 1981 velocity has tended to decline. Both of these have been periods in which controls on the banking system have been lifted. The decline of the early 1970s was reversed after controls were re-established at the end of 1973. But there is no immediate likelihood of controls being reintroduced now, and thus the second decline in velocity is probably reasonably permanent.

The relationship between growth in £M3 and growth in bank lending to the public and private sectors is shown in Figure 1.2.[4] During the 1960s growth in the money stock was driven by both public and private lending.

The importance of lending to the private sector as a source of increasing money supply is shown clearly in the events of 1972–3.[5] The nominal level of lending in these years was not surpassed until 1979 when prices were 2.6 times their 1972 level. Consideration of the events which made this expansion possible, and an analysis of their consequences for the financial system, forms an important part of this book.

In 1975 much of the slowdown in the velocity of circulation was recouped as a consequence of the severity of the price inflation of

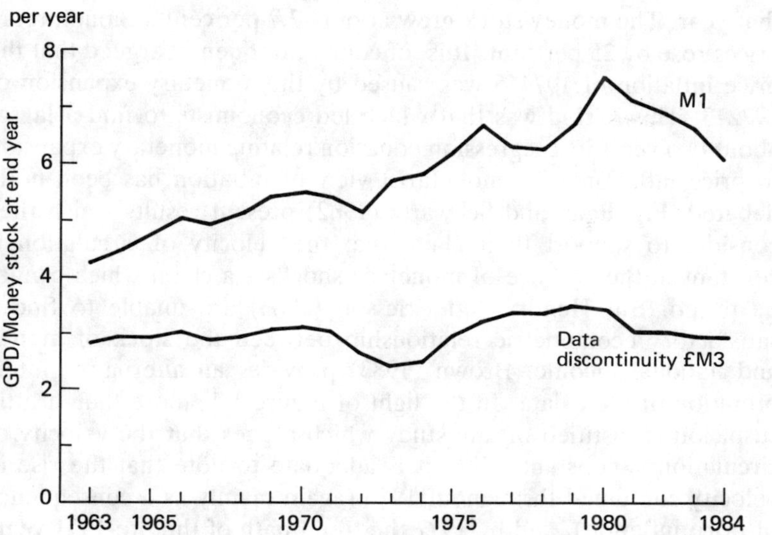

FIGURE 1.1 *Velocity of circulation of M1 and £M3*

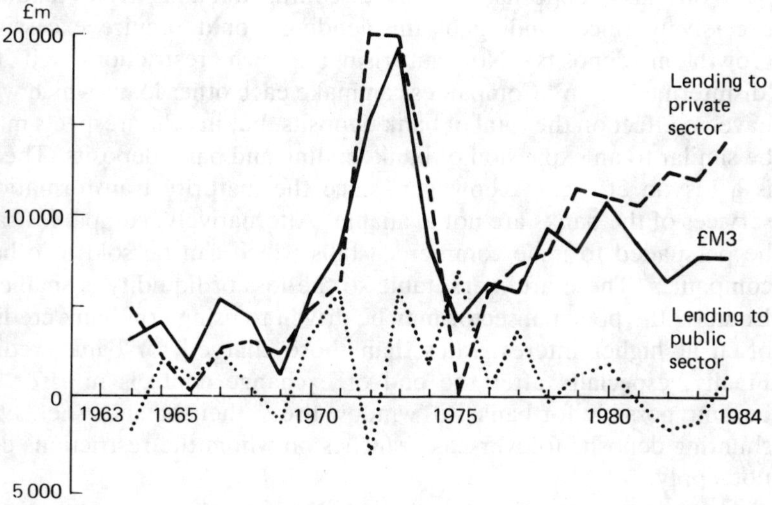

FIGURE 1.2 *Changes in bank lending and £M3*

that year. The money stock grew at only 7.7 per cent although retail prices rose by 25 per cent. It is, of course, frequently argued that the price inflation of 1974–5 was caused by the monetary expansion of 1972–3. This period was that which led economists to find a lag of about two years in a regression equation relating monetary expansion to price inflation. The monetarist view of inflation has been hotly debated. Friedman and Schwartz (1982) present results which they consider to support their claim that the velocity of circulation is constant in the absence of monetary shocks – a claim which cannot be tested. But Hendry and Ericsson (1983) are unable to find a satisfactory econometric relationship between the stock of money and national income. Brown (1983) provides an alternative interpretation of their data. In the light of Figure 1.1, more than a little suspicion is justified of any study which argues that the velocity of circulation is constant. Here it is adequate to note that the rise in velocity continued throughout 1976 (again mainly as a consequence of price inflation), and by 1977 the trend path of the pre-1971 years had broadly been regained.

However, this restoration of the 'status quo ante' had been achieved partly by means of the corset. This scheme of supplementary special deposits (considered in detail in Chapter 3) required banks to deposit with the Bank of England a fraction of their deposits if these grew at faster than a specified rate. No interest was paid on these deposits. It thus discouraged banks from lending excessively since funding of this lending would require excessive growth in deposits. Not surprisingly, such restrictions led to 'disintermediation'. Companies can make each other loans which will have no effect on the total of bank deposits, but in other respects may be similar to an expansion of bank lending and bank deposits. There is a loss in efficiency, however, since the maturity transformation services of the banks are not available. Alternatively, companies can be persuaded to issue commercial bills which can be sold to other companies. These are marketable so the loss of liquidity is smaller. Equally, the personal sector may be driven to using non-bank credit, often at higher interest rates than those charged for bank credit. Finally, especially after the end of exchange controls in 1979, it became possible for banks to 'window-dress' their balance sheets by shunting deposits to overseas branches on whom the restrictions did not apply.

These observations suggest that the corset restrictions were partially and increasingly cosmetic; indeed, when they were lifted in

1980 rapid monetary growth resumed. However, it seems likely that the demand for credit by the industrial sector was very high then, because high interest rates led, in the short term, to an increase in borrowing as firms attempted to finance their overdrafts. Meanwhile the holders of bank deposits had a 'non-permanent' increase in their income which was quite likely to be held on deposit rather than in long-term assets, especially since the rate on deposits was unusually high. A simultaneous expansion of bank lending and bank deposits took place as a result of high interest rates.

The expansion of the money stock associated with the lifting of the corset led commentators to argue that price inflation could be expected to remain at its 1980 level (17 per cent pa) into 1982–3. This was drawn directly from the previous experience of the early- to mid-1970s, and was argued despite the fact that the money stock was only expanding at the same rate as which prices were rising. In fact, the rate of inflation dropped to a 15-year low in the spring of 1983. However, the money stock has continued to grow rather faster than national income. Although there may be a variety of factors at work, it is possible that the increasing velocity of the period 1963–80 was at least partly a consequence of the various controls which had operated for most of the period.

While this view has its appealing aspects it cannot be said to cover the whole picture. For the monetary inflation of 1972–3, when controls were also lifted, was associated with abnormal behaviour in other financial markets, connected with speculative excesses at the end of the boom. One cannot argue that the history is merely one of simple substitution between 'money' and 'near money' with the sum of the two remaining constant. But it is almost inevitable that, because banks are different from non-bank credit institutions they will, if de-regulated, not merely regain disintermediated business but actually generate an expansion in the over-all lending which takes place. Thus the reduction in velocity in 1972–3, and the reduction after 1980, are not merely consequences of reintermediation but do probably also represent new business.

The new business in the first period of rapid monetary expansion was of a rather different character from that in the second. In the first banks saw few constraints on their lending since they were able to find the necessary deposits ex post. Certainly there seems to have been little official pressure to discourage lending. But in the early 1980s the Bank of England may have actually encouraged lending beyond a point commercial banks would otherwise have chosen. For a number of companies faced severe liquidity problems under the combined force of a high exchange rate and high interest rates. To have refused to lend to these would have had the effect of destroying firms some of which would become profitable again when interest rates and the exchange rate fell. By encouraging banks to lend, the Bank was effectively protecting its own position as a lender of last resort. For, had the commercial banks faced substantial losses, this could have led to a withdrawal of deposits from them. In the event profitability did recover, and the judgement of the Bank in encouraging this lending proved sound. The rather different nature of this expansion of credit had therefore neither the inflationary consequences nor the same ending as the first expansion; it reflected an increased need for credit by industrial and commercial companies rather than a speculative demand.

Such behaviour of the money stock followed a long-established pattern. Feavearyear (1963) points out that, by the end of the eighteenth century, the Bank of England had discovered that, if speculation was believed excessive, it should restrict credit. But once a contraction had started it should lend freely so as to soften the fall.

Throughout the period the behaviour of the banking system was regarded as having important implications for events in the rest of the economy. In the 1960s attention focused on bank lending to the private sector. Emphasis gradually changed, and since 1976 monetary targets have been a feature of the economic environment.[6] Initially the monetary indicator selected was £M3[7] on the grounds that this was the best monetary indicator of future changes in the price level. Ideally an announced target for £M3 would lead to appropriate inflationary expectations, and thus ensure that the demand for money did not exceed the announced target. However, there are a number of reasons why the process is unlikely to be so simple. If £M3 were controlled directly, by means, for example, of the corset, lending would be driven to non-bank financial intermediaries and the achievement of the monetary target would no longer indicate anything about the state of the economy. Goodhart's Law, that a monetary indicator loses its meaning once it is controlled (Goodhart, 1984, Chapter 3), summarises this point.

In any case, not only is the velocity of circulation not constant in the long run but in the short run there are good reasons why changes in 'liquidity', however measured, may not be associated with changes in nominal demand. Thus in 1979 interest rates were raised so as to bring the money supply under control. It has already been pointed out that this raised both money supply and money demand, at least in the short run. Such behaviour will make movements in £M3 difficult to interpret; in particular there is no reason to regard a policy of raising interest rates 'automatically' whenever £M3 exceeds its target as a sensible way of achieving the target.

Over the longer run monetary control is more likely to be achieved by a policy of fiscal management which restricts nominal income to a level at which the demand for credit and the demand for money are compatible with the monetary target. But since nominal income or gross domestic product (GDP) is the variable which is ultimately intended to be controlled[8] monetary targets under such a policy framework lose much of their importance.

1.4 INTEREST RATES AND ASSET RETURNS

This brief historical sketch of the economy should be completed by surveying movements to interest rates. These are of considerable importance for the operation of the financial institutions. During the 1960s the bank rate was used as an instrument both to regulate the state of domestic credit, and more importantly to attract foreign exhange at a time when sterling came under pressure. Thus it was raised to 5 per cent during a sterling crisis in 1961. The years leading up to devaluation saw it at 6 per cent or 7 per cent as the parity of $2.8 became harder to sustain and it was raised to 8 per cent at the time of devaluation.

Until 1968 the Bank of England pursued a policy of stabilising yields on gilt-edged securities as well as fixing the bank rate. Although yields were higher than they had been in the 1950s, there was no obvious upward trend during most of the decade. The maintenance of stable interest rates probably made it easier for the Bank to refund maturing debt. And low interest rates on the national debt had an obvious and immediate gain for the tax-payer. However, by 1968 these considerations had become less important; as the national debt declined relative to GDP, it was possible to begin to consider other policy objectives which might override funding needs. Although yields brushed 10 per cent in 1970–1, they had dropped back by 1972 and the bank rate was, at 5 per cent, at its lowest level since 1964.

The relatively low returns on gilts were contrasted by large profits available on property speculation; planning controls had restricted commercial development for some years. This led to substantial capital gains on property and a speculative boom developed in the early 1970s. It is possible that the authorities would have liked to raise interest rates at this stage as a response, not only to the property boom, but also to the rapid growth of the rest of the economy. But a voluntary prices policy had been agreed with the Confederation of British Industry (CBI), and it seemed difficult to add to industrial costs by raising interest rates (Moran, 1984, Chapter 4).

The rise in interest rates was thus delayed into 1973, and was probably as a consequence larger than it would have otherwise been. The minimum lending rate (MLR) (which had replaced the bank rate)[9] reached 13 per cent in November 1973. This increase, and associated tax penalties on property gains in the December 1973 budget, finally stopped the property boom of the previous four or five years. The end of the boom was associated with a run on many small banks as doubts about their ability to repay deposits developed.

This aspect of the financial crisis was accompanied by another problem which added to its intensity. For during 1974 inflationary expectations gathered pace, and it became clear that an associated squeeze on both the profitability and the liquidity of the industrial sector was taking place. The fall in both share and long-term gilts prices continued throughout 1974. By the end of the year the yield on Treasury bills, at 13.25 per cent was lower than it had been in 1973, but the 20-year gilt yield had risen to 17.2 per cent from 12.5 per cent at the end of 1973, producing a yield curve of unparallelled steepness. *The Financial Times* 30-share index reached a low point of 140.8 some 73 per cent below its previous peak. This fall in prices probably would have cast doubt on the solvency of some of the investing institutions had it not been dramatically reversed in early 1975 as a result of a bear squeeze in the gilt-edged market, engineered by the government broker, and share support by five insurance companies. These had built up liquidity in 1974 instead of investing their receipts as they came in.

Short-term interest rates have continued to be used as a policy instrument, predominantly with reference to the exchange rate. In October 1976 minimum lending rate was raised to 15 per cent in order to support sterling, and as the pressure eased in 1977 minimum lending rate fell. It had dropped to 5 per cent by October 1977. For a period of about four years after that, internal objectives dominated interest rate policy. minimum lending rate was used in an attempt to restrain growth in the monetary aggregates. As noted above, this is by no means a precise process. A rate of 17 per cent in November 1979 did not restrain monetary growth to its target range.

The high interest rates were probably one factor behind the rise in the exchange rate in the late 1970s, and it was natural that it should decline as they were reduced (despite the fact that the behaviour of the monetary indicators was not satisfactory). But in late 1981 the decline accelerated and was arrested by a rise in base rates from 12 to 16 per cent (minimum lending rate was discontinued in August 1981). In late 1982 a rise from 9.75 to 12 per cent was necessary for the same reason. In the summer of 1984 and again in early 1985 interest rates rose to a higher level than would have otherwise been desirable in order to support the exchange rate. Furthermore, the decline in inflation since 1980 left real interest rates at unusually high levels.

Despite the fact that inflation peaked in 1975, long-term interest rates turned down at the end of 1974. Indeed 1974 can be said to make the end of the upward drift in long-term rates which had taken place steadily since 1947 (although with pauses such as that in much of the 1960s). Since then, although there have been two other periods of very high long-term rates, at the end of 1976 and at the end of 1981 the levels of late 1974 have not been reached again. The stock market, too, has shown an almost continual bull market since early 1975, although there have been brief periods of decline.

The high long-term interest rates observed in the 1970s cannot satisfactorily be regarded as a 'crowding out' phenomenon. The stock disequilibrium induced by the national debt was less severe in the 1970s than it had been in the 1960s. If one follows Hicks (1939) in regarding long-term interest rates as reflecting the expected pattern of future short-term rates, some insight can be gained. However, in 1973 the market did not seem to be anticipating the rise in short-term rates which occurred; in 1976–7 minimum lending rate was raised to the highest level yet of 15 per cent in order to stop the run on sterling, and the yield on long securities exceeded it; this behaviour was quite incompatible with the subsequent fall in minimum lending rate to 5 per cent by October 1977. Similarly long-dated redemption yields reached a local peak of around 16 per cent pa at the end of 1981, at a time when short-term interest rates had been raised briefly to 16 per cent as a consequence of a fall in sterling. But they had already begun their trend descent from the level of 17 per cent p.a. reached in November 1979, a level imposed as a response to monetary expansion, rather than exchange rate problems. By this time more attention was paid to real yields (the rate of interest less the rate of inflation) than had been the case in the 1970s. On the assumption that real yields would be slightly positive, only pessimistic projections of inflation could have justified the level of long yields at the end of 1981.

Given the interest rate volatility over the period, it is perhaps surprising that there were not more casualties in the financial sector. Most financial institutions have some assets on fixed rates of interest. They are squeezed when interest rates rise, provided the average maturity of their assets is longer than that of their liabilities. For any bank with large non-interest bearing deposits this effect is more than offset by the extra profit that can be earned lending them out, and for banks with a large amount of variable-rate lending, the spread between borrowing and lending rates is likely to be more important than the consequences of owning fixed-rate assets. But subsequent chapters make clear the losses which arose from investment in property, whose value is sensitive to interest rates.[10]

1.5 SUMMARY

The period under study was thus one almost bisected by the events of the early 1970s which finally marked the end of the post-war boom and the start of a period of considerable instability in both financial and real economies.

Some measure of this instability in both financial and real economies may be gauged by comparing the peaks and troughs of various indicators for various financial and real indicators over the two periods 1960–71 and 1972–84, as shown in Table 1.1.

Although the date of the split has some importance, in that if 1972 were included in the first period some indicators like the rate of monetary growth might show more variability in the first period, nevertheless, the view of an economy more unstable in the 1970s and 1980s than it was in the 1960s is strongly supported. To attribute this instability to any particular cause or policy is difficult. One would rather blame the policies adopted to fight inflation, than inflation itself. But it is not clear that any particular policy has aggravated the instability over the past ten years, even if some of the policies adopted have, with the benefit of hindsight, seemed somewhat inappropriate. This point could be made of the defence of sterling

TABLE 1.1 *Indicators of economic instability, 1960–84*

	1960–71		*1972–84*	
	Lowest	*Highest*	*Lowest*	*Highest*
GDP growth (1980 prices) % pa	1.1	5.6	−2.5	6.9
Unemployment ('000 mid-year)	281.0	724.0	528.0	3 030.0
Relative unit labour costs (1980=100)	70.0	83.8	65.9	107.8
Inflation rate (increase in GDP deflator on previous year)	2.1	9.2	5.2	27.0
Yield on Treasury Bills (% pa end year)	3.76	7.80	6.39	16.49
Yield on 20-year gilt (% pa average)	5.98	9.25	8.97	14.77
FT 30-share index (average)	285.5	463.3	251.2	854.9
Growth in money stock (% change in end-year £M3)	2.1	12.9	6.7	26.8
$ exchange rate	2.385	2.81	1.19	2.48

SOURCES *Economic Trends Annual Supplement,* 1985; *Financial Statistics.*

before the 1967 devaluation, the monetary framework adopted in 1971, the dash for growth in 1972–3, and the more recent policies of tight monetary control.

2 Risk and Financial Institutions

The modern theory of risk owes its origins to Keynes (1936) and Hicks (1939). They propounded the theory of liquidity preference, arguing that, other things including return being equal, investors prefer liquid assets of certain value to illiquid assets of uncertain value. This allows them to meet potential and unforeseeable demands for funds. Thus investors require an additional return, known as a risk premium, on assets whose price varies, in order to compensate for the uncertainty about the price that such assets may command at any time. It was also argued that borrowers would prefer long-dated liabilities which require fixed interest payments for the duration of the debt. This means that, for the life of the loan, they face known interest payments and that they can make, well in advance, the arrangements necessary for its repayment. Indeed, if borrowers did not have reasons for preferring long-term debt, there would be no market in such debt. Private borrowers must be prepared to pay the premium demanded by the lenders.

While Keynes argued that investors would prefer liquid assets there are clearly some investors who show counter-liquidity preference. Life assurance and pension funds hold large proportions of long gilts and equities in their portfolios, not because the managers enjoy volatile portfolio performance but because they are concerned about the long-run performance of their assets which have to meet the long-run liabilities arising from pensions and maturing life policies. Matthews (1963) was probably the first to discuss the implications of this in a systematic way although actuaries had been concerned about the problem of immunisation – that is, matching of assets and liabilities, for many years. This aspect became of some macro-economic importance in 1982 and had some bearing on more recent monetary control arrangements. It facilitated the sale of long-term government debt (Chapter 3).

While notions of risk-premia go back to the 1930s, the first quantification of the theory of risk and uncertainty is due to Tobin

(1958). Keynes had argued that investors would be either bulls or bears and thus different investors would hold different assets depending on whether they were bullish or bearish. Tobin attempted to explain the more complex problem of why an investor would hold a mixed portfolio. He developed the theory of risk aversion which argued that, while investors prefer a high yield to a low one, they prefer a stable return to a risky one, and are prepared to trade off yield for stability. Thus a mixed portfolio of consols and money may tend to have a more stable return than either consols or money. When interest rates rise the high yield on money will compensate for the capital loss on consols, while the converse is true if interest rates fall. But money also provides transaction services and thus more money will be held than either of these considerations would suggest. Tobin's theory becomes difficult to apply in a situation where some investors (Hicks' widows and orphans) are predominantly concerned with the stability of their income. For these investors consols or their modern equivalent, indexed gilts, are safe and money or Treasury bills are risky.

In a market where different institutions and individuals have different degrees of risk-aversion, those who are very averse to risk will be prepared to pay others to bear it. Thus two individuals may expect the same gain on a given asset. One is prepared to hold it and the other is not. Tobin's model implies that the working of the market will not bring the return on all assets to equality. The return on assets which are risky will rise to the point where the extra yield is just attractive enough for a marginal risk-taker to own it. The expected yield on fixed assets will be larger than that on money since the real assets are illiquid. If an extra investor, who is increasingly willing to take risks, emerges, there will be two effects. First, the investor may earn potentially large profits, which may tempt others into the field and secondly, the return on risky assets will decline towards that on safe assets. If an investor has a different perception of risk from the market as a whole, because either he or the market has an incorrect perception of the risk involved, he may be able to make large profits on a particular line of business, at least for a time. If his view is correct and that of the market remains incorrect he is likely to go on making profit. But if his estimate is inaccurate, it is likely that sooner or later he will face bankruptcy, not necessarily because he is wrong about long-run movements but because he does not have the reserves to cover adverse short-run oscillations.

Thus risk-taking can lead to insolvency, which is why those

institutions in the business of taking risk are strictly regulated; insurance companies have to observe solvency margins so as to protect policy-holders. Risk-taking and speculation are much discussed by a wide range of economists and form the basis of the capital-asset pricing model (Brealey, 1983). Kindleberger (1981) and Galbraith (1955) provide excellent historic accounts of various speculative booms, while a more theoretical approach is adopted by, for example, Tirole (1982).

2.1 FINANCIAL INSTITUTIONS

Financial institutions can be classed broadly as maturity matching or maturity transforming. The former include life assurance and pension funds. They have long-term liabilities and tend to match them with long-term assets. They make their profits because investment through them is either mandatory or has tax advantages; they are thought to offer investing skills which individuals may not have, and, because they command a pool of resources, they are able to offer a wider spread of investments than individual small investors could hope to own, thus protecting the investors from poor performance by any particular asset.[1]

Maturity transforming institutions such as banks, building societies and finance houses play a different role in the economy. For they are prepared to borrow (take deposits) on terms which none of the people who borrow from them would be willing to accept. Building societies make secured loans and can use straightforward principles in deciding whether to make advances or not. Banks make mainly unsecured loans and indeed Cooper (1984, Chapter 4) argues that the key to successful banking is the judgement of credit risk. However, all maturity transformers make their profit out of the liquidity premium, since depositors accept low rates of return in exchange for liquidity, while borrowers pay high rates of return in exchange for illiquidity of their debts. A large proportion of deposits with these institutions, mainly banks and building societies are deposits withdrawable on demand. Many of those deposits, even if not withdrawable on demand, require only seven days notice. A bank could never hope to call in its loans at the speed at which deposits can melt away, and has instead to rely on the fact that, over the short run withdrawals and deposits will normally be roughly in balance. This remains true if many of the loans are overdrafts with no particular

TABLE 2.1 *Assets of major financial institutions*

£bn	*Maturity matching*		*Maturity transforming*		
	Life assurance funds	*Pension funds*	*Building societies*	*Finance houses*	*Banks (sterling only) 1975 and after)*
1960	5.4	3.3	3.1	0.9	13.8
1965	9.4	5.3	5.6	1.1	18.5
1970	14.5	7.8	10.9	1.2	42.0
1975	23.3	15.9	24.3	1.2	58.8
1980	53.7	54.0	54.3	6.3	108.0
1984	95.9	106.2	101.1	4.1	213.4

NOTE At the end of 1981 many finance houses were reclassified as part of the monetary sector. However the total for banks does not include the assets of these finance houses. Data discontinuities are indicated by underlining.

SOURCES Revell (1967) and *Financial Statistics*.

maturity attached to them. The relative growth of the major maturity matching and maturity transforming institutions in the British economy is indicated by Table 2.1.

An indication of the maturity transformation of the domestic banking system as a whole is given by Table 2.2, drawn from data available for the first time in 1985. It shows that one half of the system's sterling liabilities fall due in less than eight days, while a comparable amount of assets have a life of up to six months. The importance of lending with a life of more than 3 years is notable.

TABLE 2.2 *Bank sterling assets and liabilities by maturity (February 1985)*

Maturity	*Liabilities*	*Claims*	*Net position (£bn)*
<8 days	96.7	26.5	−70.2
8 days to <1 month	29.6	18.3	−11.3
1 month to <3 months	30.3	29.4	−0.9
3 months to <6 months	13.5	16.4	2.9
6 months to <1 year	8.3	15.1	6.8
1 year to <3 years	2.7	20.4	17.7
3 years and over	4.7	80.5	75.9
Total	185.8	206.6	20.8

SOURCE *Bank of England Quarterly Bulletin.*

2.2 THE BALANCE SHEET OF A BANK

The nature of a financial institution is shown by the structure of its assets and liabilities. Thus before assessing the way in which banks carry out their business and the nature of the risks this entails, it is helpful to sketch out a schematic bank balance sheet for future reference, as shown in Table 2.3.

TABLE 2.3 *A schematic bank balance sheet*

Liabilities	*Sterling*	*Foreign currency*
Notes issued	L11	
Deposits by UK banks	L12	L22
by other UK residents	L13	L23
from overseas	L14	L24
Certificates of deposit	L15	L25
Sums due (dividends, etc.)	L16	L26
Loan capital	L17	L27
Share capital and reserves including minority interests and general provisions	L18	
Total	TL1	TL2
Assets		
Notes and coin+balances with central bank (L)	A11	
Special and cash ratio deposits	A12	
Deposits with discount market (L)	A13	
UK Treasury bills (L)	A14	
Other bills (L)	A15	A25
UK gov. securities	A16	
Balances with UK banks (L)	A17	A27
Certificates of deposit (L)	A18	A28
Loans to local authorities	A19	
Investments	A110	A210
Fixed assets, goodwill and investment in subsidiaries	A111	A211
Advances	A112	A212
Creditors etc.	A113	A213
Total	TA1	TA2

NOTE (L) indicates assets regarded as liquid by convention.

This shows rather more detail than is published in most company annual reports. The aggregated bank balance sheets produced by the Bank of England also consolidate some items, but balance sheets considered subsequently are in broadly this format.

It is important to note that share capital and reserves are defined as a balancing item which ensures that liabilities equal assets:

$$TL1+TL2=TA1+TA2$$

Despite their residual nature they can, of course, be increased by share issues or retained profits. Retained or raised funds will also add to holdings of one or more assets. The published aggregate data on banks do not show share capital and reserves. Before 1975 complete balance sheets were not published. After 1975 a balancing item, net non-deposit liabilities was introduced. This is equal to:

$$L16+L26+L17+L27+L18-A111-A211-A113-A213$$

2.3 ILLIQUIDITY

Banks and other maturity transforming institutions face three distinct types of hazard. First, they may be faced with a sudden withdrawal of deposits, which they lack the liquidity to meet. Secondly, they may make advances which cannot be repaid, leading to a position in which liabilities exceed assets and thirdly, they may face losses arising from taking deposits in one currency and lending out in a different one, or from other adverse movements in the price of their assets. Both the second and the third can lead to insolvency and are discussed subsequently.

There are in fact two aspects to maturity transformation. If loans are made at a fixed rate of interest for a long period on the basis of short-term deposits, a bank is susceptible to loss if interest rates rise. If it lends at a variable rate of interest it is protected against losses arising from interest rate movement. But variable rates of interest do not make long-term loans liquid. There is a difference between a mortgage and a bill of exchange even if the mortgage is, like most mortgages nowadays, at a variable rate of interest. Maturity transforming on variable rate loans does nothing to reduce the risk of illiquidity.

In a world of perfect capital markets all bank assets (such as loans to individuals or firms) would be easily marketable and liquidity crises would not happen. In practice, some assets can be realised much more readily than others. A withdrawal of deposits (L12 to L15 and L22 to L25) must be met by the realisation of liquid assets and cannot be covered by the withdrawal of advances or the sale of fixed assets (except at disadvantageous prices). There is no clear boundary between those liquid assets which can be realised immediately and those illiquid ones which cannot. Assets conventionally regarded as liquid are indicated in Table 2.1. But it should be noted that some instruments, notably the liabilities of other banks, may become illiquid in a banking crisis.

The need of any bank for liquid assets is uncertain, depending on future events which cannot be foreseen, and for which there may be no known probability distribution. Faced with uncertainty, banks are likely to adopt fairly simple prudential rules rather than actuarial calculations in order to protect themselves, even at the cost of immediate profits. In Tobin's framework it is possible to talk of utility maximisation as an investor trades off expected profit for stability of return. But in a framework of uncertainty the precise trade-off is unknown and it is much harder to talk satisfactorily of profit maximisation or utility maximisation.

2.4 MOVEMENTS IN LIQUIDITY

A useful measure of the liquidity of a group of banks is the ratio of advances to that of non-bank deposits. If a bank has a high ratio of advances to non-bank deposits it is exposed to the hazard that some of these will be withdrawn at the same time as funds are scarce in the interbank market. A bank with a high ratio of advances to non-bank deposits does not improve its liquidity position very much by borrowing on the interbank market, or issuing certificates of deposit (CDs) and redepositing in, for example, the local authority market (Chapter 6). The assets and liabilities are likely to fall due at a similar time although such a move would depress the over-all ratio of advances to deposits. Indeed, transactions of this type have no impact on the liquidity of the banking system as a whole. Table 2.4 presents the ratio of sterling advances to non-bank deposits, A112/(L13+L14), for the clearers and two other types of British bank since 1960.

The traditional deposit base of the clearing banks is a mixture of current accounts and seven-day deposits and this base was, for many years, very stable. More recently the development of competition with the building societies has reduced the stability of the interest-bearing retail deposit base. Current accounts are probably also more interest sensitive now, and sight deposits bearing high interest rates

TABLE 2.4 *The ratio of sterling advances to sterling deposits (end year)*

	Clearing banks	*Accepting houses*	*Other British banks*
1960	0.47	data not	data not
1961	0.46	available	available
1962	0.48	0.40	1.02
1963	0.51	0.43	0.94
1964	0.55	0.44	0.82
1965	0.53	0.41	0.60
1966	0.52	0.40	0.71
1967	0.51	0.34	0.49
1968	0.51	0.31	0.38
1969	0.53	0.31	0.28
1970	0.56	0.31	0.35
1971	0.54	0.42	0.56
1972	0.72	0.53	1.03
1973	0.75	0.51	1.08
1974	0.71	0.73	1.57
1975	0.65	0.59	0.90
1976	0.67	0.54	0.90
1977	0.70	0.49	0.92
1978	0.72	0.50	0.89
1979	0.73	0.63	0.85
1980	0.74	0.55	0.80
1981	0.78	0.61	1.01
1982	0.89	0.61	1.10
1983	0.85	0.54	1.32
1984	0.85	0.52	1.35

NOTE The ratios relate to deposits and advances outside the banking system. Certificates of deposit are not included because they are held mainly within the banking system. The definition of 'Other British banks' changed in 1975. All retail banks are included with clearing banks from 1981 onwards. Underlining indicates a data discontinuity.

SOURCES *Bank of England Statistical Abstract*, nos 1 and 2; *Bank of England Quarterly Bulletin*.

have become widespread. Despite this there has been a marked decline in liquidity cover since the 1960s.

Accepting houses have always tended to receive larger deposits from companies and wealthy individuals, paying a higher return than the rate on 7-day clearing bank deposits. They often take deposits of fixed maturity. Such deposits tend to be less stable than traditional clearing bank deposits, and thus the accepting houses have observed a lower ratio of advances to deposits than that of the clearing banks. The accepting houses' relatively cautious approach is shown in the liquidity ratios of Table 2.1. To some extent the accepting houses were more exposed than the figures suggest because accepting houses issue many more acceptances, relative to their other business, than do the other banks. These (Chapter 6) represent notional liabilities which are charged on customers self-liquidating transactions. But under some circumstances they can become actual liabilities (p. 97) imposing a burden on both liquidity and solvency.

The lending of the other non-clearing banks to speculative sectors of the economy increased in the early 1970s, and they paid decreasing attention to liquidity margins. The figures of Table 2.1 suggest that the other non-clearing banks relied substantially on the interbank markets for their liquidity needs. To the extent that the larger non-clearing banks are subsidiaries of the clearers,[2] there is access to a secondary source of liquidity. But independent non-clearing banks also operated without much regard to liquidity requirements. The anticipated profitability of the loans was such that these banks advanced as much as possible. Although the figures for the ratio of sterling advances to sterling deposits by non-banks show considerable fluctuation, especially in the early years, arising from discontinuities in the series, they show a much less cautious approach than that of the accepting houses in lending out deposits. The very high figure for 1974 reflects the consequences of that lack of caution discussed in Chapter 7.

Clearly the liquidity of the whole system has fallen markedly over the period. The banking system now is less liquid than it was before the 1973–5 crisis. The direct entry of the clearing banks into the wholesale money markets has increased their vulnerability; as the secondary banks[3] found in 1973, wholesale money does not have the stability of retail deposits. The development of the new money markets (Chapter 6) has increased the risk of instability since these markets offer a source of funds much less stable than traditional current and deposit accounts. These observations illustrate that the liquidity needs of a bank depend not only on the magnitude, but also the nature of its liabilities; the new markets can meet normal liquidity needs, but wholesale funds can be withdrawn very rapidly if any doubts about solvency arise.

2.5 INSOLVENCY

Insolvency can be caused by adverse interest rate movements leading to capital losses, but the hazard also arises if a bank's creditors default on their loans. Any bank expects to have to make provision out of its profit for bad debts. But if the bad debts not provided for are larger than the value of the bank's share capital and reserves the bank becomes insolvent. In the notation of the balance sheet, reductions in the value of assets, either because of capital losses or due to bad debts, lead to a fall in the value of L18. When this becomes negative the bank is insolvent in that it cannot repay its debts. But the position of depositors is secured provided L17+L18+L27>0 if, as is usually the case, deposits represent a claim prior to loans. Just as a liquidity margin based on convention may be adopted as protection against the risk of illiquidity, so a bank will typically also focus on its capital margin. The larger its capital and reserves are relative to its advances, the lower is the risk of insolvency arising from bad debts.

A bank which is insolvent does not have to 'close its doors' in the way that an illiquid bank is obliged to do. Thus the Penn Square Bank which became insolvent in 1982 had probably been insolvent for some time before its position was discovered. Equally the Schroeder, Muenchmeyer and Hengst Bank which was found to have DM900m of doubtful loans all to one company against capital reserves of DM70–80m had not run into liquidity problems. And the First National Finance Corporation (Chapter 7) had a large capital deficiency in 1975, which it had cleared by 1982, through ploughing back trading profits. On the other hand a general banking run can force the sale of assets at adverse prices and thus result in insolvency. If the run is met through adequate supplies of liquidity, insolvency can be avoided. The Bank of England seems to have been influenced by these considerations at the time of the secondary banking crisis, 1973–5. As Hirsch (1977) points out, liquidity problems may themselves be rooted in fears about solvency and thus, to some extent, such fears can become self-fulfilling.

There is clearly a risk, under any circumstances, that some loans will not be repaid. An individual depositing with a bank is in a much safer position than if he lent to one or two other individuals. For although the expected loss may be the same, the variability about this figure is much reduced. If a bank makes a large number of loans the expected loss can be predicted with reasonable accuracy and the bank can set its profit margin accordingly. But in fact the possibility of default on one loan is not independent of that on another loan. During a depression more people will default than in a boom. Or a bank may specialise in lending to a particular sector which starts to perform badly. Thus the accepting houses suffered simultaneous losses in 1931 when many of the bills they had accepted became actual liabilities as a result of the debt moratorium. Equally the popularity of lending to the Third World in the late 1970s was a source of potential difficulty for banks which had a major interest in this line of business. Even though they may have had a number of loans outstanding the loans all became suspect simultaneously. The secondary banks which had become heavily involved in lending to property firms faced this problem in 1973. As the market turned down, many of their loans became simultaneously doubtful. The position was quite different from that of an individual bankruptcy arising through careless or unfortunate management of a firm to which a bank has lent.

If non-clearing banks use interbank markets as an important means of attracting deposits and tend to pursue rather more specialised business, such as lending to companies of a particular type, or indeed merely lending to companies rather than individuals, the implication is that they need both larger capital reserves and a higher liquidity ratio than clearing banks. For if the variability of default on loans is higher for a non-clearing bank it needs a higher capital base in order to have the same risk of insolvency as a clearing bank. Similarly, if the variability of deposit demand is greater for a non-clearing bank it needs greater liquidity in order to have the same risk of illiquidity as a clearing bank. If there is doubt about the existence of a lender of last resort the liquidity requirements are raised further, although it is unlikely that any liquidity margin, which allows profitable trading, would be adequate to protect a bank in the event of a general panic. Because of the relationship between illiquidity and insolvency, arguably the capital base requirements are also raised again. It is not possible to derive a time series of capital ratios similar to Table 2.4 because of the way in which the data are consolidated. However, the capital positions of individual banking groups are discussed subsequently.

2.6 ATTITUDES TO RISK AND UNCERTAINTY

The clearing banks sought to protect themselves against illiquidity by observing standard liquidity ratios which they had found quite adequate in normal circumstances. There is a strong tendency for one bank to have a surplus of liquidity at a time when another one is in deficit, because the funds withdrawn from one bank will, to a considerable extent be redeposited with another one. The discount market served as a buffer; the bank in deficit could withdraw its call money while the bank in surplus redeposited and the system in aggregate was scarcely affected. Problems would only arise if funds were withdrawn from the system as a whole or if the bank faced withdrawal of such proportions that its liquid reserves proved inadequate. The latter has not happened to a clearing bank in the UK for many decades. The clearing banks were, of course, also concerned about the risk of bad debts leading to capital losses. The wide spread of their business offered considerable protection, and of course they tended to avoid business they regarded as risky.

During the period of study different non-clearing banks responded in different ways to the problems they faced. Some bankers, uncertain but mistrustful of the future, decided to limit their role as maturity transformers and instead tried to match their portfolios of assets with those of liabilities. Such an approach, followed by most accepting houses, avoids the risk of problems arising from a loss of confidence in the bank itself, but it does not protect the bank from the inability of the borrower to pay. Losses through adverse interest rate movements are avoided and liquidity will not prove a problem under normal trading conditions. But if the borrower has borrowed for a purpose, which is not self-liquidating, in the expectation of being able to renew the credit, and is then unable to renew it, the bank will still face the problems of a doubtful debt. Rescheduling may mean that the debt can eventually be paid, but it breaks the match of maturities which the banker has built up.

The bankers who pursued this cautious policy[4] were probably aware that they were losing the potential profits of maturity transformation but considered the extra security an adequate compensation. In Tobin's terms they were risk-averse, perhaps because they saw their careers as dependent on the future of the institution employing them and their own perceived success or failure as measured by the ability to cope with a crisis should it arise. Other bankers took an opposite view. There were large profits to be made by speculation and they were confident that they could always obtain, in the interbank market, the finance necessary while funds were tied up in speculation. These bankers were not concerned about the ability of their organisations to weather a storm. They believed they could always stay one step ahead of the market and realise the gains their speculation was designed to achieve.

The accepting houses were also concerned to minimise the danger of default on loans. The normal practice was to restrict their exposure by placing financial limits on the amounts that could be traded with every potential borrower and regularly to review these limits, the amounts outstanding and the names with whom they were willing to trade. The information used to determine these limits was the balance sheets of the institutions concerned, coupled with knowledge in the market of the assumed credit-worthiness of the borrowers. These safeguards could not protect an accepting house if a chain of borrowers emerged, including some which had not been approved by that house. Nor were the safeguards necessarily adequate when reputedly first-class borrowers in the market, like Mersey Docks and Harbour Board and Rolls-Royce, collapsed in 1970 and 1971 respectively. Despite these general principles, it became obvious during the banking crisis in 1973–5 that not all accepting houses had been as prudent as they might have been in making advances, particularly to property companies.

Accepting houses were also exposed to the risks inherent in foreign exchange dealing since they have always been large operators in the foreign exchange markets. As with advances, attention was paid to the quality of the counterparty involved, since the soundness of the counterparty determined its ability to fulfil the contract. Regular credit reviews of potential counterparties were normal procedure for foreign exchange dealers, whether the business to be transacted was the purchase of foreign currency or re-depositing in order to gain the interest yield prior to settlement. As became abundantly clear during the crisis period between 1973 and 1975, banks can fail as easily as firms, and for this reason it was not unusual for an accepting house to spread its risk by re-depositing with several counterparties. In addition to counterparty risk, there is a country risk since, if a country exhausts its foreign exchange reserves, defaults or delay in payment can occur. This is considered in much greater detail in Chapter 8 in relation to the international debt crisis. Liquidity, too, was as great a problem in foreign exchange dealing as in sterling banking and accepting houses watched their nostro accounts (see page 214) and their over-bought or over-sold positions closely. In theory, accepting houses should always have been able to obtain the foreign currency they needed to satisfy their contracts, albeit at a price, but in practice banks have to accept the uncertainty that markets may close or may be one-way and that central banks may impose controls on foreign exchange transactions.

If, on the whole, accepting houses acted prudently during the period to mitigate the risks inherent in their type of banking, the same cannot be said of some of the other British non-clearing banks in the period up to 1975. The involvement of the banks in one particular sector of the market grew alarmingly. Although it is not possible to disentangle the accepting houses from the other non-clearing banks, we note (*Bank of England Quarterly Bulletin*) that advances to the non-bank financial sector by all non-clearing banks in the UK rose from 28 per cent of all advances in August 1968 to 46 per cent of the total by November 1973. The increase in lending to property companies (which are a part of the financial sector) was equally dramatic; in 1968 it took up 6 per cent of advances while by November 1973 this had risen to 13.6 per cent. This was at a time when the activities of the non-clearing banks were expanding rapidly anyway. Thus loans to property companies rose 4.8 times between August 1968 and November 1972 and a further 2.5 times between then and November 1973. If some banks pursued the cautious policies thought to have been adopted by most of the accepting houses and maintained their traditional role of financing trade and industrial investment, the implication is that other banks will have been very committed to a particular sector of the market. Property speculation has been common throughout history;[5] there was no reason to believe that investing in property had become safe although this argument was in fact made in the late 1960s and early 1970s. Some banks were prepared to indulge in this activity, which would generally be regarded as speculative, probably both because they were short-sighted and because they did not believe the risks were very great. They were prepared to pay higher and higher rates of interest on deposits in order to finance the speculation. Thus the increase in interest rates in July 1973 was not adequate to damp the speculation. The banks were perhaps being optimistic if they did not worry about the effect of rising interest rates on the value of their assets. But they probably also believed that they understood the market sufficiently well to withdraw from it before any crash would occur. In a market of this type the ability to refinance depends on the confidence of lenders. The sort of liquidity margin which is quite adequate to buffer day-to-day transactions becomes wholly inadequate in the situation the speculative banks faced as the crash came. The wholesale markets made speculation easy but once doubts about solvency started to arise, these banks were in a position in which they would rapidly become illiquid. The failure of these banks to act prudently has led to the Bank of England becoming much more actively involved (Chapter 3).

2.7 SUMMARY

Maturity-transforming institutions are exposed to the hazards of illiquidity and insolvency. The speculative operations of some of the British non-clearing banks led to both of these problems. The best explanation of observed behaviour in the period up to 1973 is that, while clearing banks and accepting houses understood the need for prudence, some of the other non-clearing banks did not. This was an important factor contributing to the banking crisis of 1973–5.

After the crisis a general air of prudence returned to the banking scene; the fraction of loans to property companies and other financial institutions diminished, not because these loans were wound down but more because prices generally rose in the economy. The other non-clearing banks remained much less liquid than the accepting houses, however, and some only returned to a position of solvency because a mixture of low interest rates and fairly rapid inflation over the period 1974–8 allowed them to make capital gains which repaid their losses. Arguably, as the figures of Table 2.4 suggest, they could still be vulnerable in the face of the general loss of confidence. More recently risks of bad debts have increased, particularly at the early stages of the recent depression. But this depression has not followed on from a speculative boom in one particular sector of the economy. Instead it affected a broad spread of industry, particularly manufacturing and construction. Although the banks have perhaps lent beyond limits which any individual bank might have regarded as prudent this is thought to have been done with the encouragement of the Bank of England. Losses have been spread over a wide range of institutions and not focused on specialist bodies, which had acquired an important place in the financial system. However the events leading up to the international debt crisis, discussed in Chapter 8, do illustrate again the way in which bankers can sometimes neglect the hazards of risk and uncertainty when pursuing an apparently profitable line of business.

3 Bank of England Control and Supervision

In each advanced industrialised country with a well-developed banking system, the central bank regulates both banking institutions and the flow of credit. The extent to which banks are supervised is greater than for any other sub-sector of the economy. It has gradually been recognised that, while competition and the operation of a free market generally may be desirable objectives, banking is somehow or other different. In most industries competition is encouraged because it is thought that, if the less efficient firms are forced out, the more efficient firms will survive and that this will lead in time to lower prices. But the same considerations do not apply to banks. It is believed that the social costs of failure outweigh any advantages that untramelled competition might bring. When a bank fails, it is not only its staff, its shareholders and its suppliers who suffer but also its depositors who risk losing their deposits. Moreover, only the banks can monetise debt and hence increase or decrease the credit base of the economy. This ability can clearly have macroeconomic implications of considerable importance.

Thus there are two quite distinct reasons for attempting to control the banking system.[1] One is to protect depositors from fraud, sharp practice and carelessness, and to maintain the reputation of the banking system by ensuring that depositors' money is safe. A second quite different one is in order to regulate, either the amount of credit in the economy and the sectors to which it is directed or, more recently, the stock of bank deposits in the economy in the belief that this may influence the level of activity or the price level. These two reasons have often been confused and it has not been clear which has motivated some of the policies adopted at various times; however, they both make it understandable that banks are supervised to a considerable extent. This chapter considers first the different categories of bank which have existed in the UK, and the prudential supervision to which they have been subjected at various times. It then continues by discussing regulations aimed at controlling the credit base or stock of money in the economy.

3.1 PRUDENTIAL REGULATION PRE–1979

The major part of domestic banking business since the establishment of a national banking system, has been carried out by the clearing banks, which have been monitored by the Bank of England for many years. However, banks have long existed outside the clearing system, playing important specialist roles in the economy. The British non-clearing banks at the start of the period with which we are dealing, comprised the members of the Accepting Houses' Committee, for whom a major part of business consisted of accepting and putting their names to commercial bills (Chapter 5), smaller merchant banks and other banks reporting to the Bank of England and therefore theoretically under the Bank's supervision; and a residue of financial institutions which had banking status but did not report to the Bank of England. The last-named group grew in numbers between 1960 and the early 1970s, from insignificance to some 100 or more. In 1975 a statistical change substantially further increased the number of banks in the last group. This change does not have any implications for the matters considered in this chapter. The reasons for the dichotomy between financial organisations accepted as banks so far as the Bank of England was concerned and those that were not were unique to the system of licensing and supervision operated in the United Kingdom prior to the Banking Act, 1979. The system was totally transformed by this Act.

Before the implementation of the Banking Act there were a series of steps needed for an institution to be regarded as a bank, and to advertise its services as banking services. These progressively gave that unit enhanced status. For most of the period

> any institution aspiring to become a bank [could] start a very basic banking business with no recognition at all, and aim to obtain over the years ahead the different recognitions and exemptions until eventually it would be accepted as a bank under every relevant Act, and would also be so regarded by the banking community. (British Bankers' Association, 1975).

The more important steps, starting with the minimum authorisation required, are set out below:

(a) The Board of Trade (as it then was) was empowered in 1966 to decide which 'banks' could be exempted from the provisions of the Money Lenders Acts, 1900–1927, whereby the 'bank' could reclaim loans even if it was not a licensed money lender nor classified as a bank under any other definition.

(b) Under Section 123 of the Companies Act, 1967, the Board of Trade was also empowered to issue certificates to 'banks' under (a), acknowledging them as bona fide banks solely for the purpose of the exemption mentioned. The Board of Trade certificate was conditional on such organisations fulfilling conditions laid down by the Board of Trade.

(c) Under Section 127 of the Companies Act, 1967, certain banks were exempted by the Board of Trade from the disclosure provisions of the Protection of Depositors Act, 1963, in advertising for deposits but the Board of Trade was *not* empowered to investigate or supervise the banks which it exempted.

(d) Under the Income and Corporation Taxes Act, 1970, a company had to be recognised as a bank by Inland Revenue before it could pay or receive interest gross of tax. This recognition usually followed the granting of a Section 123 certificate.

(e) Under Schedule 8 of the Companies Act, 1948, certain banks were permitted by the Registrar of Companies to maintain reserves which did not appear in their published accounts. Such banks always reported to the Bank of England and were subject to the Bank's supervision since they were clearly bona fide banks.

(f) Under the Exchange Control Act, 1947, a number of banks were authorised to deal in foreign exchange and to carry out functions delegated to them by the Bank of England. These banks were known as 'authorised banks'.

Many difficulties were created by this ramshackle system of authorisation. The Bank of England regarded itself as having a responsibility only for those banks which reported to it (initially those under (e) and (f) above). As the 1960s wore on, the Bank brought more banks into its reporting net, but at no time in the period did it regard itself as having any supervisory role as far as the Section 123 banks (those under (a) and (b)) were concerned. Indeed these banks were only recognised as such for the very narrow purpose of Money Lenders' Acts exemption.

The Bank's methods of control and supervision varied according to the financial institution concerned, and it only gradually extended its scrutiny over the banking sector as a whole. The impression that is given by the Bank of England's actions during the period before 1973 is that it reacted to events rather than anticipating them, but the extent to which this was due to indecision on the part of government rather than of the Bank is difficult to judge. Nevertheless, when swift response was needed, the Bank of England acted quickly and its efforts to prevent a major financial crisis in 1973 onwards and to reorganise itself to deal with the problems arising from the failure of some financial intermediaries were notably successful. For some non-clearing banks, in particular the accepting houses, the Bank of England maintained a watch on the composition of balance sheets through meetings between the Discount Office and the individual banks. This was presumably done with a view to ensuring that prudential limits were observed by those banks in the ratio of liabilities to assets and the composition of those liabilities and assets. The effectiveness of the supervision by the Bank of England of the non-clearing banks is debatable. In the discussions which regularly took place with representatives, of, say, the accepting houses, much depended on the information available to the Bank of England or disclosed to it by the banks. If the banks wished not to furnish details of the business which they regarded as sensitive, there was little that the Bank of England could do to elicit such information unless it was already aware of its existence. Furthermore, a former merchant banker has stated in discussion that there was no evidence that the statistical evidence furnished to the Bank of England, on the basis of which detailed investigations by the Bank might have been possible, was ever analysed and presented to those who were responsible for the periodic discussions with the non-clearing banks. In his view, these discussions were largely nugatory because the Discount Office did not possess the necessary information to probe effectively the financial viability of the non-clearing banks.

Even for those banks which made returns to the Bank of England, the Bank did not use such powers of inspection as it possessed. It could, under Section 4 of the Bank of England Act, 1946, direct a bank to make its books and records available for inspection, but such a power was never used. For banks which did not report to the Bank of England, particularly the Section 123 banks whose problems initiated the crisis in 1973, the Board of Trade theoretically had a supervisory responsibility but the department never had the resources adequate to undertake its duties. Hence, there was a fairly large number of financial organisations, enjoying some banking status including the power to advertise for deposits. They were neither supervised by nor made statistical returns to the Bank of England or to anyone else.

The situation in the United Kingdom compared unfavourably with the other countries in the European Economic Community. In each of these there was a banking law or corpus of banking laws governing the establishment and operation of financial units which were authorised to carry on the business of banking (British Bankers' Association, 1975). In most countries a licence was required before a bank could be established and in all countries *every* bank so established was subject to the control and supervision of a central agency, either the central bank or a commission/government department set up for the purpose. Inspections of banks were a regular feature in most countries, whether carried out as a routine matter or after reports had been made to the central agency by the banks' auditors. Liquidity or reserve ratios and controls over large advances were a normal feature of the supervisory system. This is not meant to imply that the arrangements for the supervision and control of banks in other EEC countries were by any means perfect. Weaknesses in the German system, for example, were revealed by the collapse of the Herstatt Bank and crises affecting other banks in 1974, and the German Banking Law of 1961 was amended after 1974 to increase the amount of information available to the central agency which was also given greater supervisory powers.

3.2 THE BANKING ACT, 1979

The 1979 Act was passed so as to allow the Bank of England to take the regulatory powers needed to ensure that a crisis like that of 1973–4 did not recur. It gave the Bank, for the first time, the formal power to supervise the banking system. It should perhaps be seen in the general regulatory environment, which is perhaps best summarised by the Gower Report (Gower, 1984) stating that regulation is necessary, 'to prevent reasonable people being made fools of, but not to protect fools from the consequences of their own folly'.

Walker (*Bank of England Quarterly Bulletin*, 1983c) summarises the methods of regulation which are available. He identifies three means. Restrictions have the effect of reducing freedom of choice, and these should be balanced against disclosure provisions which increase freedom of choice. But considerable reliance should be placed as far as possible on self-regulation and a desire of the institutions concerned to maintain their reputation.

In a banking perspective it is clear that the scope for disclosure is very limited. For individual depositors to assess whether a bank offered an unusually good return because it specialises in risky business, rather than because it is efficient, would require information about borrowers which is normally confidential, for obvious reasons. An excessive reliance on self-regulation was one of the factors which led to the 1973–5 banking crisis. So the balance inevitably falls on supervision and restriction.

The Act recognised two types of financial institution, banks and licensed deposit takers. The latter were allowed to take deposits but were not regarded as offering a sufficient range of services to be described as banks. They immediately began to acquire inferior status although the Bank repeatedly asserted that there was no reason why licensed deposit takers should have to pay more for their money than banks do. (A recent review suggests that this distinction be abolished (p. 168).)

The banks were to be subjected to a variety of 'controls' on their activities although these controls were couched in non-mandatory terms. They were designed to protect the banking system and individual banks from both insolvency and illiquidity. Any maturity transforming institution faces both of these hazards (Chapter 2); the guidelines of the Bank of England are designed to ensure that they never materialise on any significant scale, and to give early warnings of any incipient financial crisis. The proposals initially announced by the Bank of England suggested general liquidity ratios relating to particular types of liability. Thus deposits of no particular maturity such as current and 7-day deposit accounts would require liquid backing to 25 per cent of their value while interbank deposits of less than one month maturity would need 100 per cent backing. This latter requirement was designed to prevent the internal generation of liquidity in the banking system. Although there are occasions when the system as a whole is short of liquidity, perhaps because of large corporate tax payments to the government, there are also occasions when individual banks are short of liquidity. This second type of shortage can be met by reallocating liquidity from one part of the system to another provided questions of insolvency do not arise.

As noted in Chapter 2, banks' assets are of varying liquidity. It is not satisfactory to describe some as liquid and others as illiquid. The nearer a security is to maturity the greater its liquidity, and the Bank of England therefore proposed a weighting system where assets which are some way from maturity, and therefore have considerable scope for price variation, do not count towards the stock of liquidity at their full market value. Thus the value of gilts with a life of more than one but less than five years might be discounted by 5 per cent while gilts with a life of more than five years could be discounted by 10 per cent. The idea that different assets have different degrees of liquidity was noted by the Radcliffe Committee (Introduction, p. 3) but is formally used for the first time in this calculation; while the discounts are sensible in the light of the price volatility of the instruments, the weights adopted by the bank are arbitrary; even if based on working experience, they have little theoretical foundation.

The proposed general liquidity requirements advocated by the Bank met considerable opposition from the merchant banks who argued that the requirements suggested were suitable for a clearing bank with a large base of stable retail deposits, but was quite unsuited to the business of merchant banking. Banks, a large part of whose business was making markets in particular types of bond would have been particularly hard hit (*The Banker,* 1980). Thus the Bank withdrew the general liquidity requirement and instead settled for the imposition of requirements suited to the business of each institution, although it did hope to provide some general indicator of the liquidity of the banking system (*Bank of England Quarterly Bulletin,* 1981a).

The capital requirements proposed by the Bank of England (1980) were regarded as aiming:

1) to ensure that the capital position of an institution is regarded as acceptable by its depositors and other creditors
and
2) to test the adequacy of capital in relation to the risk of losses which may be sustained.

The Bank regards the first requirement as being tested by the ratio of free capital, L17+L27+L18−A111−A211 in Table 2.1, to deposits and non-capital liabilities, TL1+TL2−L17−L18−L27. This gearing ratio is typically of the order of 5 per cent for the major clearing banks. It can be calculated from published information. However it does not reflect the fact that the assets backing deposit liabilities may be very risky. The risk–asset ratio, constructed as the ratio of free capital plus premises to a risk-weighted sum of assets is designed to indicate riskiness. In principle the weights reflect price volatility or risk of default. Bank of England notes have a weight of zero, UK Treasury bills a weight of 0.1, advances a weight of 1 and property a weight of 2. This ratio cannot be calculated by the public. In any case it is only a rough guide because it does not take into account the quality of particular borrowers.

One concern arising from this emphasis on capital ratios is that it encourages 'asset-less' banking. If, instead of making advances, banks offer underwriting and guarantee services for which they receive fees, their capital ratios are raised, although they are taking on risks. Another arises from the popularity of subordinated loan capital, which is not available to meet losses in the same way as equity. Recently the Bank has encouraged the issue of what appear to be almost floating rate preference shares (perpetual loan capital) as a way of meeting this objection.

A third requirement is imposed on banks in order to take account of the particular hazards of foreign exchange and precious metal dealing (*Bank of England Quarterly Bulletin,* 1981b). For currencies can at times be quite as volatile as shares or other securities, which would normally only form a very small part of any bank's assets. Thus open positions in all foreign currencies are normally restricted to 15 per cent of a bank's capital base, while no single currency should be held to more than 10 per cent of the capital base. Special arrangements are made for foreign banks which make markets in 'exotic' currencies.

As well as giving the Bank of England power to supervise the banks in this way, the Act set up a fund, administered by senior officers of the Bank of England, to cover the losses of small depositors. A small levy has been made on recognised banks in order to raise a sum of just under £6 million which will be used to repay 75 per cent of deposits below £10 000 in the event of a banking failure. Noting that the 'lifeboat' (which consisted of loans rather than deposit compensation) reached £1200 million at its maximum, the fund does seem so small as to be insignificant, if a banking crisis occurs despite the precautions embodied in the supervision system.[2]

The Committee of London Clearing Bankers (1977), in their

evidence to the Committee to Review the Functioning of Financial Institutions, criticised this fund as an encouragement for an imprudent instititon 'to flourish, since it will be able to induce depositors to seek high returns without any regard for the associated risks'. Hirsch (1977) makes a similar and more general point, arguing that the provision of lender of last resort facilities which guarantee liquidity is also a stimulus to 'over-production' of banking services, in much the same way as a free health service may encourage unnecessary medical treatment.

On the other hand, it can be argued that, if there is no supervision the competitive outcome is unlikely to be optimal in any sense; over-production of banking may be better than an unregulated market. In any case a free market may, because of the hazards of banking, actually lead to underproduction. Certainly the provision of lender of last resort facilities, which guarantee the liquidity of solvent banks, is much more likely to lead to over-production than a deposit insurance fund. The fund protects depositors and not the institution. But the bankers employed by any particular bank will probably want to keep their jobs. Even where lender of last resort facilities exist, Bagehot (1873) thought that, provided the lender of last resort lends at a penal rate, this hazard too would be avoided.

In summary, therefore, before the implementation of the 1979 Banking Act, the British banks comprised the accepting houses, other banks reporting to the Bank of England and banks which were neither controlled nor supervised by the Bank. Since then all banks have been brought within one supervisory framework although a keynote of the framework has been flexibility, recognising the different characteristics of different types of banks. Those deposit-takers who are not recognisable banks are classified instead as licensed deposit-takers, but are still subject to the supervision of the Bank of England. The implementation of the Banking Act initially made slow progress due to late applications by a number of organisations wishing to be licensed as banks and the need for the Bank of England to investigate in detail the standing and soundness of the applicants – by early April 1980 only 241 institutions out of 610 on the Bank of England list had been approved (*Bank of England Annual Report,* 1980). Since 1980 the recognition procedure has speeded up, and by March 1985 there were 290 recognised banks and 315 licensed deposit takers. Of these 250 are overseas banks with UK branches (*Bank of England Annual Report*, 1985).

3.3 REGULATION OF THE CREDIT BASE AND THE MONEY STOCK

Central banks differ in the degree to which they act independently of the government in regulating credit conditions. There are two conflicting arguments. In favour of the greatest possible independence for the central bank is the argument that the political process in democratic societies tends to generate policies that are harmful to long-term welfare. Therefore the central bank should be isolated from the political scene and should be left to pursue the long-term objective of maintaining price stability. The contrary argument is that the loss function of the central bank should be the same as that of the elected government and that, since the financial community anyway enjoys excessive political power, the central bank should be exposed to political direction by the government. It is fair to say that, as might be expected, most central bankers desire the degree of independence which would allow them to pursue policies which their alleged non-partisan approach would favour. Nevertheless, it is difficult to envisage a central bank that would be allowed to adopt a policy stance radically different from that of the government of the day. As far as the United Kingdom is concerned, the Bank of England Act, 1946, section 4, provides that 'the Treasury may from time to time give such directions to the Bank as, after consultation with the Governor of the Bank, they think necessary in the public interest'. Power therefore resides in Treasury ministers although, so far as is known, such power has never been formally exercised.

3.4 CREDIT CONTROL IN THE 1960s

The conventional system of liquidity control gave the authorities the power to regulate both interest rates and the stock of money (Keynes, 1931).[3] Interest rates were related by convention to the bank rate in a rigid fashion (section 4.11). A minimum ratio of cash and balances with the Bank of England to deposits, gave control over the money stock. For the open-market sale of government stock led, directly or indirectly, to a fall in the cash balances of the clearing banks. The repayment of existing loans, happening all the time, was accompanied by a natural contraction in bank deposits; the contraction in cash balances prevented the banks making new advances. This then had the effect of constraining deposits. The system relied on free open market operations and thus implicitly a variable price for gilt-edged stock. It was more effective if the interest elasticity of demand for cash by the public was low; it also relied on a fringe of unsatisfied borrowers and the absence of arbitrage between different types of credit.

The controls imposed up to 1971 on the clearing banks by the Bank of England, which were intended to restrict the expansion of their lending, were of two kinds: (a) liquidity controls and (b) quantitative and qualitative controls. Both types of control were exercised through requests from the Governor of the Bank of England to the clearing banks (and, in the case of qualitative and quantitative controls, later to other banks) which, although not framed as formal directions under the Bank of England Act, 1946, had much the same force since the banks were anxious not to lose the goodwill of the Bank and knew that failure to comply with such requests could lead to more formal directions.[4] As far as liquidity controls were concerned, in 1960 the clearing banks were expected to maintain 8 per cent of deposits in the form of coin and notes in their tills and balances at the Bank of England, and a total of 30 per cent of deposits in the form of till money, cash balances with the Bank of England, money at call or short notice with the discount market, and commercial and British government Treasury bills. These liquidity ratios were those which the clearing banks had originally maintained as a matter of prudence and the request from the Bank of England did little more than regularise conventional practice. However, they had become transformed from a prudential regulation to an instrument available, at least in principle, for control of the credit base. Once a mandatory ratio was imposed, the liquid assets were no longer available to meet abnormal liquidity needs.

In 1963 the over-all liquidity ratio was reduced from 30 per cent to 28 per cent when, as the Governor of the Bank of England put it, the Bank desired 'to co-operate in ensuring that the banks are in a position to assist . . . to sustain the economic expansion that we wish to see at the present time' (*Bank of England Quarterly Bulletin*, 1963). Since only the clearing banks were controlled in the early 1960s, there was a natural tendency for non-clearing banks to fill the gap. But throughout the period up to 1971 they advanced a relatively small part of total bank lending. In 1971 lending by non-clearing banks to manufacturing and services was only just over one-quarter of clearing bank lending, and lending to the personal sector was only one-sixth of clearing bank advances. But non-clearing banks accounted for about one-third of new sterling lending to UK residents between 1960 and 1971. Rapid growth also occurred in lending overseas but this was probably done mainly by offices of foreign banks in London. It had relatively little to do with the domestic monetary scene.

In April 1960 the special deposits scheme was introduced by the Bank of England as a method of mopping up what the authorities regarded as excess liquidity in the economy. Banks were required to deposit a percentage of their deposits at the Bank of England. These special deposits earned interest but did not count as liquid assets and the system was thus similar to a variable reserve ratio. The special deposits scheme has remained in existence throughout the period since 1960, although deposits have not always been required. Morgan (1963), writing soon after the inception of the scheme, suggested that the Bank of England had finally discovered how to regulate the banking system without quantitative controls. But his view proved optimistic. The size of special deposits is shown in Figure 3.1. The non-clearing banks were not covered by the scheme initially, although they were warned that it might be extended to them if that proved necessary.

The policy of the authorities from 1960 until 1971 was directed towards an attempt to control the level of clearing bank advances, initially through liquidity constraints coupled with calls for special deposits, and later through limits on the growth and direction of lending. Special deposits were intended to absorb excess liquidity in the system but they were never called on a sufficient scale to make them an effective instrument. The clearing banks could always liquidate their holdings of gilt-edged securities to make up the difference. Requests to limit lending, which were associated with calls for special deposits were limited to sterling transactions. The public sector was excluded from lending ceilings as were shipbuilding credits and export finance in the first six months of 1968 and again after November 1968. There is little doubt, however, that the authorities were hampered in their policies by conflicts between targets and instruments. The orthodox view in the mid-1960s has been described much as follows (Fletcher, 1976). If the authorities wished to control long and short interest rates, the money supply would be perfectly elastic at the chosen rates. If they wished to control the money supply, they would have either to abandon interest rate stabilisation of market interest rates and operate on the supply of cash or Treasury bills or any other nominal quantity they chose. The

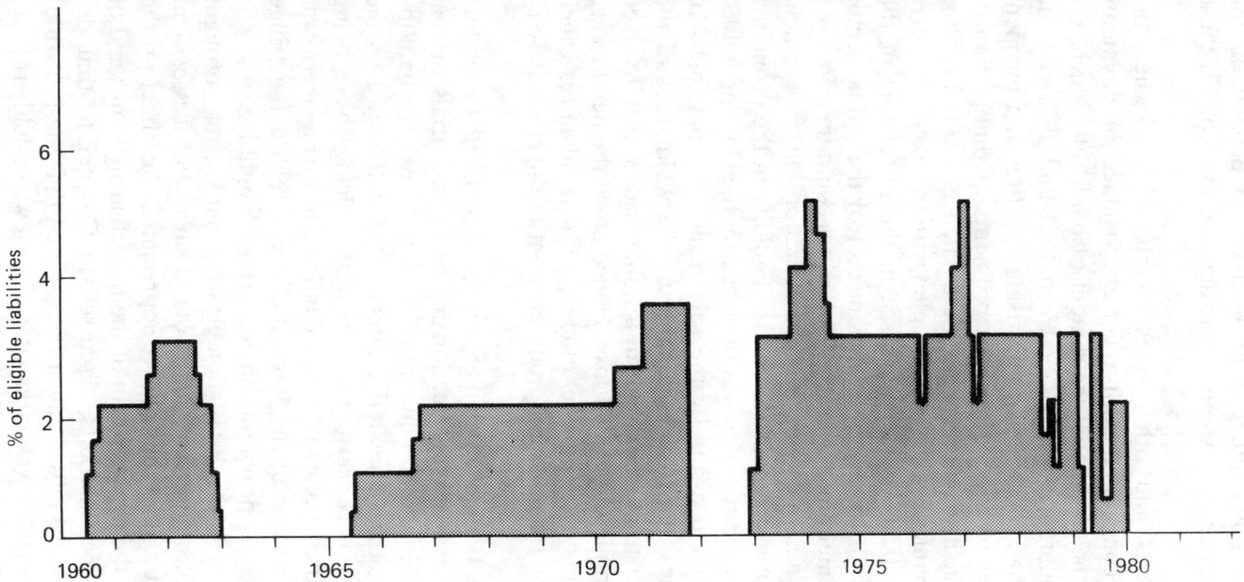

FIGURE 3.1 *Special deposits from 1960*

NOTE These are the special deposits of the London clearing banks. Until 1972 none were levied on the non-clearing banks, and before 1965 a lower rate was imposed on Scottish banks.

precision of the control and the size of the multiplier linking the money stock to the magnitude controlled would depend on the predictability and interest elasticity of the demand function for those assets.

But interest rates had other roles to play. Thus, when the authorities were confronted with recurrent balance of payments crises, they used the traditional instrument of bank rate which was changed on 40 separate occasions between 1951 and 1971. At the same time, they had to face periodic rising inflation and incipient recession. In order to cope with these problems a combination of fiscal and monetary instruments were used. Their desire to limit the rate of growth of bank advances was coupled with the need for a level of interest rates which would both assist in the re-funding of the national debt and also keep the recurrent cost of the public sector borrowing requirement in check. The authorities could therefore use neither interest rates nor open market operations in government stock as their main instruments to control liquidity in the economy, whilst the use of liquidity ratios was thwarted by the clearing banks' ability to create liquid assets by the sale from their portfolios of gilt-edged securities, itself made possible by the willingness of the government broker to purchase gilts at a stable price which involved the banks in the minimum capital loss. Hence arose the need to use quantitative controls over the level of clearing bank advances which were believed to be the most important element in the credit base of the economy.

A request by the Bank of England to banks in the United Kingdom not to make advances for speculation in shares, materials or real estate was made in 1958 when quantitative controls over the banking system were lifted; it was repeated at intervals thereafter. In 1961 the Bank of England was concerned that bills of exchange were being used to frustrate their policy of credit control and this concern was repeated in 1962 and again in 1965; it did not regard the fringe non-clearing banks as providing an important loophole.

From 1965 onwards the listed non-clearing banks were brought within the scope of quantitative limits on advances but it is evident that the Bank of England only slowly appreciated the effect on the financial sector of the rapid growth of the non-clearing banks and of the competing money markets, discussed in Chapter 6, that developed from the late 1950s. It must be assumed that the growth of the local authority market was anticipated since it was a deliberate act of policy by the authorities that brought the market into being in the mid-1950s. The local authority market developed in parallel with the discount market and differed radically from the interbank market since all borrowing, although not financing self-liquidating transactions, was backed by local rates. But the consequences of the development of a huge market in which the non-clearing banks freely loaned to and borrowed from each other without security, in sterling and other currencies, was probably not appreciated by the Bank of England until late in the 1960s.

In 1965 the Bank requested all listed banks to restrict their lending for the year to March 1966 to a level no higher than 105 per cent of that for the financial year to March 1965. The accepting houses were concerned to know if advances and acceptances were to be aggregated for the purposes of the limit on lending, since acceptances were not only a very important part of their over-all business but were also, in their view, a necessary facility for the development of trade. By the autumn of 1965 it was evident that acceptances had risen materially, and the Bank of England reiterated its concern that lending limits were being evaded. It was explained that the reason for the increase in acceptances was that lines of credit had been extended and that this had inevitably led to an increase in commitments, which couldn't be refused. The Bank of England insisted, however, that advances and acceptances must be aggregated if its credit rationing policy was to succeed. In February 1967 the Bank issued a further request that advances, acceptances and the holding of commercial bills should not be allowed to rise above the March 1966 levels.

By 1967 the Bank of England, clearly by now concerned at the rapid growth of British non-clearing banks,[5] had decided that a more comprehensive system of control over these banks was needed than the *ad hoc* requests to limit lending to specified levels. In April 1967 the Bank announced that quantitative controls over lending would be removed once acceptable alternative arrangements were worked out. By February 1968 those alternative arrangements had been devised and were proposed to the listed non-clearing banks. The objective of the new scheme was described by the Bank of England in the following terms:

> to secure an adequate degree of official influence over lending in sterling by banks operating in the United Kingdom (other than the clearing and Scottish banks covered by the special deposits scheme) to customers in the United Kingdom private sector and overseas, in situations where some restraint is required but a rigid

quantitative ceiling is not thought appropriate. (*Bank of England Quarterly Bulletin,* 1968a)

The reason for the introduction of the scheme was explained as the rapid growth in lending by the 'other banks'. In the light of the substantial increase in the importance of the non-clearing banks, ceilings on lending could not be cast aside without an effective system of control in their place. But because there was so much diversity amongst non-clearing banks, a common liquidity ratio similar to that observed by the clearing banks would not be a suitable method of control. Instead, the Bank of England proposed a system of variable cash deposits which the non-clearing banks would place with the Bank; a decision would be made at the time whether or not interest would be paid on such deposits. In preliminary discussions during 1967, the Bank of England suggested that, if interest was to be paid, it would probably be materially below the Treasury bill rate. The cash deposits were to represent percentages of (i) sterling deposit liabilities of United Kingdom residents; (ii) sterling deposits of overseas residents and (iii) foreign currency deposits to the extent that they were switched into sterling. The percentages might be uniform for all banks but the Bank of England reserved the right to apply differing percentages if this were considered appropriate.

The accepting houses did not welcome the scheme with open arms since they saw it as a tax on their profits if the interest paid, if any, on cash deposits was a penal one, and as a possible means of driving deposits away from the 'listed' banks to those banks which were not supervised and controlled by the Bank of England. The merchant banks were not opposed in principle to a more effective control over bank lending, but they were concerned that any scheme introduced should be a workable one and, in particular, should be applicable to *all* non-clearing banks including those not reporting to the Bank of England. The Bank's reply was that some similar scheme would be worked out for the 'non-listed' banks and for hire purchase companies as soon as practicable. After discussions between the Bank of England and the non-clearing banks, it had been agreed by the beginning of 1968 that interest on cash deposits would be paid at the Treasury bill rate provided that restraint was exercised over bank lending. The Bank was anxious that the scheme should be formalised as soon as possible but, in the time between proposing the scheme and agreement on its provisions, the economic situation had worsened and quantitative controls on bank lending were reimposed late in 1967, as part of the economic package associated with devaluation. In this climate the introduction of the cash deposits scheme, under which quantitative controls would be abolished, had to be postponed.

By 1970 the financial position had recovered; there was a budget surplus and the balance of payments deficit had been eliminated. A Conservative government was returned to power in 1970 with different financial objectives from those of the preceding Labour government and in these circumstances it was perhaps inevitable that the cash deposits scheme was not disinterred. As early as the autumn of 1969, lending by the clearing banks was exceeding the ceiling laid down by the Bank of England, but in February 1970 the Bank reported that the authorities were taking a lenient view of the excess. In April 1971 the new Chancellor of the Exchequer referred in his budget speech to the need for a gradual and moderate increase in bank lending in order to reflate the economy which was showing signs of recession. The accepting houses welcomed the slight easing of credit rationing but were still unhappy at what they regarded as the discriminatory treatment of fine bank bills of exchange which the Bank of England insisted on interpreting as advances. The merchant banks argued that the result was that the clearing banks were deprived of access to bills from the discount market causing the cost of borrowing by traditional bill finance to rise steeply above the cost of clearing bank overdrafts. The Bank of England was not convinced by these arguments.

3.5 COMPETITION AND CREDIT CONTROL

In May 1971 the Bank of England announced the proposals (*Bank of England Quarterly Bulletin*, 1971a) which they called 'Competition and Credit Control' and which replaced the cash deposits scheme put into cold storage in 1968. Competition and credit control was designed to apply to all listed banks; it replaced the liquidity ratio requirements imposed on the clearing banks and the quantitative controls imposed on all listed banks by a new system under which all reporting banks were to maintain a minimum of defined reserve assets at a level in value of 12.5 per cent of defined eligible liabilities. Reserve assets as finally defined were to comprise:

(i) Balances held at the Bank of England (to at least 1.5 per cent of London Clearing Bank eligible liabilities).

(ii) Treasury bills.
(iii) Tax reserve certificates.
(iv) Secured money at call with the London money market.
(v) Government stocks with one year or less to run to maturity.
(vi) Local authority bills eligible for discount at the Bank of England.
(vii) Commercial bills eligible for discount at the Bank of England up to 2 per cent of eligible liabilities.

Eligible liabilities were defined as:

(i) All sterling deposits of an original maturity of two years or less from UK residents other than banks, and from overseas residents other than overseas offices.
(ii) Sterling deposits from, less sterling claims against, banks in the UK.
(iii) Sterling CDs issued, less sterling CDs held.
(iv) The net deposit liability in sterling to overseas offices.
(v) The net liability in currencies other than sterling.
(vi) A reduction equivalent to 60 per cent of the net value of items in transit.

The scheme was to come into operation as soon as possible. Banks needed time to re-arrange their portfolios of assets and liabilities to meet the reserve asset requirements.

The purpose of competition and credit control was fourfold. First, it replaced control of the money supply through quantitative controls over bank lending by control through price. The Bank of England had become convinced by the standard economic arguments against rationing, including credit rationing, namely that it merely creates black markets in which portfolios can be re-arranged, new markets can be developed and disintermediation can be introduced, thwarting the desired economic effect. As the Governor of the Bank of England said in his address to the International Banking Conference in Munich on 25 May 1971:

> It is obvious that physical rationing . . . can lead to a serious misallocation of resources, both in the economy and the financial system, and that inhibiting competition between banks can do much damage to the vigour and vitality of the entire banking system . . . Basically what we have in mind is a system under which

allocation of credit is primarily achieved by its cost [and in which] we expect to achieve our objectives through market means. (*Bank of England Quarterly Bulletin,* 1971b)

The mechanism of credit control was thus to be an adjustment of the marginal cost of banks' funds which, it was assumed, would lead the banks as good profit maximisers to increase lending rates until marginal revenue was equated with marginal cost. Secondly, it allowed the clearing banks to compete more freely with the non-clearing banks and it encouraged them to compete directly with each other. Thirdly, it revived the role of the discount market, which had been downgraded by the development of rival money markets, by defining reserve assets as those in which the discount market dealt. Fourthly, it brought all listed banks directly under the control and supervision of the Bank of England through the formal and uniform imposition of a reserve assets : liabilities ratio. Goodhart (1984, Chapter 3) discusses the aims and problems of competition and credit control in detail.

The clearing banks felt that the proposals discriminated against them because they were not allowed to count till money as a reserve asset. The accepting houses, and no doubt some other non-clearing banks, also viewed the competition and credit control proposals with some concern. Their reasons were that (a) they wished to be satisfied regarding the technical treatment of interbank transactions and certificates of deposit, (b) they were not convinced that a uniform 12.5 per cent ratio should be applied to all listed banks, and (c) they were not happy about the exclusion from the proposals of the non-reporting banks. On (a), discussions with the Bank of England resolved the interpretative points at issue although not necessarily to the satisfaction of the accepting houses. On (b), the merchant banks pointed to the wide range of reserve assets ratios for different banks and suggested that a uniform ratio of 12.5 per cent would probably be too low for the clearing banks and too high for some accepting houses which would need to switch assets in order to conform, a costly and time-consuming exercise. The Bank of England, however, regarded a uniform reserve assets ratio which would be observed by all reporting banks as an essential feature of the proposals and argued that, according to the information at its disposal, the over-all average ratio for all listed banks was of the order of 12.5 per cent. This decision by the Bank appeared to be at variance with its view in 1968, when the cash deposit scheme was being discussed, that a uniform liquidity ratio was inapplicable to the non-clearing banks. On (c), the accepting houses wanted all banks, listed or not, to be brought into the scheme when competition and credit control was introduced, since the non-listed banks had grown fast and represented a danger to the stability of the banking sector. The Bank of England's reply was that (i) 'at the appropriate time, these [fringe] banks would have to be brought into the list of banks comprising the banking sector' and (ii) the non-listed banks might well be driven out of existence by the increased competition which the clearing banks and other listed banks would be able to offer. By September 1971 discussions on competition and credit control had been completed, if not to everyone's satisfaction, and the scheme was introduced.

There is no reason to doubt that, on the information available to it, the Bank of England believed that the arithmetical average of the reserve assets held by all listed banks represented about 12.5 per cent of eligible liabilities. However, the dispersion around the mean was wide, as the accepting houses explained to the Bank of England, and it seems that the Bank did not realise that, by adopting a uniform reserve assets ratio, it was inevitably creating a situation in which the ratio would considerably exceed the mean when the scheme was introduced. This created a situation in which an expansion of credit was likely. The reason was the fairly obvious one that those banks whose reserve assets fell short of the minimum of 12.5 per cent of eligible liabilities would ensure that they so re-arranged their portfolios as to ensure that they met the criterion whilst those with reserve ratios above the minimum laid down would need to make no adjustment. For example, a decided weakness in competition and credit control was that it was comparatively easy to increase reserve assets, despite the constraint on the discount houses described below.[6] Certificates of deposit could be issued and used as security for money placed with the discount market, or government stock with more than one year to maturity could be exchanged with the discount market for stock with less than one year to run. Individual banks could also reduce their eligible liabilities by increased lending in the interbank market.

The extent to which competition and credit control allowed a multiple expansion of bank credit to take place without any change in the over-all stock of marketable public sector floating debt (Treasury bills, balances of the Bank of England, gilts with life of less than a year and local authority bills) is discussed in Chapter 4. It may be, of course, that the authorities viewed the increased scope for bank lending with a degree of equanimity, bearing in mind the government's policy of economic expansion.

The reforms of competition and credit control also affected the discount houses. Since money at call in the discount market counted as a reserve asset, any reserve ratio system of monetary control would need an anchor in the discount market in order to be effective. Otherwise a multiple expansion in the discount market could circumvent the restraint which ought to be implied by a constraint on the stock of other reserve assets. When competition and credit control started the discount houses were regulated by means of a public sector lending ratio, whereby at least 50 per cent of borrowed funds had to be invested in certain public sector debt. This public sector debt included gilts with a life of less than five years and local authority deposits as well as the types of public sector debt which are reserve assets to the banks. Thus a bank which found itself short of reserve assets was able to create extra reserves by selling gilts with a life of between one and five years to the discount houses. Furthermore, the substitution of call money for shorter gilts or Treasury bills effectively doubled their reserve capacity; any increase by the discount houses in their holdings of public debt allowed them to increase their call money liabilities by twice the amount. The reserve base of the banking system was therefore considerably larger than a simple analysis of the reserves of the banks themselves suggests. A further engine for the creation of reserve assets was to be found in the shift of deposits with discount houses from time deposits to call money. This shortening of maturity was possible without conflicting with the public sector debt ratio although, of course, it left the discount market exposed to the risk of an increase in interest rates. For the yield on the assets of the discount houses would then be slower to adjust than those of their liabilities.

The requirement of a 50 per cent public sector debt ratio was found unsatisfactory, both from the point of view of the discount houses and of the Bank of England. In August 1973 an alternative procedure was introduced. The amount that discount houses were allowed to invest in assets, excluding those which had counted as public sector debt, was limited to a maximum of 20 times their capital base. This 'undefined assets multiple', as it was called, was in fact rather volatile and, in the face of large purchases of commercial bills by the discount houses was surpassed in 1982 (after competition and credit control had been abolished). A level of 21.4 was reached.

Competition and credit control was introduced at a time almost unique in Britain's post-war economic history (Gowland, 1978). There was a strong balance of payments, low international interest rates, a domestic economy which the government believed required a stimulus and a growing belief that a competitive market would lead to the efficient allocation and use of resources. The removal of quantitative controls over bank lending was a necessary corollary of a freely competitive market in which the original intention was that interest rates would find their own level. In place of bank rate, the new minimum lending rate was specifically designed to follow the market level of Treasury bill rates. With the clearing banks able to compete as both borrowers and lenders more directly in the wholesale money markets, these markets expanded considerably and this made the task of the non-clearing banks in obtaining deposits easier rather than more difficult. And it became clear that the Bank of England's belief that the non-listed banks on the fringe of banking would wither away was singularly ill-founded; the non-listed banks were able to obtain all the funds they needed quite easily after competition and credit control because there was so much money seeking a home that the higher interest rates which the non-listed banks offered to money brokers were a sufficient inducement to direct funds in their direction. As the monetary expansion of competition and credit control gathered pace the authorities responded by traditional calls for special deposits. But these had the effect of pushing up rates in the parallel markets (Chapter 6) and did not restrain the growth in bank credit.

The traditional system of monetary control (section 3.4) no longer worked, because competition and credit control removed the rationing mechanism. Rates on wholesale deposits were bid up when the authorities tried to tighten monetary conditions. So high interest rates had no effect (or perhaps a perverse effect) on the demand for money, and only operated on the stock of money through their effect on the demand for bank credit. This effect was by no means precise and, as noted earlier (section 1.3), could also be perverse in the short run.

The substantial increase in the £M3 definition of the money supply (of 26 per cent in 1972 and 27 per cent in 1973), which so alarmed both the authorities and commentators, may not have reflected the true position. There was a substantial divergence between the M1 and £M3 rates of increase, as Figure 1.2 (p. 11) shows, and this may have been due to a number of factors, including the following:

(a) There was probably a switch from demand deposits and from deposits with non-monetary institutions to time deposits as interest rates on money rose, reducing M1.
(b) The constraints on bank lending prior to competition and credit control may have encouraged substantially more inter-company loans than most estimates suggest, loans which reverted to the banks when lending ceilings were abolished.
(c) Competition and credit control encouraged major banks to attract wholesale deposits at market rates of interest. This encouraged investors to hold more rather than less money at a time of higher interest rates, and was an entirely new phenomenon.
(d) The expectation that ceilings on bank lending would be reintroduced as inflation gathered pace may have induced customers of the banks, as a precaution, to borrow to the limit of their credit facilities.
(e) A perverse relationship developed between bank borrowing and market lending rates (Chapter 6). This may have encouraged corporate treasurers to borrow on overdraft and re-invest the proceeds in, say, certificates of deposit.

The last four factors resulted in the £M3 definition of the money supply in the period from 1971 to 1975 being a poor indicator. Indeed, Morgan Grenfell estimated that the published £M3 growth may have been inflated by as much as 50 per cent (*The Economist,* 18 May 1974), although this seems an unduly high estimate in view of the relative size of the factors involved. What appears to be certain is that, as Artis (1978) has suggested, 'the most likely explanation seems to be that, following the release of controls, a large part of the expansion in bank advances accommodated a reshuffling of asset (and debt) portfolios, which involved the substitution of bank credit for less preferred forms of debt'. This was made possible by the existence of a variety of markets which allowed financial intermediaries to exploit the suppressed demand for credit which existed in the economy. 'For all banks operating under competition and credit control the way to boost bank profits was to lend as much money to as many borrowers as possible. More and more of this lending was carried out by non-clearing banks' (Johnson, 1977).

3.6 THE SUPPLEMENTARY SPECIAL DEPOSITS SCHEME

The monetary expansion made possible by competition and credit control finally led to action in December 1973 when the Bank of England imposed the supplementary special deposits scheme. This scheme, described initially in the *Bank of England Quarterly Bulletin,* (1974) and more fully considered in an obituary notice (*Bank of England Quarterly Bulletin,* 1982a), operated by requiring banks to make non-interest-bearing deposits with the Bank of England if their interest-bearing deposits grew at more than a specified rate. Such a deposit imposed a penalty on any bank which took in too much business and thus tended to restrain periods of rapid monetary growth. It was recognised that it would tend to inhibit the competition which competition and credit control was designed to promote, but since it was hoped that the scheme would only operate for short periods this was not considered to be a major disadvantage. The 'corset' as the scheme rapidly became known was thought to be less distortionary than various other approaches to monetary restraint. Interest rate ceilings were thought to have considerable drawbacks and were not regarded as a viable alternative.

Although the scheme was intended to be short lived, it in fact operated for four of the next six and a half years before its final abolition in June 1980. The growth rates allowed by the scheme in the various periods of operation over the stock of deposits in the base period are shown in Table 3.1. A comparison with the growth rate in money GDP over the same period gives an indication of the tightness of the corset on each occasion.

TABLE 3.1 *The supplementary special deposits scheme*

Period	*Growth rate in interest-bearing eligible liabilities*	*Monthly growth rate in money GDP (%)*
Dec. 1973 – Feb. 1975	8% over first six months then 1.5% per month	1.7
Nov. 1976 – Aug. 1977	3% over first six months then 0.5% per month	1.1
June 1978 – June 1980	4% over Aug.–Oct 1978 then 1% per month	1.3

SOURCE *Bank of England Quarterly Bulletin,* 1982a.

The penalty itself was on a sliding scale. Until November 1974 banks had to make a supplementary deposit of 5 per cent of any excess of up to 1 per cent of interest-bearing eligible liabilities. A 25 per cent deposit was required on an excess of between 1 per cent and 3 per cent while an excess over 3 per cent required a 50 per cent deposit. After November 1974 the boundaries were raised from 1 to 3 per cent and 3 to 5 per cent but the scheme was otherwise unaltered.

The corset was lifted in February 1975 as speculative demand for credit eased and, with the revival in the stock market, other capital markets reopened. It was reimposed in November 1976 as part of the measures adopted to end the run on sterling and lifted in August 1977 after a sharp change in Britain's external position. Finally it was reimposed in August 1978, because monetary expansion appeared excessive, and not as a consequence of any external pressure. Not until 1980 did it lead to significant supplementary deposits at the Bank of England. By then its life was expected to be short, and banks probably did not mind paying a penalty for a while, in order to retain business which would outlast the corset.

When the financial system was well stocked with reserve assets the corset had little effect because banks were allowed to offset against their interest-bearing eligible liabilities deposits with other banks and deposits with discount houses, provided these were not reserve assets. Thus, provided they had adequate reserves, they could turn call money into time deposits, with the discount houses generating room to take in extra deposits which would finance extra lending. But this could not go on indefinitely because the discount houses were constrained, in the end, by the undefined assets multiple, which limited the ability of the system as a whole to generate reserves. Thus the corset was often operated in conjunction with the special deposits scheme (a means of draining excess reserves) to ensure that it was able to bite. For most of the four years from 1974 to 1978 the special deposit call was held at 3 per cent. Reductions were made when banks were expected to be short of liquidity, for example, because of seasonal tax payments. And in 1976 the call was briefly raised to 6 per cent as part of the measures designed to arrest the fall in sterling. From mid-1979 to mid-1980 the level was reduced to 2 per cent and deposits were then repaid in order to facilitate the short-term corporate borrowing made necessary by high interest rates and the depression.

The efficacy of the corset is difficult to judge. It does appear to have retarded the growth of interest-bearing eligible liabilities, but there is thought to have been considerable disintermediation; the most important means was the 'bill leak' whereby banks accepted bills of large firms and marketed them with the same ease as certificates of deposit. This leak grew to £2700 million in the first quarter of 1980 when interest-bearing eligible liabilities were around £35 000 million. There will also have been other forms of disintermediation such as a market in trade bills which had not been accepted by any bank, but these were unlikely to have been so important. The abolition of exchange controls in October 1979 allowed banks to book all excess deposits offshore; it is not clear how much was driven offshore but in any case freedom of capital movement made the corset unworkable and it was abolished in June 1980.

In retrospect, most commentators would agree that competition and credit control did not work well; the Bank of England announced its abandonment from 20 August 1981. The major reason for the failure was that success depended on the existence of an elastic and stable demand function for credit for which there was no econometric or other evidence. All demand for money regressions produced for periods before 1970 consistently under-predicted demand post-1970, and both the supply of, and the demand for, money proved inelastic in relation to actual changes in interest rates (Goodhart, 1984, Chapter 3). There was, for example, a marked increase in the velocity of circulation of money over the period before 1971 (Figure 1.2, Chapter 1). Brown (1983) draws attention to the extent to which velocity of circulation is variable both cyclically and over long periods.

Moreover, the theoretical view that banks will try to maximise profits by equating marginal revenue and marginal cost is not the way in which banks act in practice by trading-off balance sheet size liquidity, risk and expected return. The Bank of England believed that an increase in the cost of funds to banks would correspondingly lead to an increase in lending rates. It could influence this through the discount market in which call money was an essential element of reserve assets. But the major banks were always prepared to take on additional business in order to increase their market share, and the marginal cost of such business to the clearing banks fell as base rates rose due to the endowment factor of current account deposits.

The purpose of the reserve asset ratio is still not entirely clear. In its paper on 'Competition and Credit Control' issued on 14 May 1971, the Bank of England stated that 'the minimum reserve assets ratio is intended to provide the authorities with a known firm base for the operation of monetary policy'. But in a Green Paper (*Monetary Control,* 1980) on monetary control, the Bank affirmed that:

> the choice of definition (of qualifying reserve assets) reflected the decision not to seek to control strictly the supply of reserve assets. The lack of control has not been of particular concern because . . . the authorities regard the datum point of control over short-term interest rates as being the 1.5 per cent of their eligible liabilities kept by the London Clearing Banks at the Bank of England.

The best explanation is perhaps that offered by Moran (1984, Chapter 3). The magnitude and composition of the reserve requirement was determined by political forces rather than by any economic logic.

Perhaps the circumstances surrounding the introduction of competition and credit control were unfortunate. It began at a time when there was a political reluctance to raise interest rates as a major boom developed. So the end of quantitive controls and the cartel were not replaced by any other active means of control. There is always the possibility that the authorities believed that the reserve asset ratio gave them control in rather the same way as the old liquidity ratios could have. But subsequently, in Chapter 4, the ability of the system to generate its own reserves is clearly demonstrated.

3.7 MONETARY CONTROL IN THE 1980s

At the time the corset was abolished there was much discussion of an appropriate means of monetary control. The discussion was stimulated by the Green Paper (*Monetary Control*) of March 1980. Monetary control was no longer seen as important because of the need to restrict credit (which had been the Radcliffe position) but because there was believed to be a clear link between the money stock and the price level. The debate thus became considerably heightened in importance, given the inflationary experience of the 1970s.

The Green Paper essentially compared a system of control of the monetary base as against an alternative whereby interest rates were used as a control mechanism. The Treasury and Civil Service Committee (1980) received a wide body of evidence considering the consequences and the mechanisms of monetary control. Friedman

(1980) and Minford (1980) argued strongly the case for monetary control as a means of reducing inflation and supported the idea that the money stock should be regulated through control of the monetary base, the sum of coin, Bank of England notes and bank deposits at the Bank of England. The idea that there is a stable relationship between the monetary base and the money stock is an old one, which can be traced back to Ricardo (1809). But Kaldor (1981), in his critique of both monetarism and monetary base control, pointed out that there is a large stock of banknotes held outside the banks. Since the ratio of monetary base held by the banks to bank deposits is necessarily low, bank deposits can expand considerably if notes held outside the banks return to the banking sector. There is no reason for the aggregate relationship between the money stock and the monetary base to be well-defined. Furthermore, the adoption of monetary base control would imply that the Bank of England was abandoning its role as lender of last resort. Such a move would be likely to add to financial instability.

The alternative scheme mentioned by the Green Paper relies on the use of interest rates to control the stock of money. High interest rates are intended to restrict the demand for money and thus control the stock of money. As noted in Chapter 1, the effect of high rates can be perverse in at least the short run and this mechanism will at best work imperfectly. But an associated policy of debt management may allow the short-term control of the money stock to proceed reasonably smoothly (Coleby, 1982).

This approach was in fact adopted by the Bank of England (*Bank of England Quarterly Bulletin,* 1981c), which believed a small cash ratio requirement was adequate to rapidly enforce changes in interest rates, by generating cash shortages and forcing the banks to borrow at higher interest rates. Banks and licensed deposit takers were therefore required to hold cash equal to 0.5 per cent of their eligible liabilities. Those banks whose bills were eligible (see below and Chapter 5) for rediscount at the Bank of England were also required to hold an average of 6 per cent and a minimum of 4 per cent of their eligible liabilities in the London discount market. The new system began on 20 August 1981. From 18 August 1983 it was amended. The average ratio of funds held on the discount market was reduced to 5 per cent with a minimum of 2.5 per cent because it was felt (*Bank of England Quarterly Bulletin,* 1983b) that rapid growth in eligible liabilities led to excess funds being deposited on the discount market, and this forced the depositors to accept poor interest rates.

An essential feature of monetary control turned out to be overfunding. This implied that the Bank of England sold more long-term debt than was needed to cover the budget deficit. With the balance it bought commercial bills. It thereby lent to commercial borrowers directly. This reduced bank lending and therefore eased pressure on the money supply (Bain, 1982). Overfunding has been carried on to such an extent that much of the Bank of England note issue is now secured on commercial bills instead of government paper.

Fortunately the Bank was able to effect this change of policy easily. For many years it had undertaken to rediscount, at the bank rate, bills underwritten by the accepting houses. In 1979, in order to comply with EEC regulations, this facility was extended to any bank which could show that its bills traded at only a small discount on Treasury bills. This created plenty of scope for the Bank of England to take over bank lending by discounting accepted bills. However, as the table below shows, scope for overfunding within the traditional framework is limited by the size of the note issue.

TABLE 3.2 *Issue department of the Bank of England, 1981–4*

£million	*Liabilities* *Notes issued*	*Assets* *Government securities*	*Other securities*
September 1981	10 675	8 740	1 935
December 1981	11 025	6 329	4 696
December 1982	11 275	3 217	8 058
December 1983	12 160	4 699	7 461
December 1984	12 620	1 888	10 732

SOURCE *Bank of England Quarterly Bulletin.*

Until the passing of the 1982 Finance Act there was no other convenient mechanism by which overfunding could take place. This Act allowed the banking department of the Bank of England to hold commercial bills as security for deposits by the National Loans Fund. Such deposits would typically arise if gilts were issued in excess of any budgetary need. This mechanism offers unlimited scope for overfunding. Deposits by the public sector have, since 1982, not been included in measures of the money supply; overfunding can therefore be used as a means of financing commercial borrowing without disturbing the monetary statistics. The mechanism was used in the spring of 1983 and 1984 when tax payments made the banking system very short of cash. But in the first half of 1985 public sector deposits with the banking department (including National Loans Fund deposits) averaged £4993 million compared with £412 million in the first half of the previous year. Banking department bill holdings seem to have become a permanent feature of the monetary scene.

In October 1985 an end to overfunding was announced together with the suspension of a target for £M3. Any attempt to reduce the 'bill mountain' will lead to an increase in the money stock. It is not obvious that the real economy will be much affected if households hold their wealth in bank deposits instead of long-term securities.

3.8 SUMMARY

This survey of Bank of England regulation may be summarised by observing that the monetary policy of the authorities in the period from 1960 to the introduction of competition and credit control in 1971 rested on the assumed dominance of the clearing banks and the discount market in the transmission mechanism. The control of credit could not be implemented solely through liquidity ratios imposed on the clearing banks because there was not, as the Radcliffe Committee had assumed, a strong causal relationship between the supply of Treasury bills and the quantity of bank deposit liabilities (Crouch, 1964). An active resale market in Treasury bills provided liquid assets for the clearing banks outside the allocation of bills at the weekly tender by the Bank of England, whilst the increasing availability of commercial bills and call money for the discount market diminished the importance of Treasury bills issued as an instrument of control. The clearing banks could increase their holdings of liquid assets much more easily than the orthodox control mechanism suggested and, if the authorities wished to impose credit rationing, direct controls on bank lending were necessary. Hence, quantitative ceilings were imposed on clearing bank advances, and extended in 1965 to non-clearing banks. Throughout the period up to 1971, monetary policy was directed towards controlling credit flows in various sectors of the economy. The Radcliffe Committee had assumed that monetary policy would be mainly permissive with severe shocks administered only in an emergency. But the economic problems of balance of payments deficits and inflation were becoming more and more difficult to solve. The authorities decided that it was necessary to maintain stringent controls on credit expansion and for this purpose interest rates were ineffective for two main reasons. First, short-term interest rates were varied primarily with reference to the state of the foreign exchanges; they could not also be used to regulate credit. Secondly, the authorities needed an orderly market in government securities to cope with their refunding problems, and believed that the market's reaction to interest rate changes could be either perverse or unpredictable: an increase in interest rates that might have inhibited borrowing from the clearing banks might have made it more, not less, difficult to sell government debt.

The major feature of the 1960s was, however, the growth of non-clearing banks and rival money markets. This led to the introduction of competition and credit control in 1971, a system which proved incapable of restraining credit at a time of high demand and was soon amended by the introduction of the corset. The clearing banks gradually increased their participation in these new markets at the expense of the discount market; the new system of monetary control introduced in 1981 appeared to support the continuing existence of the discount houses. But the subsequent reduction of the necessary holding of 'club money', as the deposits with the London Discount Market Association are known, might perhaps be taken as an indicator that the authorities would like, eventually, to remove the support offered by club money holdings.

Outside this framework of monetary management, a brief reference should be made to the theoretical discussion of the relationship between monetary and fiscal policy (McCallum, 1984). Many of the models used to explore this issue are couched in a framework in which the only money is banknote money: that either it or bond issues are the means by which a government finances its deficit. The fact that bond issues imply future interest payments, while banknote issues do not, is of major practical importance in the solution of such models. But, in practice, the way budget deficits lead to monetary expansion is by the sale of bills or bonds to the banking sector, which then seeks deposits to cover them. Both monetary and non-monetary finance of deficits imply future interest payments. This strengthens the observation that monetary restraint will be difficult to achieve if the government is a major borrower. Thus a relatively tight fiscal policy has made it easier for the new system of monetary control to become established. But it is not clear that the new system will be any more successful than competition and credit control was in restraining a major monetary expansion if interest rates are held down while circumstances in the rest of the economy favour such an expansion.

4 The Traditional Banking System

The traditional banking system in 1960 comprised the London clearing banks, the Scottish and Northern Irish banks and the London discount market. In the early 1960s the clearing banks (including those in Scotland) and the Northern Irish banks accounted for some 95 per cent of the bank deposit liabilities of United Kingdom residents. By the end of the decade this proportion had fallen to less than 80 per cent as a result of the increasing competition from the non-clearing banks and the constraints exercised by the Bank of England on the clearing banks (Committee of London Clearing Bankers, 1977). The role of the discount market also changed radically in the period after 1960, largely due to the emergence of other money markets which quickly exceeded the traditional market in size. Excellent accounts of the evolution of the system are given by Sayers (1960), Griffiths (1973) and Rowan (1973).

4.1 THE CLEARING BANKS

In 1960 there were eleven London clearing banks, but mergers in the 1960s reduced the number to six: Barclays, Lloyds, National Westminster, Midland, Coutts and Co. (a wholly-owned subsidiary of National Westminster) and Williams and Glyns (owned by the Royal Bank of Scotland and merged with it in September 1985). A proposed merger between Barclays, Lloyds and Martins in 1968 was thwarted by a majority decision of the Monopolies Commission (1968), which considered that competition would be unreasonably reduced if a single bank accounted for more than 50 per cent of all clearing bank business, although no objection was raised to a merger between Barclays and Martins which was duly effected. In 1975 the Co-op and Trustee Savings Banks joined the London Clearing House and the National Girobank was admitted in 1980. The Bank of England also has access to the clearing system. Other banks use the services of the

London clearers. The Royal Bank of Scotland is itself partly owned by Lloyds Bank. The other Scottish and Northern Irish banks are also wholly or partly owned by the London clearing banks. Those banks which do not have direct access to the clearing system but operate a branch system as small retail banks such as the Yorkshire Bank are now usually included with the clearers. Throughout this book unless otherwise indicated the clearing banks are taken to include London and Scottish clearing banks and Northern Irish banks. After 1981 the term is taken to include all retail banks.

At the end of 1984 the size of the clearing banks, including their subsidiary companies, was as shown in Table 4.1.

TABLE 4.1 *The retail banks in 1984*

£ million	*Assets*	*Net Profit*
Barclays Bank	73 623	291
National Westminster Bank	71 517	385
Midland Bank	61 483	−88
Lloyds Bank	44 009	230
Royal Bank of Scotland	13 382	64
Bank of Scotland	7 217	40
Williams and Glyns Bank	5 878	35
Clydesdale Bank	2 516	13
Ulster Bank	2 196	15
Trustee Savings Bank	1 675	11
Coutts & Co.	1 667	5
Yorkshire Bank	1 532	22
Northern Bank	1 521	7
Co-operative Bank	1 195	8
National Girobank	1 091	11

NOTE Coutts & Co. is a wholly-owned subsidiary of National Westminster Bank, Williams and Glyns was a wholly-owned subsidiary of the Royal Bank of Scotland and has now merged with it. Midland Bank owns the Clydesdale Bank.

SOURCE *The Times 1000*, 1985–6.

Some other banks (for example, Standard and Chartered and Citibank) have applied for clearing status. In 1985 reforms to the clearing system, which would allow such an expansion, were announced (page 83).

4.2 BALANCE SHEET STRUCTURE

The changing nature of clearing bank business is illustrated by balance sheet data for four years of the period of this study (see Table 4.2). Despite the much-discussed monetary expansion of the early

TABLE 4.2 *Clearing banks' balance sheet (December)*

		Liabilities (£ million)					
		1960	*1966*	*1975*		*1984*	
Currency		*All*	*All*	£	*Other*	£	*Other*
Current & deposit accounts	UK banks	7 806	9 890	833	1 008	10 100	6 352
	Other UK			22 889	406	73 860	4 330
	Overseas			1 256	2 558	6 930	21 630
CDs		—	—	651	436	5 684	1 906
Banknotes		134	140	315	—	917	—
Net non-deposit liabilities		190	264	5 478	168	18 608	2 666
Total		8 130	10 293	31 422	4 576	116 099	36 884

	Assets (£ million)					
	1960	*1966*	*1975*		*1984*	
Currency	*All*	*All*	£	*Other*	£	*Other*
Notes and coin and working deposits at the Bank of England (L)	771	975	1 439	—	2 159	—
Balances with UK banks (L)	57	83	3 186	1 257	11 079	13 235
Call money (L)	709	1 286	807	—	4 177	—
CDs (L)	—	—	334	33	2 002	177

Local authority loans	—	—	435	—	1 906	—
Treasury bills (L)	1 027	703	1 053	—	201	—
Other bills (L)	162	493	534	22	3 038	82
UK government securities	1 437	1 265	1 915	—	5 120	—
Advances & loans: UK residents	3 652	5 105	13 749	1 144	65 375	3 977
Advances & loans: Other	—	—	1 990	1 961	4 626	17 413
Other assets	164	185	5 359	159	16 072	2 000
Special and cash ratio deposits	151	198	621	—	344	—
Total	8 130	10 293	31 422	4 576	116 099	36 884
Acceptances	—	—	167		2 708	
Ratios						
Liquid assets/Deposits	0.35	0.36	0.29	0.30	0.23	0.39
Advances/Deposits	0.56	0.52	0.61	0.70	0.72	0.63

NOTE These data relate to London and Scottish clearing banks and the Northern Ireland banks. The 1984 data relate to all retail banks.

(L) Liquid Asset as defined by the Bank of England before 1971. Of course British government securities and local authority loans have a high degree of liquidity. Non-deposit liabilities are a balancing item.

The 1984 figures for UK banks relate to monetary sector institutions.

SOURCES *Bank of England Statistical Abstract Nos. 1 and 2; Bank of England Quarterly Bulletin.*

1970s, it should be noted that the liabilities of clearers to non-banks grew faster after 1975 than they did between 1966 and 1975. Interbank borrowing and foreign currency deposit-taking are developments of the 1970s. They are perhaps best seen as a response to the growth of other British and foreign banks.

The asset side has, of course, grown broadly in line with the liability side. But perhaps the most interesting feature here is the increasing importance of advances, balanced against the declining importance of holdings of British government securities, local authority deposits and Treasury bills. In total these declined from 30 per cent of sterling assets in 1960 to 7 per cent in 1984. This reflects the declining importance of the national debt and illustrates how bank advances can grow relative to bank deposits by displacing public debt.

These changes in balance sheet structure also implied changes in the sources from which the clearing banks drew their deposits. Data presented in the clearing bank annual reports show how wholesale deposits had grown to 47 per cent of sterling deposits by 1984 while interest-free current accounts declined in importance. This reflects the willingness and the necessity of the clearing banks to enter the wholesale market.

4.3 CLEARING BANKS IN THE 1960s

The clearing banks provided in 1960 almost the whole of the money transmission services and deposit banking facilities in the United Kingdom except, of course, those provided by the Post Office remittance services, the Post Office Savings Bank and the Trustee Savings Banks. As deposit takers, their major competitors appeared to be building societies to whom they have since lost a considerable share of new money deposits (section 4.6). The clearing banks relied on a very large number of individual accounts to provide the deposits on the basis of which they could extend lines of credit to their customers. Since about 55 per cent of all deposits by value were in current accounts on which no interest was paid (*Bank of England Statistical Abstract No. 1,* 1970) the economic rent that could be earned on advances made to clearing bank customers was sufficient to meet the costs of an extensive branch network and to leave a satisfactory profit for the banks' shareholders. By agreement between them, each of the clearing banks paid the same rate of interest on time deposits and, in general, charged the same rate of interest on advances to selected groups of customers. These rates of interest were traditionally related to the bank rate. The higher the level of bank rate, the greater the profits accruing to the clearing banks due to the 'endowment factor' of demand deposits on which no interest was paid, compared with advances on which interest was charged at bank rate plus a margin depending on the category of borrower. The increase in clearing bank profits resulting from an increase in interest rates imposed by the Bank of England and not due to any action by the banks themselves has continually been the subject of criticism leading to demands for a tax to cream off 'surplus' profits, demands which were met in the 1981 Finance Act which levied a 'windfall tax' on bank profits.

The cartel agreement between the clearing banks on the rates of interest paid on time deposits, and charged to customers on advances, attracted increasing criticism during the 1960s from the Monopolies Commission (1968), the National Board for Prices and Incomes and academic writers, on the grounds that there was insufficient competition between the banks in providing the services they rendered to their customers. The National Board for Prices and Incomes, in its 1967 report on clearing bank charges, also drew attention to the evidence of 'over-banking' from the duplication of branch banking: it recommended that the branch network of the clearing banks should be rationalised since it did not believe that the most effective form of competition was for each clearing bank to open more and more branches of doubtful profitability. It was argued that the clearing banks were too passive in not bidding actively for deposits and seeking new clients, and that efficiency would be improved if there was a much greater degree of competition. There was some inconsistency in these criticisms since it was argued on the one hand that there was too little competition, and on the other hand that there was too much through the opening of more and more branches. But the criticisms did lead to the system of competition and credit control introduced in 1971. At this stage the point that needs to be emphasised is that, at the time the Radcliffe Committee reported in 1959, the clearing banks regarded themselves essentially as providing a public service to their customers: indeed, one of the criticisms was that they behaved too much like public utilities. It is only fair to point out that the authorities were by no means consistent in their attitudes to the clearing banks. When, in October 1963, the clearing banks suggested a greater measure of competition in rates of interest to attract deposits coupled with an increase in overdraft rates, the then Chancellor of the Exchequer argued that this could only lead to an undesirable increase in short-term rates (Tew, 1978). It is also pertinent that the quantitative controls exercised by the Bank of England over the level of clearing bank lending almost continuously from 1960 to 1971 made it pointless for the banks to compete with each other for interest-bearing deposits.

The imposition of a minimum liquidity ratio (the preferred method of control recommended by the Radcliffe Committee) did not inhibit growth in lending by the clearing banks, given the requisite demand, for reasons which illustrate the dilemma faced by the authorities in attempting to control the supply of credit. The clearing banks had emerged from the post-Second World War era with substantial holdings of government stocks, totalling over £1500 million at the start of 1960 (*Bank of England Quarterly Bulletin*, 1962), and liquid assets could always be created by selling such stocks and putting the proceeds into the discount market, provided the profits to be earned from the additional advances, which such liquid assets made possible, exceeded the net loss of interest or capital depreciation on the government securities surrendered. In theory this should not have been possible in a freely competitive market, since substantial sales of gilt-edged stocks by the clearing banks would only have been feasible at a price which would have involved the banks in a capital loss. In practice, however, the market was not a freely competitive one because the Bank of England, on behalf of the government, was concerned to maintain an orderly market in government stocks in order to ease the refunding problem arising from the substantial maturing of gilt-edged securities during the 1960s. The end of Bank support for the gilts market, in 1968, did not immediately lead to a lifting of controls, but it was a necessary precursor for the introduction of competition and credit control.

4.4 THE CLEARING BANKS, COMPETITION AND CREDIT CONTROL AND AFTER

The reserve asset ratio of competition and credit control was set sufficiently low to allow almost all banks to meet it, and when the scheme started in September 1971 the clearing banks had a reserve ratio of 16.3 per cent. Thus a 30 per cent increase in deposits could take place without any change in reserve assets. By August of 1973 the ratio had fallen to 13 per cent and at the same time the stock of reserve assets had risen by 10 per cent.

As is seen from Table 4.3 the bulk of the expansion in reserve assets between October 1971 and December 1973 occurred through an increase in call money held in the discount market. The nature of this is described subsequently when the discount houses are discussed. The main point is that both this increase and the extra commercial bills held were generated by the private sector and not as a direct consequence of monetary policy operations.

TABLE 4.3 *Reserve asset growth under competition and credit control, 1971–3 (£ million)*

	Oct. 1971	*Dec. 1973*
Balances with Bank of England	219	193
Treasury bills	206	422
Tax reserve certificates	53	12
Call money	1 727	2 542
Gilts <1 year	309	355
Local authority bills	42	70
Commercial bills	165	532
Other (1)	—	5
Total	2 721	4 131
Held by clearing banks (2)	1 960	2 664

(1) Other assets include Irish Republic and South African government securities with maturity of less than one year.
(2) Including holdings by other deposit banks.
SOURCE *Bank of England Quarterly Bulletins*.

From the end of 1973 until the end of 1980 the clearing banks operated with a reserve ratio of around 13 per cent, although on occasions it dropped close to its minimum level. For most of the period their expansion was constrained by the corset. The major operational changes of this period were an increasing flexibility in interest rates and a shift to a pattern where clearing bank lending rates followed those in the wholesale markets. This marked the first stage of the integration between the wholesale and retail markets. The second stage, allowing access to wholesale markets by retail depositors, came in the first half of the 1980s.

At the end of 1980 the policy of overfunding started to have its effects (section 3.7). The decline in the Treasury bill issue, and the fact that the Bank of England had been buying in commercial bills, created a shortage of reserve assets in the discount market; this reduced the availability of reserve assets to the banks. Holdings of reserve assets by clearing banks dropped by 18 per cent between December 1980 and January 1981. Loans to the private sector were substituted for holdings of reserve assets. The Bank of England reduced the reserve asset ratio to 10 per cent in order to avoid a severe credit squeeze. The draining of liquidity in the discount market combined with the reduction in the reserve asset ratio thus had the effect of allowing an increase in private sector lending without leading to any increase in deposits. Extra bank lending was thus created in a fashion compatible with observance of monetary targets. This process can be seen as a form of non-bank intermediation. Personal sector saving was at a high level; the government recycled these savings to the corporate sector by buying bills instead of allowing the banks to intermediate. Later in 1981 the minimum reserve ratio was reduced further to 8 per cent, but in fact it never dropped below the figure of 9.4 per cent reached in March 1981, before being abolished as a control variable in August 1981.

However, in June and July of 1981 the lower reserve ratio had a more conventional role. The end of the corset meant that the banks could take back into the system those deposits the corset had prevented them from taking. The lower ratio thus allowed for an increase in deposits after the end of the corset, particularly since the reserve asset position of the banks rose again after April 1981 as holdings of call money on the discount market increased. These effects are shown in the movement of reserve assets at the end of competition and credit control (see Table 4.4).

The new system of monetary control replaced the reserve asset requirement with a cash requirement that 0.5 per cent of eligible liabilities should be held with the Bank of England, and a rolling average of 6 per cent, reduced to 5 per cent of eligible liabilities should be held on the discount market. Although the deposits in the discount market are liquid, and although the ratio can fall as low as 2.5 per cent, nevertheless, a mandatory deposit requirement of this nature is incompatible with the idea of a prudential reserve. The system, perhaps deliberately, forces the banks to maintain an extra liquid buffer over and above the discount market deposit and it is perhaps, therefore, not surprising that the ratio of old reserve assets

TABLE 4.4 *Reserve asset movement at the end of competition and credit control (£ million)*

	Mar. 1980	*Dec. 1980*	*Mar. 1981*	*Aug. 1981*
Balances with B. of E.	370	485	563	564
Treasury bills	861	1 168	454	1 163
Call money	3 939	4 896	3 594	4 396
Gilt <1 year	509	782	945	745
Local authority bills	241	502	211	339
Commercial bills	988	1 251	900	1 149
Total	6 908	9 084	6 667	8 356

SOURCE *Bank of England Quarterly Bulletins.*

to eligible liabilities has remained at roughly the same level as it was in early 1981. Thus the changes associated with the end of competition and credit control did not have the dramatic results associated with its introduction. The end of the corset lifted a constraint on the system. This led to a smaller shift in the pattern of lending than had been seen in the early 1970s, probably because less distortion had built up under the controls of the 1970s than those of the 1960s.

4.5 THE PATTERN OF LENDING

Between the beginning of 1967 and the start of 1970 (the earliest period for which there are data) clearing bank lending to manufacturing industry rose by 40 per cent. However, lending to service industries and the personal sector moved by much smaller amounts and lending to the financial sector actually declined. The direction of lending was clearly successful.

The effects of competition and credit control, and of lifting quantitative controls, may be seen by comparing the position at the start of 1970 with that at the beginning of 1973. Total clearing bank lending to manufacturing climbed by 67 per cent while the non-clearing banks achieved faster growth of 131 per cent to £1425m. The non-clearing banks similarly shared much faster growth in personal sector lending, gaining by nearly 650 per cent to £1102m while the clearing banks 'only' managed to expand by 242 per cent. But it was in lending to the financial sector, and in particular to property companies, that the most dramatic growth was shown. Here clearing bank lending rose by 255 per cent and non-clearing bank lending rose by 757 per cent to £4130m, with even higher growth rates applying to lending to the property sectors.

There is perhaps something of a paradox in these figures. For if the clearing banks had been controlled up to 1971 one might expect them, rather than the non-clearers, to show the more rapid growth rates after 1971 as they were in a position to regain lost businsess. In fact the non-clearers grew more rapidly, partly reflecting merely a growing-up process, but also perhaps suggesting that non-clearing banks were more willing to take risks, and that the developing money markets encouraged the rapid growth of the non-clearing banks.

The period after November 1973 saw the corset in operation for much of the time. This penalised excess growth in deposits at any bank (not just clearing banks) by obliging them to make non-interest-bearing deposits with the Bank of England if their growth rate of deposits exceeded specified limits. The details of the restrictions themselves were presented in Chapter 3. In 1980 for the first time there were significant holdings of supplementary special deposits at the Bank of England, although these cannot easily be apportioned between clearers and non-clearers. Between 1973 and 1979 the pattern of lending altered, with the relatively depressed manufacturing sector increasing its borrowing fairly slowly, and the financial sector showing even less demand for clearing bank credit. The major growth areas were lending to the personal sector, despite the high level of savings in the mid- and late-1970s, and services, which were less affected by the slow growth of the economy.

The end of the corset in 1980 again provided clearing banks with the opportunity to look for new business, and seek the necessary deposits. In the early 1980s manufacturing faced cash flow problems and had to borrow. Personal sector credit demand was also buoyant. By 1982 the position of manufacturing had improved, relatively reducing its need for credit. Lending to the personal and financial sectors, on the other hand, grew at a rate between 1982 and 1985 not much lower than that of the early 1970s.

There was a major lending market in which the clearing banks had taken little interest until the 1980s. Clearing banks had left the mortgage market predominantly to the building societies, allowing home loans to decline as a share of personal sector lending. Indeed, the government had made a considerable attempt to keep the building societies, with their politically sensitive mortgage rate, relatively distinct from the rest of the financial economy.

However, there was a clear decision by the banks in 1981 to compete in the market for mortgages. Loans for house purchase quadrupled between May 1981 to February 1983, rising from 6 to 10 per cent of total bank advances to UK residents, leading to a position where they had captured at times over one-third of the market in new mortgages (see Table 4.5). This increase in lending was almost entirely attributable to the clearing banks. For a period the clearing banks tended to withdraw from this market, feeling that they could not compete satisfactorily with the building societies, perhaps because of the way building societies were taxed. However by 1985 their mortgage advances had reached 20 per cent of those of the building societies.

The other major change taking place in the 1980s relates to clearing bank participation in the securities market. It represents an attempt to provide a wider range of services but does not directly offer access to a new source of deposits. However such participation will be carried out mainly through subsidiaries and is discussed in Chapters 5 and 7.

The two periods of decontrol have thus seen the clearing banks behave in rather similar ways. In both there was a tendency to expand more rapidly than had been the case during the period of control. But in the first case the growth took place in an atmosphere of expansion and was associated with the speculative excesses of 1972–3. During the second period the demand for loans came, initially not from property companies and highly geared financial institutions, but from firms facing liquidity problems under high interest rates and from expansion in the market for personal sector loans. Bank lending also rose as commercial borrowing, which had been squeezed out by the corset, re-entered the system. By the mid-1980s the pattern of expansion was more similar to that of the early 1970s. The competition for deposits took place rather more in the retail market than in the wholesale market, and clearing bank advances rose relatively faster than those of the British non-clearing banks. However in 1982 and 1983 the development of interest-bearing sight deposits with non-clearing banks, offering some cheque-book facilities and paying a higher return than deposits with clearing banks led to a potential deposit loss by the clearing banks. They were forced to offer similar facilities. The process of innovation seemed to have accelerated with the ending of the corset in 1980. This must be seen as a success for the policy of decontrol.

TABLE 4.5 *London and Scottish clearing bank lending to UK residents*

£ million February	*1967*	*1970*	*1973*	*1976*	*1979*	*1982*	*1985*
Manufacturing	1 801	2 521	4 219	3 702	5 858	9 064	12 600
Other production	809	883	1 737	2 077	3 183	5 941	11 394
Personal sector	701	739	2 527	2 974	4 493	10 812	25 027
(of which house purchase)	(288)	(318)	(745)	(1 035)	(1 384)	(4 435)	(11 763)
Services	1 203	1 351	2 537	3 969	6 356	11 411	17 800
Financial	518	461	1 639	2 302	2 265	2 430	8 345
(of which property)	(254)	(233)	(764)	(1 012)	(867)	(1 291)	(2 943)
Total	5 031	5 955	12 659	15 023	22 154	39 657	75 165

NOTE The figures for 1985 cover all retail banks and include acceptances. The classification in 1985 differs from that of earlier years.

SOURCES *Financial Statistics* and *Bank of England.*

4.6 THE CAPITAL BASE OF THE CLEARING BANKS

It is clear from the aggregate balance sheet (Table 4.2) that the non-deposit liabilities of the clearing banks have expanded considerably from £190 million in 1960 to £21,274 million by 1984, although statistical changes prevent this being interpreted precisely. A reasonably good idea of the sources of this expansion can be obtained by looking at the growth in shareholders' funds and loan capital for the 'big four' clearing bank groups. Data are only available since 1970 when the clearing banks stopped holding hidden reserves (see Table 4.6).

The figures of Table 4.6 cannot be reconciled with those of the aggregate balance sheet. This is partly because they relate to clearing bank groups and not the clearing banks themselves, but also because not all the clearing banks are shown and because the net non-deposit liabilities include other items apart from share capital, reserves and loan capital. Two major points can be drawn. First, the major expansion in the capital base has been achieved through retained profits. A part of this includes capital gains on the fixed assets of the banks, since in any historic cost accounting framework such gains have to be financed. Secondly, relatively recently there has been a major increase in the importance of loan capital. The view that this has been forced on banks because low profitability makes equity issue less attractive may not be correct. Loan capital has to be financed out of profits.

Much of the reason for the increased importance of loan finance lies in the international nature of the operations of the clearing bank groups. There are obvious attractions in financing overseas operations by foreign currency borrowing; as Table 4.7 shows, only a relatively small part of the total loan issue is in sterling. Furthermore, the attraction of floating rate subordinated loan issues is clear. These often carry an interest rate only slightly above that on comparable deposits. But they expand the capital base of the bank and thus allow a multiple expansion of its operations. Despite these points, the magnitude of the sterling debt, at interest rates of up to 16 per cent p.a. and stretching into the twenty-first century, is surprising. If inflation remains relatively low, and interest rates adjust to this, the debt will seem a very expensive form of capital finance.

4.7 COMPETITION IN RETAIL BANKING

During the period, the environment in which the banks competed for deposits changed very markedly. In section 4.3 attention focused on

TABLE 4.6 *The capital base of the 'big four' banks (£ million)*

		Issued capital	*Reserves*	*Loan capital*	*Minority interests*	*Total*
1970	Barclays	83	304	58	67	512
	Lloyds	65	214	—	—	279
	Midland	65	193	—	—	258
	National Westminster	104	225	61	4	394
	Total	317	936	119	71	1 443
1975	Barclays	201	571	121	59	952
	Lloyds	130	438	126	2	696
	Midland	132	432	151	10	725
	National Westminster	197	662	134	14	1 007
	Total	660	2 103	532	85	3 380
1980	Barclays	282	1 710	323	102	2 417
	Lloyds	171	1 224	236	9	1 640
	Midland	164	1 184	441	33	1 822
	National Westminster	249	1 566	331	19	2 165
	Total	866	5 684	1 331	163	8 044
1984	Barclays	343	2 258	2 063	173	4 837
	Lloyds	235	1 817	865	15	2 932
	Midland	230	1 455	1 294	486	3 465
	National Westminster	373	2 276	1 623	39	4 311
	Total	1 181	7 806	5 845	713	15 545

SOURCE Clearing Bank Annual Reports.

TABLE 4.7 *Clearing bank long-term debt in 1984 (£ million)*

Currency	*Fixed rate*	*Floating rate*
£	640	200
DM	243	—
SF	36	—
US$	1 391	3 335
Total	2 310	3 535

SOURCE Clearing Bank Annual Reports.

influences on competition between the clearing banks. Here competition with other intermediaries is discussed. Since 1960 the competition offered by the building societies has much increased (*Report of Committee on the Functioning of Financial Institutions,* 1980), and the establishment of National Girobank in 1968 obliged the banks to improve their cash transmission mechanisms. More recently they have expanded so as to attempt to attract deposits of customers who would, traditionally, have been paid in cash, and at the same time to develop images as 'money-shops' offering a wide range of financial services. But competition has also emerged from the non-clearing banks as technical progress has cut the cost of handling transactions and given access to wholesale deposit rates for relatively small sums of money.

The magnitude of competition with the building societies and National Girobank is best indicated by a comparison of deposits (excluding interbank deposits) with the two types of institution (see Table 4.8).

Until recently the competition hinged on the interest rates offered by building societies which were almost always higher than bank 7-day deposit rates after allowing for standard rate tax; it was primarily for savings deposits. Building societies opened on Saturdays; the banks stopped this in 1968 and are only now beginning to restart. An account with a building society provided privileged access to mortgage funds, but on the other hand building societies were not allowed to make unsecured loans. And of course banks offered cheque-books and from the mid-1960s guarantee cards, while the building societies would only issue cheques to third parties on special application.

But in the last few years the competition has extended from the

TABLE 4.8 *Deposits with clearing banks, building societies and national giro (£ million, December)*

	Clearing banks	*Building societies*	*National Girobank*
1960	7 806	2 952	—
1965	9 748	5 159	—
1970	11 423	10 142	58
1975	24 145	22 696	192
1980	44 339	49 950	632
1984	80 790	91 305	1 140

NOTE Only sterling items (excluding interbank deposits) are shown. The 1984 clearing bank figure covers all retail banks. National Girobank figures relate to the following March.

SOURCE *Financial Statistics* and Post Office Annual Reports.

deposit-taking service to the money-transmission service. Several building societies now offer interest-bearing cheque accounts which differ from bank accounts mainly in that cheque guarantee cards do not exist and overdraft facilities are not available. A recent Green Paper (HM Treasury, 1984) suggests that building societies should be allowed to make unsecured loans. This will have the effect of increasing competition between the two still further.

Competition for retail deposits has led to banks offering to take sight deposits at rates determined by those in the wholesale money markets, and higher than those on 7-day deposits. Such accounts were pioneered by the accepting houses such as Robert Fleming and Kleinwort Benson (in co-operation with the M & G unit trust group). The clearing banks then felt obliged to offer similar services. This move was stimulated when banks became obliged, like building societies, to pay interest net of standard rate tax. Although such accounts do often include cheque-book facilities, cheques may only be written for a relatively large minimum sum (by the standard of most household day-to-day transactions). Thus they compete more with deposit than current accounts.

Associated with this increased competition has been a technical change in the nature of the banking services offered. Most visible to the customer has been the introduction of automatic teller machines. Competitive pressures are likely to speed up the introduction of such new technologies. Other important changes at a wholesale level have been the introduction of CHAPS (Clearing House Automatic Payment System) which allows same-day clearing of cheques for over

£10 000, and the establishment of BACS (Bankers' Automated Clearing Services) to allow electronic bulk clearing.

The introduction of National Girobank in 1968 was expected to make money transmission facilities available to a wider range of the public than had hitherto been the case. But deposits with it have grown less rapidly than those with the clearing banks, and perhaps the system has not been as successful as was hoped. It did have the immediate consequence of encouraging the clearing banks to introduce their own giro system, allowing the payment of several bills by one debit. But this grew increasingly costly. Since the competition has been less than might have been expected from National Girobank, the banks felt able to introduce a charge, in 1982, to customers receiving payment of bills in this way.

A change which seems likely to have a larger impact is the redesign of the English clearing house structure. This was prompted by applications for membership from Standard Chartered and Citicorp. In future there will be three clearing companies covering general and credit clearing, CHAPS and town clearing and BACS. Participants will be able to join some or all of these provided they are suitably regulated, appear able to manage the technology of the system, have settlement facilities at the Bank of England, cover their share of the costs and have the prospect of accounting for at least ½ per cent of the total volume cleared (*The Banker,* January 1985). The Bank of England retains control of the system since it must agree to the establishment of settlement facilities, but this reform clearly lays the way open for expansion and further competition in money transmission services.

A brief reference should be made to bank charges. The clearing banks have always charged different amounts for their services. At periods of very high interest rates they have tended to offer 'free banking', while on other occasions they have moved from having a charge per debit, to a system which offers free banking to customers with more than a minimum, or minimum average amount, in their account. Recently Barclays and National Westminster have begun to charge customers a flat fee for having a bank account unless it contains more than a minimum or minimum average amount; the Midland has abolished charges to customers in credit. The extent to which customers move accounts in response to this is unclear.

Goodhart (1984, Chapter 5) argues that the nature of retail banking, which was broadly stable for the first 80 years of the century, is now changing very rapidly; this change is a consequence of the rapid technical progress in the sector. The increasing competition this generates, not only among the clearing banks, but also between the clearing banks and other deposit-taking institutions such as building societies, has had the effect of integrating credit markets. It has broken down the distinction between administered and market-determined interest rates, creating a position in which the formally administered rates are now set with reference to market rates. This is seen not only in the behaviour of the clearing banks. The building societies now change their interest rates more frequently than in the past and an administered cartel system has broken down there too.

4.8 THE DISCOUNT MARKET

The discount market, comprising the members of the London Discount Market Association, provided an essential link in the mechanism used by the authorities for the control of credit, a link that was unique to the United Kingdom. The discount houses in 1984–5 were as shown in Table 4.9.

TABLE 4.9 *Discount houses and their total assets in 1984–5*

£ million	*Assets*	*Net profit*
Gerrard & National	4 191	5.2
Union Discount Co. of London	3 124	7.9
Cater Allen Holdings	1 795	3.7
Alexanders Discount	706	−3.9
King & Shaxson	598	0.8
Clive Discount	368	−0.8
Smith St Aubyn	344	−0.6
Seccombe, Marshal & Campion	163	0.3
Gerald Quin, Cope	54	0.1
Total	11 343	12.7

SOURCE *The Times 1000,* 1985–6.

By convention, a clearing bank neither borrowed from nor loaned to other clearing banks: instead, the smoothing operation for the clearing bank's temporary deficits or surpluses was carried out by the discount houses. Nor, by agreement, did the clearing banks tender direct for Treasury bills. The discount market performed this function for them at one remove. The clearing banks loaned their surplus funds to the discount market at call or short notice, receiving as collateral from the market Treasury and commercial bills and government bonds to the value of the funds loaned plus a margin (5 per cent for bonds and a percentage on bills to cover the discount at current market rates). The margin was met by the discount houses from their capital and reserves. When funds were required by a clearing bank, it recalled its loans to the discount market. Thus, the market in call money which the discount houses provided was used by the clearing banks to adjust their liquidity on a continuing basis, and the movements in discount market funds provided the Bank of England with the information it believed it required to implement its monetary policy. Since call money was an important element in the clearing banks' liquidity and since the discount houses used call money to purchase the bonds and bills which were used as collateral, it could be said that the Treasury and commercial bills and government stocks held by the discount houses were, in effect, held on behalf of the clearing banks.

The discount houses also played an important and essential role in the gilt-edged market by acting as professional dealers and jobbers, and assisting the government broker to preserve an orderly market regarded as necessary for the management of the national debt. So far as floating debt was concerned, the market undertook that it would take up the whole of the Treasury bills tendered each week by the Bank of England and thus ensured a relative degree of stability in Treasury bill rates. Provided Treasury bills remained a dominant element in the discount houses' and clearing banks' portfolios of liquid assets, the Bank of England could create any monetary effect it desired through its role as 'lender of last resort' to the market. The policy of the Bank of England was therefore to control short-term rates of interest, particularly the Treasury bill rate, by acting as the residual supplier of finance to the discount houses. For example, when the clearing banks were short of funds (when, for instance, their customers made their tax payments to the Inland Revenue), they called back money from the discount market. If the Bank of England did not relieve the resultant shortage in the discount market, it could force the discount houses to borrow at the bank rate from the Bank. The whole basis of Bank of England policy was to retain the initiative by creating shortages in the traditional money market which it could relieve on terms that the Bank considered appropriate. So, it offered more Treasury bills, which the discount market had to cover, than were required to meet the central government borrowing requirement when it wished to absorb surplus funds from the market, and provided bills which would mature on days when money was expected to be short. This gave the Bank of England the decisive say in the rates of interest on the basis of which it was prepared to sell Treasury bills. Moreover, since bank rate was the keystone in 1960 for the structure of short-term interest rates, and was also the effective rate which the discount houses were forced to pay when borrowing from the Bank of England to relieve shortages in the market, by controlling the volume and frequency of such borrowing the authorities could directly influence any chosen structure of rates in the short-term market.[1]

The above is a necessarily abbreviated description of the traditional money market in which the discount houses acted as a transmission agency between the authorities and the clearing banks. The discount market also took call and short-notice money from non-clearing banks and from non-bank lenders, who could earn at least ⅜ per cent more for 7-day money than from the clearing banks' deposit rates. From 1960 to 1971, however, the proportion of discount houses' borrowed funds represented by the non-clearing bank sources steadily declined with the growth of rival money markets (see Chapter 6). One merchant banker stated in discussion that, from the early 1960s onwards, only the minimum quantity of funds was put into the discount market to maintain an appearance of support, simply because higher yields could be obtained in other markets.

The discount market found it necessary to participate in the new money markets that developed fast in the 1960s. With the declining importance of Treasury bills, and the possibility of capital losses on government stock, a loss that actually occurred in 1964, the discount houses needed to find alternative sources of profit and these they found in the newer markets. Commercial bills formed a close substitute for Treasury bills. As the commercial bill issue expanded it was natural that the discount houses would be major holders of them. When negotiable sterling certificates of deposit were introduced in 1968, the discount houses played a prominent part in making a market in them. By 1971 and the introduction of competition and credit control, the discount houses held a very wide range of securities in their portfolios of assets, including Treasury bills, government bonds, bank and fine trade bills, local authority securities, promissory notes, and dollar and sterling certificates of deposit. As Channon (1979) has pointed out:

> The extensive use of certificates of deposit as security in the

discount market meant, however, that there was a risk of insecurity in the event of any future economic pressure.[2] This was coupled with the fact that, in covering their forward positions . . . they had no way of knowing on what source they might ultimately be depending for funds in terms of certificates of deposit.

4.9 THE BALANCE SHEET OF THE DISCOUNT HOUSES

The declining importance and changing nature of the discount market is summarised by the evolution of its balance sheet. Total liabilities grew eight-fold as against a nineteen-fold increase in those of the clearing banks in the same period. The decline in the importance of public debt, visible in the clearing bank balance sheet, can also be seen here. The dominant position of Treasury bills and British government securities in 1960 has been taken by other bills, most of which are probably eligible for rediscount at the Bank of England, and certificates of deposit, which are not. The discount market has not entered foreign currency business to any significant extent (see Table 4.10).

TABLE 4.10 *Discount market balance sheet (December)*

	Liabilities (£ million)					
	1960	*1966*	*1975*		*1984*	
Currency	*All*	*All*	*£*	*Other*	*£*	*Other*
Bank of England	—	82	—		48	
UK banks*	857	1 284	2 262	84	6 124	293
Other	140	119	274	59	1 263	90
Total	997	1 484	2 536	143	7 435	383
	Assets (£ million)					
	1960	*1966*	*1975*		*1984*	
Currency	*All*	*All*	*£*	*Other*	*£*	*Other*
Treasury bills	458	424	819	—	99	—
Other bills	108	404	980	129	2 944	77
UK gov. securities	451	542	96	—	401	—
CDs	—	—	303	14	2 701	302
Other	36	195	472	1	1 568	4
Total	1 054	1 565	2 670	144	7 713	383

*Monetary Sector in 1984.
SOURCE *Bank of England Quarterly Bulletin.*

4.10 THE DISCOUNT MARKET AND COMPETITION AND CREDIT CONTROL

After the introduction of competition and credit control, the mechanism of reserve asset generation (Chapter 3) began to work powerfully. The reserve asset base of the whole banking system rose from £2721m in October 1971 to £4131m by December 1973 (*Bank of England Quarterly Bulletin*). Money at call in the discount market (with money and discount brokers as well as with discount houses), rose from £1727m to £2542m over the same period. The changes in the discount market itself are summarised in Table 4.11.

TABLE 4.11 *Sterling assets and liabilities of discount houses, 1971–3*

£ million	*October 1971*	*December 1973*
UK government securities	432	25
Treasury bills	292	269
Other bills	477	628
Local authority securities	341	387
CDs	368	923
Other	273	285
Total	2 182	2 517
Borrowed funds	2 070	2 456
Call money	1 727	2 542

SOURCE *Bank of England Quarterly Bulletin.*

The borrowed funds of the discount houses only showed a much more modest increase from £2070m in October 1971 to £2456m by December 1973 (Table 4.11). The balance of call money is attributable to deposits with money and discount brokers. One can infer that about half of the expansion in money at call was achieved, not by any multiple expansion of deposits, but by a shortening of maturity of deposits in the discount market. Term deposits were turned into call money.

If a change in the maturity structure of deposits with discount houses and discount brokers made possible about half of the increase in money at call between October 1971 and December 1973, the rest of the increase can be seen as arising from partially offsetting factors as Table 4.11 shows. The expansion of certificate of deposit holdings is dominant, and the most interesting development. It illustrates the possibility of multiple expansion of the reserve base since, if discount houses buy certificates of deposit from banks, the banks can deposit the funds as call money to be used as a reserve base for profitable lending and deposit-taking. The discount houses are constrained by the public sector debt ratio or the undefined assets multiple; the first could be lifted by buying public sector debt from the banks. The second could not, but the undefined assets multiple was only 13.8 when the regulation was introduced in August 1973. It rose to 17.5 by December 1973, a rise mainly attributable to an expansion in holdings of certificates of deposit. Thus, during the early stages of competition and credit control, until August 1973, the ability of the discount houses to create reserve assets was by no means fully exploited. One mechanism, that of buying public sector debt from the banks in exchange for call money, had scarcely been used; the banks held more than £1000m of gilt of maturity between one and five years, which could have provided extra reserves, although leaving the discount houses in an exposed position if interest rates rose.

After the change in the regulation of discount houses there was still some further scope for an expansion in call money. But it may be the case that the banks would not have wished to see a much larger increase in their holdings of call money after the end of 1973. Equally the discount houses might have become unwilling to expand their holdings of certificates of deposit much further, given the problems which were starting to emerge in the secondary banking sector at this time. Thus, by the time the corset was introduced, it is likely that the mechanism for expanding bank lending which had run so powerfully in the early 1970s was running out of steam.

As in the case of clearing bank lending, there are, after 1973, periods of nominal expansion of greater and lesser rapidity. But the system was increasingly constrained by the corset. The velocity of circulation of broad money (£M3)[3] rose from 2.56 at the end of 1973, to 3.75 when the corset was ended in August 1980. Similarly, the borrowed funds of discount houses rose by 70 per cent, although nominal GDP rose by 196 per cent; borrowed funds of discount houses moved roughly in line with total advances to UK residents. Thus, the general atmosphere of monetary restraint affected the discount houses.

The ending of the corset, too, led to an increase in the demand for reserve assets by the banks, as notional deposits suppressed by the corset re-entered the system. This was initially achieved by shortening the maturity of bank deposits with the discount houses. As the reintermediation process continued, the discount houses expanded their borrowing matched by increased holdings of Treasury bills, short gilts and certificates of deposit. Holdings of commercial bills declined. The switch from commercial bill holdings to certificates of deposit holdings did not affect the undefined assets multiple, while the increase in holdings of public sector debt allowed the extra borrowing.

The instability in the stock of reserve assets affected the discount market. Table 4.12 summarises the position of the discount houses at the end of competition and credit control. The effect of Bank of England bill purchases is shown here as in Table 4.5. The failure of borrowed funds to recover to their end 1980 level in 1981 reflects the lower reserve asset ratio of the banking system.

TABLE 4.12 *Sterling assets and liabilities of discount houses, 1980–1 (£ million)*

	December 1980	*March 1981*	*August 1981*
Government securities	956	1 254	797
Treasury bills	556	77	495
Other bills	2 485	1 849	2 089
Local authority securities	377	385	303
CDs	613	594	515
Other	234	279	486
Total	5 221	4 438	4 685
Borrowed funds			
Call money	4 845	3 850*	4 446
Other	255	455	145
Total	5 100	4 305	4 591

*Including £218 million from the Bank of England.
SOURCE *Bank of England Quarterly Bulletin.*

The changes in the regulations concerning banks also affected the discount houses. The undefined asset multiple ceased to apply as a constraint. This made it easier for the Bank of England to continue its policy of buying in bills of all types, as a means of bypassing the banking system. But growth in bank liabilities to the rest of the economy continued, albeit at a slower rate than in 1981. Call money deposits were still required even though the reserve requirement had ended, and the expansion was secured against an increase in holdings of certificates of deposit. By 1983 the undefined assets multiple would have been well above 20 and the public sector debt ratio below 20 per cent, reflecting the magnitude of the changes that had taken place since the early 1970s.

The imminent changes in the structure of the gilt-edged market (*Bank of England Quarterly Bulletin,* 1984b, c) have more fundamental implications for the nature of the discount houses. While the Bank of England seems keen that they should maintain their traditional role of discounting bills, the reforms to the gilt-edged market allow them ample opportunity to develop as market makers in competition with other securities dealers. It seems not improbable that the 'club money' requirement will be withdrawn when the Bank of England considers they have had sufficient time to adjust to this role.

4.11 INTEREST RATES IN THE TRADITIONAL MARKETS

The principle influences on the broad pattern of short-term interest rates have been considered in section 1.4 of Chapter 1. Here the relationship between bank rate or the minimum lending rate and other interest rates in the traditional banking system is considered.

As noted the clearing banks had conventionally set their interest rates with reference to the bank rate. This principle, together with the fact that most clearing bank customers had access to no other source of credit, had given the Bank of England the power to control both bank lending and interest rates (Chapter 3, p. 44). Only first-class borrowers could rely on bills and on alternative sources of finance. For the traditional system to work, the bill market rate had to be below the administered bank rate. Call money with the discount houses fitted into this structure. The rate on call money was between 3/8 and 1 3/8 per cent higher than that on 7-day deposits which was itself 2 per cent lower than the bank rate. Thus, when clearing banks were short of funds, the withdrawal of call money was a relatively cheap source of finance. The lowest possible rate on call money set a minimum for the market-determined bill rate.

In 1970 each clearing bank adopted its own base rate which replaced the bank rate as the rate relative to which overdraft and deposit rates were calculated. This change in convention immediately reduced the influence of the authorities on administered interest rates. Changes in the minimum lending rate, which replaced the bank rate in October 1972, might only be reflected with a lag in the administered rates. This happened, in extremis, in 1973, when for a while a gap of 3.5 points developed. The minimum lending rate was raised to 11.5 per cent in July 1973, but the clearing banks, perhaps because of the atmosphere of price control, were slow to follow suit.

Competition and credit control increased the attractiveness of call money, when the demand for money was high. It became a complement for other assets (since it was necessary to hold reserve assets to expand liabilities needed to finance asset expansion). Thus at times, before the corset was imposed, the yield on call money fell below that on 7-day deposits. The same process drove down the yield on Treasury bills. Since the minimum lending rate was related to this expansion of the demand for money tended to drive down rates throughout the traditional system. The authorities were periodically forced to suspend the formula linking the minimum lending and Treasury bill rates, and finally abandoned it in April 1978.

The process which began in 1970 has continued. The integration of traditional and parallel markets does not remove the ability of the Bank of England to fix short-term interest rates. But it does prevent the simultaneous control of interest rates and the stock of credit. Thus from 1975 a more integrated structure developed which removed the arbitrage possibilities between traditional and parallel sectors. Clearing banks began to relate base and overdraft rates to parallel market rates in order to remove arbitrage possibilities. These converged with the minimum lending rate in 1977, and a very close relationship was maintained until the latter was abolished in August 1981. Since then base rates have moved more closely in line with those in the parallel markets discussed in Chapter 6, it appears that the whole structure is closely related to the bill rate imposed in the manner described on p. 62.

4.12 SUMMARY

In the 1960s, it was argued that competition and innovation were stifled because it was fruitless for any clearing bank to attempt to attract deposits if lending was denied in excess of specified limits (Committee of London Clearing Bankers, 1977). Constraints confined largely to the clearing banks did little to achieve credit-rationing if other parts of the banking sector were left outside official controls, and, as we shall see, the non-clearing banks took every opportunity offered by the restraints imposed on the clearing banks to expand their deposit liabilities and advances on a massive scale. That this was made possible by other developments in the money markets was not incidental: the growth of markets competing with the traditional discount market was part of a major change in the financial system, which at the beginning of the period included the clearing banks as the apex of the pyramid of institutional structures. The development and importance of the parallel markets is illustrated by the fact that in 1960, as noted, current accounts were 55 per cent of clearing bank deposits and 7-day deposits accounted for the remainder. By 1984 demand deposits amount to 28 per cent, savings and 7-day deposit accounts to 23 per cent and time deposits, which are essentially parallel money, made up the remainder of domestic deposits with the big four clearing banks. The Committee of London Clearing Bankers (1977) suggests that much of this change took place in the early period of competition and credit control.

As the non-clearing banks expanded, the discount market declined in importance during the 1960s. This process continued during the 1970s despite the prop offered by competition and credit control. A parallel change, also originating in the expansion of the new markets, was the breakdown of the traditional system of administered interest rates. This was a gradual process which caused many problems in its transitional stages, and can only recently be described as complete. The changes to the gilt-edged market offer a major role for the discount houses as market makers. But they will face severe competition and it remains to be seen how they will adapt to this new environment.

5 The Accepting Houses

The membership of the Accepting Houses Committee has undergone several changes in recent years. Members must be at least 50 per cent British owned and be based in the City of London. The committee is not a formal body in the sense that there are no rules which a bank has to accept if it wishes to apply to become a member. Its members are expected to have a substantial business in acceptances which command the finest discount rates and are eligible for re-discounting at the Bank of England. Under the informal system which is so prevalent in the City of London, the Bank of England would be expected to be consulted before new members were admitted to membership of the committee. Since the end of the Second World War, six banks have been invited to join the Committee: Antony Gibbs (later forced to resign when the bank was taken over by the Hong Kong and Shanghai Banking Group); S. Japhet; S. G. Warburg; Arbuthnot, Latham (which was taken over by a consortium of foreign banks in 1982 and resigned then); Rea Brothers and Robert Fleming. It seems unlikely that many new members will join the Committee although Robert Fleming was not admitted until 1980. All the members are also members of the Issuing Houses Association and, were, during the period of exchange control, authorised foreign exchange dealers. The members of the committee are very diverse in terms of size. They are listed in order of their 1984 asset base in Table 5.1

5.1 BACKGROUND

The original business of the accepting houses was the finance of overseas trade and many had begun their existence as merchants, developing banking services as an adjunct to their merchanting activities. Barings, for example, originally specialised in the early eighteenth century in the wool trade and established close connections with the Netherlands; other houses traded in cotton, rubber and

TABLE 5.1 *The accepting houses in 1984–5*

£ million	*Total assets*	*Net profit*	*Acceptances*
Kleinwort Benson	4 098	30.3	603
Schroders	3 653	11.1	267
Morgan, Grenfell	3 481	20.4	461
Hill Samuel	3 037	31.9	158
Samuel Montagu	2 936	11.0	305
Hambros	2 710	10.2	530
N. M. Rothschild	1 894	2.8	220
S. G. Warburg	1 751	19.9	274
Lazard Bros.	1 181	4.4	114
Baring Bros.	953	1.6	255
Charterhouse Japhet	848	8.0	85
Robert Fleming	626	7.3	34
Guiness Mahon	579	1.4	50
Brown, Shipley	506	3.4	65
Singer & Friedlander	419	5.2	109
Rea Brothers	173	1.0	34
Total	28 845	169.9	3 564

SOURCE *'The Times 1000', 1985–6.*

a variety of other commodities. A few maintained their merchanting connections into the 1960s although, with the exception of bullion dealing, these had little significance in the over-all business activity of those houses. Some, notably Rothschilds, Lazards, and Morgan, Grenfell, began as bankers with strong overseas connections which they used in the nineteenth century to expand international banking services based in London as a growing centre of international finance. By a shrewd combination of seeking profits wherever they could be made and the development of trust in their integrity, they flourished in the heyday of Britain's dominance over the world's trade. Through their specialised knowledge of overseas markets, the accepting houses perfected the use of the acceptance credit for the finance of goods and produce traded internationally; the bill of exchange on London became the recognised means of credit for overseas trading transactions. The annual turnover of bills drawn on London increased from some £425 million in 1840 to over £2000 million by 1913, of which the accepting houses accounted for at least two-thirds (Rybczynski, 1973). In addition, through their wide range of overseas contracts, they established themselves as the recognised agents of foreign governments who wished to raise loans to meet both their short-term and long-term financial commitments. London before 1914 was the major financial centre in which funds could be raised to finance developments in the Americas, the British Empire and other developing territories. For example, out of some £3600 million loaned abroad between 1870 and 1913, some 40 per cent was raised by London accepting houses (Rybczynski, 1973).

During the nineteenth century, as trade developed, so the question of finance arose. The prime means of international trade finance was the bill on London. The 1882 Bills of Exchange Act defines a bill as:

> A Bill of exchange is an unconditional order in writing, addressed by one person to another, signed by the person giving it, requiring the person to whom it is addressed to pay on demand or at a fixed or determinable time a sum certain in money to or to the order of a specified person or to bearer.

But the guarantee of payment is greater if the bill bears the name of a reputable trader. The accepting houses put their name to these bills, underwriting the default risk, and thus allowing the bills to command discount rates scarcely worse than those on Treasury bills. The accepting houses charge a commission for these acceptances which depends on the quality of the borrower. They can be better informed than those who might discount the bills; there may be economies of scale in gathering information about credit worthiness. Accepting houses may also be in a better position to bear the hazards of occasional loss. Thus the risk premium embodied in their commission is lower than that which another institution would charge on a bill which had not been accepted. Nevertheless, the acceptance is a notional liability only, unless the initial borrower defaults. Accepting houses are not the only issuers of acceptances, but acceptance has to form a major part of their business.

The development of acceptance credits and the raising of finance for foreign governments and corporations led to the accumulation of foreign deposits with the acceptance houses in London. It was normal for clients who were granted acceptance credits to maintain deposit balances with their merchant banks and, over time, these balances grew appreciably and could be used to develop foreign exchange departments and, in the case of one or two houses, bullion dealing. Until the First World War, however, sterling remained the dominant currency in which international transactions were denominated and the sterling bill of exchange remained the prime instrument for international trade. Indeed, sterling bills of exchange drawn on a London banker were often used to transfer credit from one overseas country to another, the bills being used by the overseas holder to purchase goods in the United Kingdom or to be sold to a local bank.

The decline of sterling after 1918, and with it Britain's dominance in international trade, radically changed the role of the accepting houses. The world economic depression post-1929 led to a sharp fall in international trade and to default on some foreign loans. This greatly reduced the traditional business of the accepting houses and some had to be assisted in order to survive.

> When the crisis broke, the accepting houses with some £60 million of capital resources, had £105 million deposits, nearly all foreign while £50 million of their acceptances were for countries where moratoria had been declared. Their deposits fell by 40 per cent and Schroders, Kleinworts, Hambros, Lazards, Barings and Rothschilds, who in that order held the majority of acceptances, had to take them off the market and hold them. Contingent liabilities became actual. The Bank of England intervened through the discount market and gave special facilities to houses which needed them. (Young, 1971)

Those houses which had important overseas connections maintained them against the day when they might need them again, but all the accepting houses had to find new fields of activity to compensate for the decline in acceptances and in foreign deposits and international issues. In place of their overseas business, the merchant banks readily accepted the advice of the Macmillan Committee (*Report from the Committee on Finance and Industry,* 1931) that they should turn their attention to the home market by fostering links with British industry and the use of commercial bills to extend short-term credit to domestic trade.

It was in the 1930s that a number of company amalgamations took place in the United Kingdom and the accepting houses became involved in capital issues, corporate financial advice and the raising of capital for the merged companies. For example, Lazards established close connections with English Electric and Schroders with Pressed Steel, not as 'banques d'affaires' on the European model, investing in companies with which they were associated, but as financial advisors acting as middlemen between the sources and users of funds. Acceptance facilities were provided by the merchant banks to British companies to finance the purchase of raw materials prior to processing, manufacture and sale. With bank rate at 2 per cent, and an adequate supply of funds in the discount market to re-discount bills, it was cheaper for companies to use acceptance credits, renewable on maturity, than bank overdrafts for their short-term needs. Some merchant banks developed investment management services to place the funds entrusted to them by family trusts, and launched investment trusts to tap funds in the United Kingdom and North America. All the accepting houses remained small private partnerships with a defined place in the market quite separate from that occupied by the retail deposit banks.

The controls imposed on capital issues and foreign exchange transactions during the Second World War, which were not removed until well into the 1950s, further restricted any possibility of growth for the accepting houses: they survived but that was about all. In real terms, their average deposits and acceptance credits outstanding were almost exactly the same in the period 1955–7 as they had been in 1927 (Kellet, 1967). Government policy immediately after the end of the Second World War was directed towards stringent exchange controls to prevent a depreciation of sterling; with the Exchange Control Act of 1947 and later legislation, the sterling area was established, and balances with sterling area countries were blocked. Overseas countries, which tied their domestic currencies to sterling, and pooled their gold and non-sterling currency earnings in London as sterling balances, were linked to Britain by exchange controls which discriminated against non-sterling area countries. Import quotas were established, strict controls on overseas investment were imposed and bank lending was restricted. The accepting houses were cut off from their traditional overseas markets and, as sterling declined in importance as an international currency, so too did the bill drawn on London as an instrument for international trade. Moreover, the accepting houses ceased to enjoy correspondent relationships with overseas banks since the number of transferable sterling accounts was limited by the authorities. As these relationships dwindled, overseas banks, particularly in the Commonwealth, assumed the role of financing trade in wool and other commodities. The only field of activity in which the accepting houses were able to expand was that of capital reorganisation and re-investment as the post-war spate of company mergers and acquisitions began. The bitter struggle in 1957 for control of the British Aluminium company between Reynolds Metals (jointly bidding with Tube Investments) and Alcoa, with merchant banks divided against each other in advising the respective bidders, opened new avenues for the corporate finance departments of the accepting houses. The fee income, and perhaps more important, the kudos, to be gained from a successful bid, or from a successful defence against a bid, were high and it therefore paid merchant banks to expand their staffs to provide the best professional services they could. Nevertheless, in the highly segmented financial markets of the period from 1945 to 1960, the accepting houses occupied a small but important niche in which they competed with the clearing banks neither for deposits nor in lending.

5.2 RESURGENCE

Thus, until the late 1950s the accepting houses remained the small private banks which they had been for decades past, occupying their own place in the financial intermediation process and providing advisory, acceptance credit and investment management services complementary to the services offered by the clearing banks. Then a new aggressiveness manifested itself in merchant banking with the accepting houses pursuing growth in the belief that increased profits, if not survival, depended on size of organisation and the range of services that could be offered. No attempt could obviously be made to compete with the clearing banks in retail deposit banking; the sheer cost of setting up a branch network of dubious profitabiliy made that a non-starter from the outset. What they could, and did, do was to open regional offices in order to market the services they offered. But growth of the wholesale money markets, described in the next chapter, provided the accepting houses with the opportunity massively to increase their deposit liabilities, and success in attracting deposits was likely to be dependent on the apparent strength of the houses' balance sheets. The 1960s were a period in which size of organisation was regarded as an indication of relative importance; as early as 28 May 1960, *The Economist* had argued that size was as important for the accepting houses as it was for much of industry.

From the late 1950s the period witnessed a succession of mergers, and some abortive plans for mergers, between merchant banks, and between merchant banks and insurance companies, all designed to produce organisations sufficiently large and diverse to be able to contend effectively in an increasingly competitive environment. The more important mergers were:

Warburgs and Seligman	(1957)
Philip Hill, Higginson and Erlangers	(1959)
Lazards and Edward de Stein	(1960)
Schroders and Helbert, Wagg	(1960)
Kleinworts and Robert Benson, Lonsdale	(1960)
Charterhouse and S. Japhet	(1963)
Philip Hill and M. Samuel	(1965)
Hill, Samuel and Noble Lowndes	(1969)

Hill, Samuel and Co. decided to expand even further in 1970 when the bank made a bid for Metropolitan Estates and Property Corporation (MEPC) in order 'to create a huge financial supermarket'. As Spiegelberg (1973) points put, the proposal came to nothing, largely because the other merchant banks were sufficiently alarmed at the prospect of so large a financial conglomerate that they were able to secure a different fate for MEPC by a deal with Commercial Union and Trafalgar House. In no way deterred, Hill, Samuel and Co. and Slater, Walter Ltd announced their intention to merge in 1973, a merger which, had it taken place, would bring Slater, Walter Ltd the coveted position in the City establishment which it desired. Fortunately, as it turned out for Hill, Samuel and Co., the deal fell through for reasons which were never made entirely clear.

The motivation behind some of the mergers was the obvious one of bringing together two banks, or a bank and an issuing house, with different spheres of interest. For example, a bank with strong industrial connections, like Schroders, found it advantageous to join a bank with strong overseas connections and acceptance business, like Helbert, Wagg. Moreover, the mergers opened the door to membership of the Accepting Houses Committee to banks like Warburgs, Philip Hill, Helbert, Wagg and Lonsdale, which had hitherto been closed to them. There were, however, other reasons for the mergers. In an era when it was firmly believed both by commerce and government that success depended on combining in one organisation as many economic activities as possible (however disparate those activities might be), the merchant banks, who were actively engaged in promoting mergers to their industrial clients, practised what they preached. It was the age of the conglomerate and there seemed no good reason why what was assumed to be good for industry should not also be good for the financial sector. The clearing banks were of course likewise engaged in mergers in order to reap the benefits of economies of scale. Not all accepting houses followed this path; some groups with strong family interests (Morgan, Grenfell, Hambros and Barings) retained their individual identities and managed to expand without acquiring other merchant banks. One notable exception, Warburgs, resisted the cult of growth and remained comparatively small without suffering in comparison with its competitors. In industry and commerce the merger movement began to gather strength in the late 1950s. It was perhaps fuelled by the Restrictive Practices Act, 1956, which outlawed agreements between separate producers. The economic consequences of the boom have been much discussed and remain controversial. Meeks (1977) found that mergers did not seem to produce the results hoped for, although his results have since been criticised by, for example, Cosh, Hughes and Singh (1980). The accepting houses recruited teams of accountants, lawyers and business school graduates in order to provide advice needed by companies intending to merge, or involved in takeover battles.

A further factor which helped the accepting houses to expand in other than their traditional banking and acceptance business was the substantial increase in the investment funds of the insurance companies, pension funds, investment trusts and unit trusts. By 1970 about one-half of the total issued capital of all quoted companies was held by such institutions as a result of a substantial growth in savings, and the increased attractiveness of equity shares with rising and expected inflation. The accepting houses competed strongly to act as advisors to institutional investors, again not so much for the fee income, which often barely covered a very labour-intensive service, as for the prestige which appointment to a pension fund or similar investing institution would bring.[1] They were also attracted by the profits that could certainly be made from managing a successful unit trust or investment trust.

Statistics of the value of funds managed by the accepting houses are not available for most of the period covered by this study, and even for the most recent year it is not possible to build up a fully comprehensive picture. However Table 5.2 does give an idea of the importance of fund management to the accepting houses.

There were obviously dangers of which the well-conducted accepting houses were well aware and which needed to be averted if justifiable criticism was to be avoided. When a share issue was

TABLE 5.2 *Funds managed by accepting houses 1984 (£ million)*

Morgan, Grenfell	7 272
Robert Fleming	5 753
Lazard Bros.	5 300
Hill Samuel	5 115
N. M. Rothschild	5 000
S. G. Warburg	4 500
Schroders	4 000
Baring Bros.	2 541
Kleinwort Benson	2 262
Samuel Montagu	2 000
Hambros	1 098
Charterhouse Japhet	848
Singer & Friedlander	250
Brown & Shipley	75
Guiness Mahon	75
Rea Bros.	n.a.
Total	46 089

NOTE This table probably understates the value of funds managed. In some cases the data relate only to the value of UK pension funds managed and do not include other funds managed or funds advised.

SOURCE *Pension Funds and their Advisors*, 1984.

underwritten by an accepting house, there was the temptation to use the investment funds under management as repository for shares left on the hands of the house whether or not the shares were a proper investment to meet the funds' objectives. (This temptation becomes much more acute as the accepting houses develop as equity market-makers on a large scale; p. 103.)

For this reason, most houses took pains to ensure that the corporate advisory department and the investment management department were kept at arm's length. This was more difficult to achieve in practice than in theory, as the Takeover Panel discovered in 1969 when they concluded that it was not feasible in real life to separate the investment management functions from the corporate advice function.[2]

It was not only in investment management for United Kingdom institutions that the accepting houses expanded their services. Some also acted as selling or paying agents for North American mutual funds and other overseas unit trusts, and took an active part in British-based unit trusts. Kleinwort, Benson own part of the M. & G.

Group of unit trusts and Robert Fleming own the Save and Prosper Group, whilst other accepting houses have launched their own unit trusts either alone or in association with an insurance company.

Investment management and investment advice lead naturally to an attempt to cut the cost of dealing in securities. The London stock market was expensive to trade in compared with other markets such as the Frankfurt exchange. In 1972 the accepting houses established ARIEL (Automated Real-time Investments Exchange) which was designed as a computer clearing house for subscribers who would enter securities they wished to buy and sell so as to allow bargains to be struck without going through the conventional medium of the stock market. Initially all members of the accepting houses committee held capital in ARIEL but after a reorganisation in 1980 the capital was held by eleven banks and seven insurance companies. Although the system never did a large amount of business, and its custom, after initial growth, dwindled back to the level of 1974 (when it started trading), it did lead to a cut in stock exchange commission even before it began operations.

The establishment of ARIEL pointed the way to another development now taking place. In 1986 fixed commissions on the stock exchange will end. At the same time the distinction between brokers and jobbers is being abolished and outsiders will be able to buy up stock exchange members completely (instead of facing the current limit of 29.9 per cent). This opens the way for banks to become market makers. As a prelude to this the accepting houses have been in the van of forming links with stockbrokers and jobbers. Baring Bros, Guiness Mahon, Hambros, Hill Samuel, Kleinwort Benson, Morgan, Grenfell, N. M. Rothschild, Samuel Montagu and Warburgs have all bought stakes in jobbers or brokers, moving to total ownership when this is permitted. Schroders chose to set up a new venture, believing that the other accepting houses paid unreasonable prices for their jobbers and brokers. Robert Fleming is attempting to establish itself as a market maker, initially outside the stock exchange. In 1984 it anticipated the forthcoming reforms by beginning to make markets in a number of electrical and electronic shares.

The accepting houses also established insurance broking or life assurance links either directly or by incorporating insurance companies in the holding companies of which they were part. Montagu Trust, for example, the holding company for Samuel Montagu and Co., included Bland Welch, one of the largest British insurance brokers and E. W. Payne. Morgan, Grenfell associated with Willis, Faber and Dumas, the largest Lloyds broking house in 1967, whilst Kleinwort, Benson acquired a 20 per cent stake in Wright, Deer and Company. Warburgs and Lazards also took substantial equity stakes in insurance broking firms. Hill, Samuel acquired Lambert Brothers in 1968, and followed this by acquiring Noble Lowndes and Partners in 1969, and Hamilton Smith and Company and L. Hammond and Company in 1971 and 1972. For Singer and Friedlander the entry into insurance broking was achieved by a reverse takeover when C. T. Bowring acquired the accepting house in 1973. The principal reasons for establishing such insurance links have been explained as follows (Clay and Wheble, 1983):

(a) Insurance, like banking, had considerable financial power.
(b) Many activities in insurance required little capital as they expanded.
(c) Most clients of the accepting houses needed insurance services of one kind or another, and if an accepting house could provide such services it would gain and retain important customers.
(d) The accepting houses could often provide the expertise in managing cash flow which the insurance companies required,
(e) Insurance tended to grow consistently and not to be subject to the cyclical pattern of merchant banking.

All the accepting houses bar two had subsidiary or associated companies by 1975 acting as insurance brokers, including most of the largest houses. In addition, some six houses had important links with life assurance companies.

In addition to insurance links, most of the accepting houses expanded into leasing and factoring through subsidiary or associated companies. Leasing of capital equipment had become more attractive than purchase for parts of manufacturing equipment for a variety of reasons. The predominant one arose from the system of corporate taxation in operation before 1984–5 in Britain. After 1974, 100 per cent first year depreciation relief was allowed on plant and machinery. But low profits meant that in many cases firms' tax relief was fully exhausted (Goudie, 1984), and so marginal investment did not enable the potential relief to be used. A financial institution which bought capital equipment was able to offset the relief against its normal profit and the rent charged to the lessee took account of this. So the financial institution was able to make some return and the manufacturing firm found it spent less than if it had financed the purchase of capital equipment directly. The 1984 Budget substantially reformed Corporation Tax in a manner which removed much of the attraction of leasing.

The accepting houses also expanded overseas, in the United States of America where Barings, Hambros and Schroders established subsidiaries, in Australia where Schroders formed a link with Darling and Co., and in Switzerland, where Montagu Trust acquired Guyerzeller Zurmont. Needless to say, the houses which dealt in bullion (Rothschilds, Samuel Montagu, Hambros through Mocatta and Goldsmid and Kleinwort, Benson through Sharps, Pixley) retained those activities and found in them an increasing source of profit.

The accepting houses expanded, therefore, into every field which was likely to add to their prestige and, hopefully, to their profits. It was firmly believed by a number of merchant bankers that the future for their banks lay in the provision of as many services as possible under one roof, creating, as one banker put it, financial supermarkets in which their clients could find any service they required from the provision of term loans to financial advice, the insurance of their assets, the management of their pension funds and even the collection of their outstanding debts. Not all the additional activities proved profitable, particularly as expansion involved a substantial increase in overhead costs. By far, however, the most important aspect of the accepting houses' expansion was that it was made possible by the development, for which they were largely responsible, of a complete banking sector which grew up side by side with the traditional sector.

5.3 ACCEPTANCE HOUSE BANKING

In 1958 the transferable and American sterling accounts were consolidated as the first major move towards full convertibility of sterling; in 1961 full convertibility was formalised when Britain accepted Article 8 of the International Monetary Fund Agreement. At the same time Britain and most other countries allowed direct capital flows for both portfolio and other investment as one of the measures considered necessary to stimulate economic growth. The removal of some financial constraints created a climate in which

TABLE 5.3 *Accepting houses' balance sheet (December)*

	1960	1966		1975		1984	
Liabilities (£ million)							
Currency	*All*	£	*Other*	£	*Other*	£	*Other*
Current & deposit accounts: UK banks	173.6	107.4	119.2	496	844	1 677	3 888
Current & deposit accounts: Other UK		449.0	25.3	1 444	246	6 212	2 028
Current & deposit accounts: Overseas	249.9	130.0	304.3	153	1 639	1 158	7 425
CDs	—	—	—	170	73	753	322
Net non-deposit liabilities	48.5	127.2	20.8	743	2	3 319	−173
Total	472.0	813.6	469.6	3 006	2 804	13 119	13 490

	1960	1966		1975		1984	
Assets (£ million)							
Currency	*All*	£	*Other*	£	*Other*	£	*Other*
Notes and coin and working deposits at the Bank of England (L)	0.7	0.9	—	2	—	4	—
Balances with UK banks (L)	25.9	108.7	141.4	485	570	4 200	3 250
Call money (L)	70.2	71.6	—	142	—	245	—
CDs (L)	—	—	—	277	178	825	798
Local authority loans	54.6	186.5	—	391	—	647	—

Treasury bills (L)	20.0	14.0	—	69	—	2	—
Other bills (L)	22.2	19.3	—	111	42	66	127
UK government securities	58.1	75.4	—	23	—	252	—
Advances & loans: UK residents	110.0	217.3	23.6	994	376	2 861	1 058
Advances & loans: Other	89.1	15.8	272.3	49	1 571	1 358	7 415
Other assets	21.2	104.1	32.3	420	67	2 637	842
Special and cash ratio deposits	—	—	—	43	—	22	—
Total	472.0	813.6	469.6	3 006	2 804	13 119	13 490
Acceptances	131.8	271.2		946		3 803	
Ratios							
Non-bank advances/Non-bank deposits	n.a.	0.40	0.90	0.65	1.03	0.57	0.90
Liquid assets/All deposits	0.33	0.31		0.38		0.41	
Non-bank advances/All deposits	0.47	0.34	0.66	0.46	0.69	0.43	0.62

NOTES A currency split for 1960 is not possible.
(L) Liquid asset as defined by the Bank of England before 1971.
Cash-ratio deposits are included with special deposits.
Net non-deposit liabilities are a balancing item.
The 1984 figures for UK banks relate to monetary sector institutions.

SOURCES *Bank of England Statistical Abstract Nos 1 and 2; Bank of England Quarterly Bulletin.*

accepting house banking could once again thrive and from 1960 the houses expanded at a remarkable rate. Previous correspondent relationships with banks overseas were renewed and the opportunity to regain their former position in currency transactions was exploited to the full. Their deposit liabilities increased from 1960 to 1974 at a compound annual rate of nearly 19 per cent, well above twice the comparable rate of increase for the clearing banks, with a substantial proportion in currencies other than sterling. Advances made by the accepting houses increased from about £200 million in 1960 to some £1800 million by 1971 and to nearly £3000 million by 1975, of which a large part went to non-United Kingdom residents.

The table of balance sheets (see Table 5.3) summarises the development of the banking side of accepting house business. In the first half of the 1960s growth was, by later standards, fairly slow. But sterling liabilities rose 3.3 times between 1966 and 1975, and grew a further 4.3 times between the end of 1975 and 1984. During the last period the accepting houses grew faster than the banking system as a whole, and thus increased their market share of sterling deposits. They rely on wholesale deposits by banks to a much greater extent than the clearing banks but non-bank sterling deposits (from outside the banking system) have tended to exceed advances made outside the banking system. The foreign currency side of accepting houses' operations is managed differently; by its very nature it lacks a large domestic non-bank deposit base and thus liabilities to UK banks are substantially larger than deposits with them. It is probable that much greater attention is paid to the matching of maturities in foreign currency business. This reduces the need for liquidity in this sector.

In 1960 the houses had issued 66 per cent of all acceptances; their share in this business declined to well under half by 1966. Although they remain more important than either the clearing banks or the other non-clearing banks in this field, their share has, in the face of competition from non-British banks, declined to 25 per cent of the total.

The accepting houses were in a prime position to exploit the opportunities that came their way. They had always dominated the foreign exchange market; indeed, until 1914 the market consisted of the accepting houses, plus a few foreign bill brokers who met on the floor of the Royal Exchange. With the development of improved methods of communication by telephone, telex and cable, many other banks and foreign exchange brokers entered the market after the Second World War to carry out dealing with financial centres around the world, but the head start which the accepting houses enjoyed enabled them to operate with the maximum flexibility in meeting the needs of their customers. They could transfer the excess funds of the international financial and trading community to any country specified and, by means of swap conversions, made these funds available to local borrowers in their own currencies.

The expansion of the accepting houses was made possible by a combination of factors which provided the opportunities which they were quick to seize. These factors can briefly be summarised as (a) the development of new money markets from which the clearing banks were excluded until September 1971, by convention or by the need to maintain a minimum liquidity ratio, (b) the general belief in the associated goals of economic growth and increasing size of organisation and (c), the extension of the traditional activities of the accepting houses into the fields of unit trusts, investment trusts and property bonds; insurance broking; leasing; factoring; and equity participation through the provision of venture capital. The last area of expansion is, of course, not reflected in the balance sheet totals, which only indicate the size of the banking business. The different nature of accepting house business from retail banking may be seen from the rather different structure of their balance sheets. These issues are considerably elaborated on later as the development of new markets is discussed, but at this stage it is worth noting that typically they have found it necessary to maintain a much higher level of liquidity than the clearing banks, with therefore a much lower ratio of advances to deposits. Equally their lending has been much more heavily directed towards the financial sector than either the clearing or the other non-clearing banks.

In the process of expansion the accepting houses ceased to confine their interest to markets which were essentially complementary to those in which the clearing banks operated, and they competed on an increasing scale with the retail deposit banks. It is fair to point out that such competition was not confined to the British non-clearing banks. The foreign banks which opened branches in London were just as competitively aggressive with the clearing banks in the range of services they offered their customers. But the major difference between the British non-clearing banks and foreign banks was that the former dealt with the same clients as did the clearing banks whilst the latter served predominantly the multinational corporations and the overseas establishments of their domestic customers.

The banking crisis in 1973–5 did not seriously damage most of the accepting houses, which were largely responsible for the growth in the 1960s of the parallel money markets. Without these the heavy borrowing to finance speculation in assets such as property, or for lending to others who were themselves speculating in such assets, would have been much more difficult. As explained above, the merchant banks were generally very conscious of the need to maintain adequate liquidity by matching deposit liabilities and advances, and to limit lending to 'good' names in the market. This is not to say that the accepting houses were unaffected by the collapse of some non-clearing banks and the over-all decline in property and equity values; some suffered a substantial fall in profits in 1974–5. Some accepting houses undoubtedly made loans to property companies and needed to write off some advances when the property market collapsed. A property company with a land bank or a large site ripe for development appeared to be able to offer adequate security for its borrowing since non-one could foresee the fall in property values that was to come. Nor were they always as prudent in diversifying their portfolios of assets as in theory they ought to have been. Hambros, for example, was later badly affected by the collapse of the bulk tanker market in which it was heavily involved through its connections with Scandinavian shipping interests. Most were able to weather the crisis through the strength of their reserves and the broader base they had established over the past decade or so.

The two exceptions were William Brandt's and Antony Gibbs. William Brandt's had to make a provision in 1975 of £14 million for loans to property companies which proved irrecoverable, a provision larger than its inner reserves and its 1974 profits (*The Economist*, 5 April 1975). It survived because it had the heavyweight backing of its owners, National and Grindlays Bank, but found it necessary to resign from the Accepting Houses Committee and to make wholesale changes in its top management. Antony Gibbs also found it necessary to resign eventually from the Accepting Houses Committee as a result of the bank's acquisition by the Hong Kong and Shanghai Bank, a direct consequence of the losses it suffered in the crisis.

Detailed information on the pattern of advances is only available after 1976. A comparison of the sector breakdown with that of the clearing banks shows that the accepting houses directed their lending more towards the financial and services sectors than the clearing banks, and that lending to the financial sector increased in importance (see Table 5.4), in the 1980s.

The accepting houses' need for liquidity did not obviously lead to

TABLE 5.4 *Accepting houses' advances and outstanding acceptances to UK residents*

£ million February *Sector*	*1976*	*1979*	*1982*	*1985*
Manufacturing	306	872	1 174	1 525
Other production	54	113	217	407
Persons	93	99	139	322
Services	289	863	1 647	1 108
Financial	563	1 132	1 788	3 310
(of which property)	(203)	(210)	(414)	(582)
Total	1 305	3 079	4 965	6 673

NOTE The 1976 figures exclude acceptances. The classification in 1985 differs from that of earlier years.

SOURCE *Financial Statistics* and Bank of England.

larger holdings of reserve assets than the clearing banks. They would naturally prefer to hold high-yielding non-reserve assets. When competition and credit control started in October 1971 their reserve asset ratio was 15.7 per cent as against 16.3 per cent for the clearing banks. Although it subsequently rose to over 20 per cent, by the end of 1973 it was at 13.7 per cent as against 13.8 per cent for the clearing banks. At the end of 1973 accepting house holdings of reserve assets were the same as they had been at the start of competition and credit control. The expansion in their eligible liabilities of 16 per cent between October 1971 and the end of 1973 was thus achieved solely by a reduction in their reserve ratio.

Despite this relatively small expansion in eligible liabilities, it is clear that they played a major role in the expansion of the banking system. For they considerably increased their deposit liabilities to non-bank depositors (from £789m in October 1971 to £1597m by December 1973) and lent the major part of money on to other banks either by purchases of certificates of deposit or through direct increases in balances. Thus the accepting houses were much more heavily involved in the monetary expansion than a simple analysis of the change in their eligible liabilities suggest; their intermediation assisted the general rise in the money stock.

Following the introduction of the corset in February 1975, and, in a period in which the companies who provide accepting house deposits found themselves short of liquidity, sterling balances held by non-banks with the accepting houses, both as normal deposits or as certificates of deposit, declined. This again was buffered by a reduction in on-lending and the accepting houses again held their eligible liabilities stable, although their reserve assets rose slightly.

The lifting of the corset allowed the accepting houses to make fairly rapid growth, and its periodic reimposition did not prevent, over the period January 1975 to July 1981, the eligible liabilities of the accepting houses growing by 177 per cent as against 136 per cent for the banking system as a whole. Although they generally maintained a higher reserve ratio than the clearing banks they were equally affected by the drain in reserves in the first half of 1981. The importance of on-lending by the houses to the other monetary institutions continued to vary erratically. Thus 1982 saw rapid growth in non-bank private sector deposits, which had only a small effect on the eligible liabilities of the houses, being mainly lent on to the rest of the banking sector again, directly or through issues of certificates of deposit. The behaviour of the accepting houses, particularly since the introduction of competition and credit control, illustrates how interbank lending can be used as a buffer in order to balance day-to-day borrowing and lending; if a bank holds excess deposits relative to either its stock of reserve assets or opportunities for lending, it can lend them on to other banks which have a surplus of reserves and a use for the money (see Table 5.3).

5.4 THE CAPITAL BASE OF THE ACCEPTING HOUSES

It is clear from Table 5.3 that there has been a substantial growth in the non-deposit liabilities of the accepting houses. Such expansion would normally be achieved from retained profits, and the accepting houses have not been any major exception to this principle. Unlike the clearing banks, individual accepting houses still do not publish their true historic cost profits. Arguably their accounts do no more than indicate broad trends. Data on the capital base of four large and one small accepting house illustrate the capital expansion which has taken place. There has been an increased tendency to rely on loan capital (as was found with the clearing banks). The major capital expansion has been in disclosed reserves (retained profits) rather than equity issues. The effect of Hambro's shipping losses are visible in its 1975 figures (Table 5.5).

5.5 SUMMARY

The accepting houses developed the business of merchant banking to include the provision of a wide range of corporate services. This

TABLE 5.5 *The capital base of five accepting houses (£ million)*

		Issued capital	*Disclosed reserves*	*Loan capital*	*Minority interests*	*Total*
1970	Brown, Shipley	2	4	1	—	7
	Hambros	6	39	13	—	58
	Hill, Samuel	12	13	16	—	41
	Kleinwort, Benson	16	16	1	—	33
	Schroders	8	13	2	3	26
1975	Brown, Shipley	6	4	1	—	13
	Hambros	6	50	52	5	113
	Hill, Samuel	12	53	30	—	95
	Kleinwort, Benson	16	49	16	—	81
	Schroders	9	18	16	3	46
1980	Brown, Shipley	6	25	—	—	31
	Hambros	6	109	34	—	149
	Hill, Samuel	17	90	41	5	153
	Kleinwort, Benson	16	139	40	3	198
	Schroders	16	45	41	4	106
1984	Brown, Shipley	14	32	—	—	46
	Hambros	6	192	58	3	259
	Hill, Samuel	23	202	127	6	358
	Kleinwort, Benson	15	236	147	2	402
	Schroders	16	148	63	7	233

SOURCE Accepting House Annual Reports.

provided them with the profits they needed to expand the scale of their banking operations at a faster rate than the clearing banks. Their share of their traditional business of writing acceptances has declined considerably since 1960, but it remains, relative to their size, more important for them than for any other type of bank.

A need for liquidity greater than that of the clearing banks has encouraged the accepting houses to make active use of the interbank market in balancing their liquidity. But their major contribution has been as market-makers rather than as large participants. The growth of the new money markets was fostered by the accepting houses and served to meet not only their own needs but also those of many other financial institutions. The accepting houses have proved of much greater importance in the evolution of the financial system than their balance sheet size alone would suggest (Cooper, 1984, Chapter 2).

6 The New Money Markets

The new money markets that came into being from about the mid-1950s are usually called 'parallel' markets because they developed alongside the traditional discount market, which they rapidly overtook in size. This term is, however, misleading since it obscures the extent to which the new markets were interlocked in a complexity of operations which it is impossible to unravel statistically. Solely for clarity of exposition, the markets can be divided into (a) the local authority markets, (b) the sterling and currency interbank market, (c) the negotiable certificate of deposit market and (d) the eurodollar and eurocurrency markets. The new markets differed considerably from the traditional discount market; all lending was unsecured, there was no lender of last resort, loans were not self-liquidating and the authorities had no direct control over the flow of funds through them. All the markets provided the non-clearing banks with an opportunity, which for most of them had not previously existed, to develop deposit banking and thus to expand their deposit liabilities on the basis of which they could engage directly in commercial lending. Statistics illustrating the rapid growth of these markets, and the related finance house market, are shown in Table 6.1.

6.1 THE LOCAL AUTHORITY MARKETS

In 1955 local authorities, which had hitherto met their borrowing requirements from the Public Works Loan Board (the PWLB), were driven on to the market, the PWLB only acting as lender of last resort. The reason for this change was that the authorities wished to exercise a closer control over the issue of Treasury bills which, in the 1950s, accounted for a sizeable proportion of the clearing banks' liquidity. If the PWLB, in order to meet local authority borrowing demands, had to draw funds from the Exchequer, this closer control would have been frustrated, particularly because the size of local authority borrowing was rising sharply as the lag in house building resulting from the Second World War was overtaken, and as the scale

End year (£ million)	Local authority deposits	Local authority mortgages	£ CDs	Other CDs	Interbank deposits £	Interbank deposits Other	Eurocurrency deposits	Finance house deposits
1960	846	2 106	—	—	270		633	n.a.
1961	1 112	2 319	—	—	312		749	n.a.
1962	1 178	2 685	—	—	244	266	960	337
1963	1 394	2 958	—	—	360	342	1 280	390
1964	1 762	3 115	—	—	404	448	1 786	494
1965	1 798	3 480	—	—	500	628	2 122	654
1966	1 807	3 843	—	81	593	835	3 002	669
1967	1 918	4 076	—	249	865	1 475	4 384	597
1968	1 952	4 667	166	597	1 180	1 848	7 139	612
1969	1 982	5 165	442	1 541	1 692	4 151	11 994	636
1970	1 982	5 659	1 089	1 650	1 880	5 431	15 283	688
1971	2 067	5 854	2 242	1 924	2 103	6 300	17 605	823
1972	2 564	5 900	4 926	3 072	4 450	8 824	25 460	437
1973	3 553	6 531	5 983	4 429	7 688	14 160	39 017	477
1974	4 258	8 063	4 318	5 088	8 596	15 612	47 451	459
1975	4 058	9 073	2 979	6 419	7 039	18 996	63 368	415
1976	4 720	9 639	3 340	9 860	8 146	23 216	87 319	1 749
1977	3 386	9 777	4 641	12 455	11 027	24 544	89 338	1 855
1978	4 346	9 884	3 809	14 132	13 093	27 989	104 566	1 901
1979	5 819	10 750	3 833	17 843	19 305	36 718	126 756	2 528
1980	5 541	12 352	5 727	20 946	17 677	42 708	144 954	2 354
1981	5 478	13 608	6 695	40 424	24 186	64 614	220 076	2 358
1982	4 041	12 637	8 525	57 229	34 429	84 887	281 868	931
1983	4 129	10 724	9 792	70 457	36 158	84 617	331 229	1 094
1984	4 898	9 877	11 230	79 648	43 239	98 692	428 945	1 212

NOTE Local authority mortgage totals are shown on 31 March of the following year. The total of eurocurrency deposits indicates only those held in the UK. It includes holdings of foreign currency CDs. Underlining indicates data discontinuities.

SOURCES *Financial Statistics* and *Bank of England Quarterly Bulletins*.

of welfare provision increased. Moreover, the government wished nationalised industries to raise their capital funds from the PWLB rather than from the market, and therefore considered that it was preferable for bodies which were not controlled so directly (that is local authorities) to meet their borrowing needs from the market.

The change in government policy created difficulties for the local authorities which had been accustomed to securing long-term funds from the PWLB against the issue of mortgages. The capital market had a long queue of would-be borrowers and, even if local authorities could have found an early place in the queue, with interest rates rising their needs could only have been made at the price of a significant increase in borrowing costs. The local authorities therefore looked to the market in short-term loans, hoping that the rise in interest rates was temporary. Short-term funds were borrowed against the issue of temporary deposit receipts pending the issue of mortgages. They also sought long-term borrowing from sources other than the PWLB.

The accepting houses found that they were able to make a market in short-term loans to local authorities largely as a result of the contemporaneous availability of deposits offered to them by foreign banks domiciled in London. Some of these foreign banks had surplus funds (both sterling and other currencies) on which they wished to earn a higher yield than the deposit rates offered by the clearing banks. In addition, the Eastern European banks (like Moscow Narodny Bank) were unwilling to place surplus US dollars in New York. If the 'Cold War' intensified these might be frozen, and many preferred to keep their surpluses in London. These banks therefore offered short-term funds, initially in amounts not less than £50 000 or £100 000, to non-clearing banks who were prepared to take them at an interest rate higher than the clearing banks' deposit rates, in order to on-lend, at a small margin above cost, to the local authorities seeking funds. The temporary deposit market grew substantially, trebling in size between 1960 and the beginning of the 1970s as Table 6.1 shows. Since then the market has been more stagnant. Its size ultimately reflects the demand for short-term credit by the local authorities, and this means it is unlikely to grow to the same extent as markets which are pure financial intermediation. The market in long-term local authority debt is larger than the market in temporary debt. Long-term debt offers borrowers the attraction of certainty as to interest costs and avoids the need for repeated refinancing. But since 1980 it too has stagnated; central government has as a matter of policy expanded its role in local authority finance at the expense of both of these markets.

The sectoral ownership of both types of local authority debt is shown in Table 6.2. The banks have a surprisingly small holding of temporary debt, given the nature of their own liabilities. On the other hand their importance in the long-term debt market has grown considerably. Many of the mortgages are at fixed interest rates and thus bank holdings of these represent pure maturity transformation.

TABLE 6.2 *The ownership of local authority debt*

		Local authority temporary debt (£ million)				
End year	*Banks*	*Other financial institutions*	*Industrial & commercial companies*	*Personal sector*	*Other*	*Total*
1962	270	—	812	—	—	1 082
1966	349	332	393	330	267	1 671
1970	420	629	220	310	241	1 820
1975	334	1 535	459	211	746	3 285
1980	435	2 476	508	321	1 043	4 783
1984	1 015	1 502	276	284	344	3 421

NOTE The 1984 bank figure includes overdrafts, while the earlier data do not. Holdings of revenue bills cannot be identified and are not included. Inter-authority debt, included in Table 6.1, is not shown here.

SOURCE *Financial Statistics.*

		Local authority long-term debt (£ million)				
31 March	*Banks*	*Other financial institutions*	*Industrial & commercial companies*	*Personal sector*	*Other*	*Total*
1962	174	969	92	884	200	2 319
1966	361	1 434	152	1 326	207	3 480
1971	1 572	1 988	106	1 733	260	5 659
1976	2 856	3 410	277	2 049	481	9 073
1981	5 881	3 702	279	1 730	760	12 352
1985	5 573	2 465	106	1 003	730	9 877

NOTE Estimates before 1976 are derived by cumulating published flows, and then scaling the results to reconcile them with published over-all stock data for the years concerned.

SOURCE *Financial Statistics.*

6.2 THE INTERBANK MARKET

From the same sources of deposits as were used by the accepting houses to provide the funds to lend to local authorities, there developed a market in wholesale deposits between non-clearing banks and from large institutions to non-clearing banks. It is clear from Table 6.1 that this is now by far the largest of the new sterling markets. The minimum size of deposit was normally £25 000 and for a loan £50 000. The clearing banks as a matter of history never lent directly to each other, but cleared their balances by placing surplus funds in the discount market, and calling in their loans to the discount market when they were short of funds as described in Chapter 4. In any case, whilst the clearing banks were constrained by liquidity minima and also subject to quantitative controls on their advances, there was little benefit to be gained from attracting large wholesale deposits on which they would have paid interest but which they would have been unable to deploy profitably. Later in the 1960s, however, the clearing banks did set up subsidiaries, described in Chapter 7, to operate in the interbank market. The non-clearing banks were not subject to the same constraints, and the accepting houses were quick to seize the opportunity to expand their deposit liabilities. They could afford to offer a higher rate of interest than the clearing banks' deposit rate since they did not have to cover the costs of a large branch network. The attractive rates of interest offered brought substantial amounts from corporate treasurers who had surplus funds which they wished to place on a comparatively short-term basis.

The interbank market developed fast, as Table 6.1 shows; the accepting houses used it as an important major source of funds and made a market not only in short-term funds but also in deposits and loans for three months, six months and longer periods. All lending was unsecured. By the mid-1960s, the accepting houses were not only using the market in order to balance their borrowing and lending to their industrial and commercial customers, but were also increasingly looking for profit opportunities from interest arbitrage. The money market dealers in the merchant banks were prepared to take a view on trends in interest rates in both the very short-term and the longer term, in order to gain profits from their dealing if their views turned out to be correct (or, of course, to suffer losses if they guessed wrongly). It was in the opportunities that the interbank market offered to build up deposits that the greatest dangers lay. Most bankers who have been consulted assert that they used the interbank market primarily to acquire deposits without necessarily having specific borrowers in mind. The accepting houses regarded it as important that they should increase their deposit liabilities since balance sheet size was a fundamental factor in demonstrating relative important in the market. The first objective was therefore to build up the deposit liability base and only afterwards to deploy those deposits to best advantage (although, of course, they knew that there were profitable opportunities to be found). Some part of the increased deposits could be used internally within the accepting house for dealing and trading in equities, foreign bonds, precious metals and so on. What was not required internally could be loaned to local authorities, always in the market for funds, to clients of the bank, or placed back in the market. Dealing in the interbank market was essentially a daily operation. The money market dealers adjusted their books as the day proceeded, and accepted or placed deposits, usually via money brokers, according to their views on the relative tightness or ease of money in the market. For this reason, statistics of money loaned and borrowed in the interbank market which are only available on a monthly basis may provide a misleading snapshot view of the scale of transactions in the market.[1]

The policy adopted by accepting houses and other non-clearing banks of building up their deposit liabilities has been dubbed 'liability management' and it represented a completely new outlook so far as the United Kingdom was concerned. As the Committee of London Clearing Bankers (1977) has put it:

> Traditionally most deposit-taking institutions, the clearing banks included, could be described as 'deposit-driven'; that is to say their main concern was to deploy the deposits received in the normal course of business as best they could . . . The development of the wholesale money markets has enabled bankers to modify the traditional approach since they can now enter lending commitments in the knowledge that any shortfall in deposits can be made good in the markets. Indeed, many non-clearing banks without retail deposits are now effectively 'advances-driven'.

It was, however, a policy with inherent dangers. However prudently banks might behave in deciding their lending policies, at times there were always likely to be excess funds in the interbank market seeking an outlet and the money brokers who thrived on the business which the market created were only too anxious to find borrowers for those funds.[2] This created greater instability in the financial system because the ultimate liability for money lent in the interbank market might be known only at the end of a chain of lenders and borrowers. Bank A might only be prepared to lend to Bank B which it regarded as a 'good name', but Bank B, with excess funds to dispose of, might be willing to lend to Bank C and so on. At the end of the chain of borrowers might be Bank X to which Bank A would under no circumstances have loaned direct and yet the sequence of unsecured lending had the effect that Bank A was to some extent dependent for the repayment of its loan to Bank B on the ability of Bank X to repay its borrowing when due. So, a failure in the chain of repayments of loans could have a domino effect on other banks stretching back to the first bank in the chain. The effect of the growth of the interbank market was therefore that banks become increasingly interdependent with the 'layering' as Minsky has dubbed it, so that weaknesses in one part of the banking sector could permeate to the sector as a whole. This risk of contagion must grow as the interdependence of the system increases. For uncertainty about how banks are affected by any particular event may provoke a general withdrawal of deposits.

In the interbank market it is not possible to separate genuine commercial business from dealings between market makers. There is no doubt that the accepting houses used the interbank market to provide their industrial and commercial customers with the advances which those customers sought and the merchant banks were able not only to advise their customers to seek term money rather than overdraft facilities for their longer-term needs, but also to provide such term money themselves. But what proportion of the total funds raised in the interbank market were directed towards meeting the requirements of industry and commerce and what proportion was devoted to speculative credit creation is unknown. Brown has suggested as a general rule that, as the number of banks in a financial centre increases, the size of interbank dealings not related to the needs of commercial customers increases (Brown, 1978). In any case, in the general atmosphere of speculation which developed as the property boom reached its height, one would expect that, as different financial institutions were prepared to participate to different degrees, and as they had differential knowledge about the opportunities for profitable speculation, so the interbank market would expand.

The growth of interbank lending relative to other banking may be seen from Table 6.3.

TABLE 6.3 *£ deposits and advances, 1960–84 (£ million)*

End year	*Deposits by non-bank UK residents*	*Balances with UK banks*	*Advances to non-bank UK residents*	*Advances: Deposits (%) (all*	*excluding banks)*
1960	Not available	Not available	4 082	—	—
1966[a]	11 864	593	6 039	54	51
1971	15 063	2 103	8 919	64	59
1973	24 915	7 688	20 057	85	81
1975	30 028	7 039	21 823	77	73
1980	56 066	17 677	48 350	89	86
1984[b]	98 076	43 239	103 339	104	105

a This may include some foreign currency items. It does not cover deposits by Scottish and Irish clearers with London clearers.
b These statistics relate to the monetary sector, which differs from the banking sector mainly in that it includes the Trustee Savings Banks.
SOURCE *Financial Statistics.*

From a small level at the start of the 1960s, interbank borrowing grew to about 30 per cent of other deposits by 1973. Indeed it was a much more important source of deposits for 'other banks' than for accepting houses. The latter typically obtained about one-sixth of their deposits in the interbank market. The end of the monetary expansion and property boom halted the growth in interbank lending; the restoration of stability after the crisis of 1973–5 maintained it at around 30 per cent of deposits by non-banks, until the end of the corset in 1980. Since then the importance of interbank lending has taken another upward turn. As was shown in Table 2.4 (page 27), the liquidity of the banking system has fallen considerably. Towards the end of the period it was provided by an excess of sterling overseas deposits over overseas lending and by the capital base of the system.

6.3 NEGOTIABLE CERTIFICATES OF DEPOSIT

In 1966 the American banks in London introduced negotiable certificates of deposit denominated in US dollars following their successful use in the United States of America as a method of attracting deposits. The incentive in America for the introduction in 1961 of CDs was not dissimilar to that which induced the clearing banks to set up their subsidiaries to compete in the interbank market. The New York banks, which in 1945 accounted for some 20 per cent of all deposits in the USA, had lost ground considerably by 1960. The interest that could be paid on time deposits was limited by Regulation Q of the Federal Reserve and, although company treasurers were increasingly looking for more profitable outlets for their liquid reserves, the New York banks were denied the opportunity to attract deposits by bidding up interest rates. The introduction of CDs, on which there was no upper limit on the interest payable, was the New York banks' solution to the problem of regaining lost deposits. Negotiable CDs proved 'outstandingly successful in reversing the trend away from the New York banks, and indeed by 1972 approximately 40 per cent of US bank deposits were held in the form of Certificates of Deposit' (Shaw, 1981). The bank CD is a negotiable instrument acknowledging the receipt of a deposit and incorporating an unconditional obligation to pay the bearer the amount of the principal together with interest at a stated date in the future. A CD can therefore be traded outside the banking system as well as within it.

The United Kingdom market in United States dollar CDs grew substantially from 1966, despite the fact that they could only be held by non-residents. Between 1966 and 1972, as a proportion of non-sterling currencies, they increased from 2 per cent of total liabilities to 8 per cent (Shaw, 1981). More recently the size of the $CD market tended to settle at between 10 per cent and 15 per cent of total overseas foreign currency liabilities of UK banks, although since 1980 its importance has risen again. The success of $CDs led First National City Bank and Allan, Harvey and Ross (a discount house) to propose, at a meeting of banks in 1967, that CDs denominated in sterling should be introduced. Not all the accepting houses present at the meeting were in favour since some foresaw the danger of replacing short-term money by the purchase of longer-term CDs on which there was always the possibility of capital loss should interest rates rise.

A market for sterling CDs opened in October 1968, and the value in issue grew rapidly as Table 6.1 shows. This market, despite being smaller than the $CD market, was obviously of greater importance as far as internal banking was concerned. The Bank of England looked on the introduction of sterling CDs with approval, 'Sterling certificates may provide companies and others with a useful additional outlet for the investment of liquid funds. From the point of view of individual banks a growth in deposits at longer terms may . . . increase the scope for longer term borrowing' (*Bank of England Quarterly Bulletin,* 1968b). Until September 1971 the clearing banks could only issue CDs through their subsidiaries; thereafter they could issue them in their own name and quickly dominated the market.

The attraction of sterling CDs was enhanced by a quirk in the tax laws which freed the interest earned on CDs not held to maturity from tax; this made CDs an attractive investment for the wealthy clients of the accepting houses which were not slow to emphasise the advantages. The loophole in the tax laws was closed in the Finance Act, 1973. This was by no means the only attraction which CDs offered to the non-clearing banks. By issuing CDs the non-clearing banks were able to assure themselves of deposits which would remain with them for the period to maturity of those CDs, a period longer than the normal deposit received via the interbank market. With a source of term deposits at their disposal, the houses were able to expand their term lending, secure in the knowledge that, with a reasonably matched book, they would be less likely to be faced with a liquidity crisis. Moreover a CD was a negotiable instrument. Some depositors were more ready to switch from clearing bank time deposits into CDs than into non-negotiable wholesale deposits.

The maturity pattern of CDs reflected the differing interests of depositors and issuers. In a world of uncertainty regarding future interest rates, expectations governed the term and size of the CD issue. If depositors expected interest rates to rise, they were unwilling to purchase CDs other than of short maturity, since more interest could be earned by re-depositing as rates rose. With the same expectations, issuers wished to issue CDs for long maturities secure in the knowledge that the deposits secured could always be profitably re-deployed in the short-term interbank or local authority markets. The converse was true, of course, if it was expected that interest rates would fall. The actual maturity pattern of CDs demonstrated the compromise between these conflicting interests. In April 1973 40 per cent of all CDs outstanding matured within three months and 90 per cent within one year (*Bank of England Quarterly Bulletin,* 1973). The Bank of England reported that there was little difference in the maturity pattern of CDs as between groups of issuing banks, although the clearing banks after 1971 preferred on the whole to use CDs to secure funds at a somewhat longer term than did the non-clearing banks.

The introduction of CDs, which were issued in minimum units of £50 000, resulted in a further stimulus to the market in wholesale deposits but, although CDs had obvious attractions for the accepting houses which issued them, and for the discount market which traded in them, the CD market contained inherent dangers. Since CDs were negotiable, the ultimate holder of a CD was dependent on the ability of the issuing bank to repay the CD with accrued interest at maturity. If the issuing bank was an accepting house, or a member of a clearing bank group, the risk of default was probably minimal, but other banks, not so creditworthy, also issued CDs. There was, of course, no lender of last resort since the Bank of England refused to extend to CDs the rediscount facilities offered on eligible bills of exchange. Some argued that without one there could be no guarantee that liquidity could be adequate in times of distress. To some extent this problem was offset, because the issuing banks undertook to make a market in each others' CDs. But there was no certainty that this would always be possible, except at very poor rediscount rates. A market developed in 'roll-over' CDs, which could be extended at the will of the issuer at the original rate of interest, and in 'forward CDs' under which banks could enter into contracts to buy or sell CDs at some date in the future. Both of these innovations involved considerable risks for operators in the market with the volatility in interest rates that was a feature of the early 1970s. These risks were amply demonstrated in 1973 when the Scottish Co-operative Society was involved in heavy losses on forward CDs and needed to be rescued by a consortium of banks. But perhaps the most cogent criticism of the CD market is that it provided an attractive means of expanding deposit liabilities given that there would be sufficient liquidity in the banking system to meet maturities as they arose. This could not be guaranteed.

The experience of banks in the United States of America in the mid-1960s demonstrated the instability which could result from over-reliance on the CD market to finance expansion of deposits. The United States banks had issued CDs on a very large scale and were heavily dependent on CD issues to maintain their positions. As interest rates moved against them, and as their liabilities ran off in 1966, they were forced to find other sources of funds (mainly in eurodollars) outside the control of the Federal Reserve. The result was a prolonged liquidity squeeze which culminated in the Penn Central bankruptcy (Minsky, 1971).

In the United Kingdom the potential instability of part of the financial system was demonstrated by the fact that the non-clearing banks, other than the accepting houses, held 55 per cent of their total liabilities in the form of CD and interbank deposits. This compared with a proportion of only 35 per cent for the accepting houses. The financial crisis in 1973–5 in the United Kingdom brought home to the banking sector the dangers of instability in the financial system as it became increasingly difficult for the CDs issued by a number of non-clearing banks to be traded at all. As a result of this and the other changes already mentioned, the volume of CDs in circulation decreased sharply from some £6000 million in 1973 to less than £3000 million by December 1975 (see Table 6.1). The changing fortunes of CDs are seen even more clearly from an analysis of their holders. While negotiable deposits have continued to play an important role in the banking system, their holdings by the non-bank institutions have declined very considerably in real terms since 1972, before the tax position changed. Typically, CDs earn a slightly lower yield than interbank deposits of similar maturity. The extra liquidity that they offer through negotiability is more likely to appeal to financial than to non-financial institutions; at the same time the financial position of the company sector has deteriorated markedly since 1973; these factors, and the tax changes already mentioned, have led to a situation where, despite the fall in the value of money since then, holdings of £CDs by industrial and commercial companies are not back to their 1972 level (see Table 6.4).

TABLE 6.4 *The ownership of sterling CDs (£ million)*

End year	*Industrial and commercial companies*	*Other financial institutions*	*Total (including bank holdings)*
1968	56	27	166
1972	1 203	355	4 926
1976	266	517	2 979
1980	488	943	5 727
1984	507	1 446	11 230

SOURCE *Financial Statistics.*

6.4 THE FINANCE HOUSES

The finance houses have operated on the fringe of the banking system, traditionally providing high-risk consumer credit, although they have gradually developed into other areas such as leasing, credit factoring (the purchase of a company's debts) and the provision of personal loans. Shaw (1981) refers to industrial and commercial lending in 1980 taking up 60 per cent of finance house lending, but repeated redefinitions of the sector make it difficult to come to any general conclusion. In 1984 loans to the personal sector amounted to 54 per cent. By comparison only 30 per cent of monetary sector domestic advances were made to the personal sector (*Financial Statistics*).

Finance houses are maturity transformers to a greater degree than banks. Their lending tends to be at fixed interest for the whole of the life of any loan, a feature of only a small part of clearing bank lending. This obviously makes them very susceptible to periods of high interest rates and encourages them to borrow for as long a term as possible.

More than any other institution their traditional business, that of consumer credit provision, has been subject to government regulation. Hire purchase controls have frequently been in force requiring minimum down-payments, and maximum repayment periods, in an effort to regulate purchases of consumer durables and thus control the state of demand in the economy. This proved necessary even during the period of competition and credit control, despite the existence of a reserve asset ratio; for it was, of course, not possible to regulate the supply of reserve assets to the finance houses independently of that to other financial intermediaries (and control over the total was hardly precise). But the traditional business of the finance houses was very much the specific type of lending, which periods of credit restriction were intended to suppress, and thus it was natural that direct controls were adopted. The statistical picture of finance house deposits is confused because the figures of Table 6.1 include, up to the end of 1971, houses also classified as banks. Further statistical changes occurred in 1976 and in 1981.

Banks participated in consumer credit business in three ways. In 1958 hire purchase controls were lifted and the clearing banks rapidly set up their own finance houses as subsidiaries. They also made loans to other finance houses and more recently they have developed 'personal loans' as a form of consumer credit.

The finance houses outside the monetary sector rely predominantly on the monetary sector as a source of funds. Table 6.5 shows their liability structure.

TABLE 6.5 *The pattern of finance house liabilities, December 1984*

	%
Commercial bills	16.0
Short-term from monetary sector	24.8
Long-term from monetary sector	30.6
Other borrowing	4.6
Other current liabilities	4.6
Capital and reserves	19.4
Total	100.0

SOURCE *Financial Statistics.*

One must note the fraction of shareholders' funds in total liabilities. This high capitalisation reflects the fact that finance house business is riskier than banking business.

The 1979 Banking Act obliged deposit-taking finance houses to apply for licences placing them in the monetary sector. It is thus inevitable that the remaining houses and consumer-credit companies have to rely on the monetary sector as their major source of finance, but that the magnitude of the market for such finance is much diminished in importance relative to the interbank market.

6.5 INTEREST RATES IN THE PARALLEL MARKETS

Figure 6.1 shows local authority temporary deposit Treasury bill rates measured relative to the bank rate/MLR/bank base rate. As can be seen there are substantial divergences in the returns offered. Local authority rates have tended to move in line with certificate of deposit rates, which are close to, but usually slightly below, interbank rates. Treasury bill rates are usually considerably lower, reflecting the extra liquidity of bills.

The relationship between institutional lending rates and market rates is of some importance. The nineteenth century tradition was that there were two interest rate structures. One set of rates was market determined while the other set was determined relative to the bank rate. This second group included overdraft and deposit rates.[3] Only during periods of crisis would the bank rate have a substantial influence on market rates. The tradition of linking clearing-bank rates to the bank rate continued. It was only in 1970 that the banks

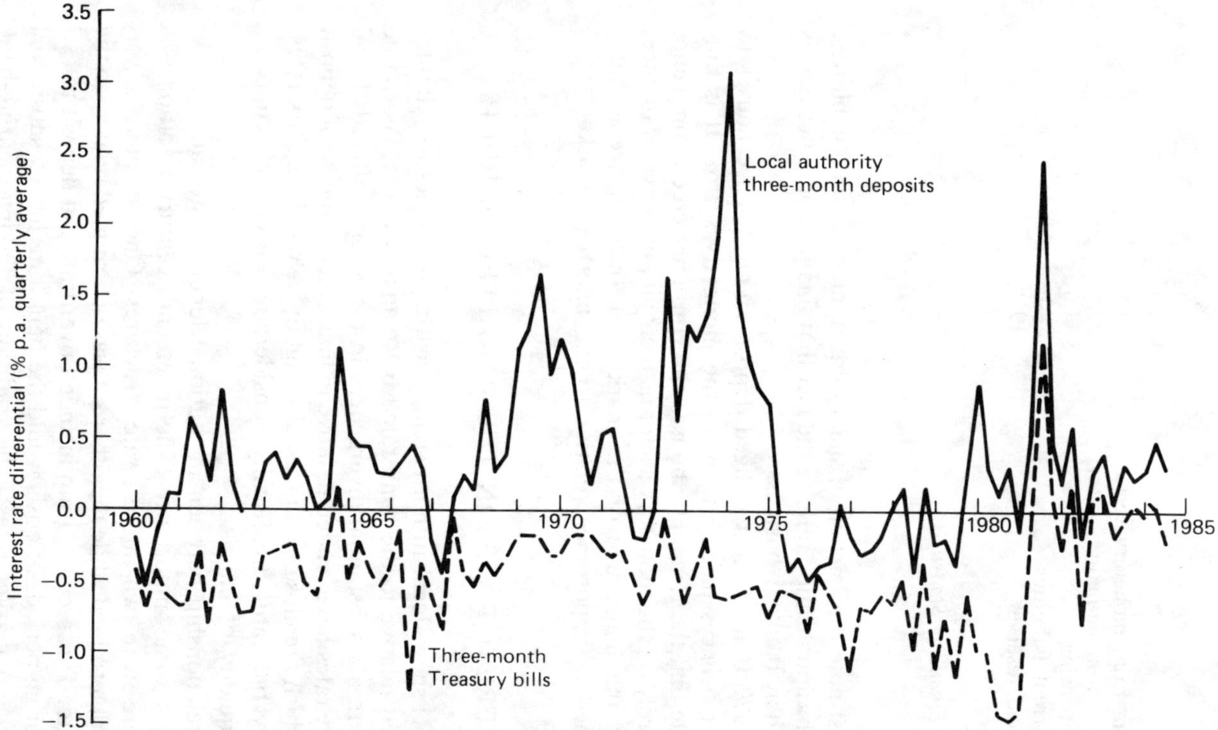

FIGURE 6.1 *Local authority and Treasury bill three-month rates relative to minimum lending rate**

*Bank Rate to October 1972, Minimum Lending Rate to August 1981 and Bank Base Rate since then.
SOURCE *Financial Statistics.*

began to set their own base rate, which then served as the reference point for overdraft and deposit rates.

The link between this and a rate set by the Bank of England was weakened further in October 1972 when the bank rate was turned into a formula-related minimum lending rate. As noted in Chapter 4, the banks were, in 1973, slow to increase their base rates when the MLR rose; since MLR, in any case, did not move with the rates in the parallel markets (p. 92) it was profitable to borrow at overdraft rates and redeposit at interbank rates.

Much of the discussion of 1972–4 stresses the interaction between reserve and non-reserve assets as the source of this differential (Spencer, 1982 and 1985). The demand for credit was high but, in order for this demand for credit to be supplied, the banks had to bid for extra deposits and buy extra reserves. The yield on reserve assets was thus forced down while yields on money rose. Calls for special deposits may have accentuated the problem by effectively making it harder for the banks to obtain the reserves they needed. A gap of up to 3½ per cent appeared between Treasury bill and three-month parallel rates.

Provided administered rates rose to some extent this process led to higher rather than lower profits for the clearing banks; in November 1973 only a quarter of their net deposits were wholesale, while over a third were non-interest-bearing current accounts. Thus a 2 per cent increase in the administered rate structure would increase profits, provided rates in the wholesale market rose by not more than 4.5 per cent. In 1972 wholesale deposits were rather less important and profits would have increased, provided wholesale rates rose by less than 10 per cent in response to a 2 per cent rise in administered rates. So although it would have been sensible for profit maximising banks to raise loan rates, there were no great financial pressures on them to do so rapidly. But the pressures on the banks which relied mainly on wholesale deposits were intensified and can be inferred from the peak differential of 1973/4. This peak may partly reflect concern that the banking crisis would lead to general illiquidity in the parallel markets.

The period since 1975 has shown a much more stable picture for two reasons. First, whenever the monetary position caused concern the authorities relied on the corset in addition to special deposits, and this effectively prevented the mechanism which created the yield differential from operating with the same vigour. Secondly, banks adjusted to the new system making administered rates move more closely in line with market rates (with the corset driving a wedge between deposit and lending rates). The ending of the corset and the new system of monetary control essentially marked the integration of the traditional and parallel markets. The only brief disturbance to this position arose in 1981 when administered rates were unresponsive to market tightness generated by the Bank of England in support of sterling.

Most attention focuses on the three-month interest rates in the parallel markets. Overnight money has played even more of a role in residual financing; the interest rate in this market has shown very great instability, fluctuating over a large range during the course of a day. But the changes on August 1981 have had a stabilising effect here. For the separate average and minimum requirements for banks' holdings in the discount market imply that call money can be used for temporary residual financing in a way that would not be possible if the average and minimum were equal. Thus, since August 1981 the fluctuations in the overnight market seem to have been reduced.

6.6 THE EURODOLLAR AND THE EUROMARKETS

The eurodollar market in London began in about 1957 when, following the Suez crisis in the preceding year, the use of sterling to finance non-British trade was restricted. In 1958 most European currencies were made convertible externally and foreign exchange controls were relaxed which allowed arbitraging of funds between US dollars and European currencies. The conventional explanation for the growth of the eurodollar market is that, since the United States of America was running a large balance of payments deficit, US dollars accumulated in those countries where balance of trade was favourable. There was a limit on the rate of interest that could be paid on time deposits by banks in the United States of America (Regulation Q of the Federal Reserve system) and US dollars were therefore not returned to the United States but held outside in countries where interest yields were higher. The large balances of US dollars held in Europe were used by the banks holding them to provide the foreign exchange needed by governments, other banks and large companies (particularly the multinational corporations). Since central banks had intervention points in US dollars, most international currency operations were quoted and dealt against US dollars.

There has been considerable debate about the nature of eurodollar deposits. Revell (1973) argues that, because they do not represent transactions' balances, the scope for a bank to lend on deposits it has received is relatively limited, and despite the absence of any formal reserve requirement, the potential for multiple expansion, was strictly limited; Hogan and Pearce (1983) make the same point. Both Revell and they regard as crucial the fact that there is no eurodollar clearing system and that eurodollar banks do not issue cheque books. If one company borrows from a eurodollar bank and makes a purchase, only a small part of the money will end up in another eurodollar account. Thus eurodollar markets can be regarded as increasing the ability of money to circulate by making markets more efficient, but not increasing the stock of money in the world economy. Some economists such as Rist (1940) attach great importance to this distinction, but, as Tobin (1963) points out, the amount of money in the economy is in any case limited by the demand for it.

The conventional explanation that the United States' balance of payments deficits accounted for the development of the eurodollar market has been challenged by Dufey and Giddy (1978). They admit that the years of growth of the eurodollar market coincided with a mounting United States balance of payments deficit and point out that 'it is not surprising that many have assumed that there is a direct causal relationship' between the two. But they argue that:

> deposits made in the eurodollar market are *quite independent* of foreigners' export earnings which (1) are not necessarily invested in dollar assets and (2) even if they are held in dollar assets, are not necessarily held in the eurodollar market. Indeed, most of the funds deposited in eurobanks are probably obtained in the foreign exchange market by individuals and institutions who may or may not be involved with US trade.

This argument is supported by the evidence. As Mendelsohn has pointed out, the eurodollar market grew rapidly when the United States balance of payments was in equilibrium or in surplus in 1966, 1968 and 1969 and very slowly even when the balance of payments was in deficit in 1971 (Mendelsohn, 1980). It was profitable for United States banks to transfer dollars from New York to branches in London and Zurich in order to take advantage of the higher interest rates available on eurodollar business.

Moreover, after 1965 the United States authorities adopted a voluntary restraint programme under which firms were asked not to shift funds abroad. United States firms wishing to expand overseas found it much more convenient to borrow the funds they needed from the overseas branches of American banks. Just as domestic expansion of the money stock may, despite arguments of reserve ratios and high-powered money multipliers, be relatively independent of government borrowing, so the expansion of dollar denominated assets and liabilities outside the United States may be relatively independent of its balance of payments deficit. This argument is all the stronger because there are no reserve requirements for off-shore banking.

The existence of London as an important financial centre, a hangover from the heyday of sterling as the dominant international currency, meant:

> that there was already a well-developed banking structure in London, complemented by the other markets in the City: the stock market, the insurance market, the shipping market and the commodities market. It was therefore natural that the new foreign currency markets should be drawn to London. (Committee of London Clearing Bankers, 1977)

This was not the only reason why London became the most important centre for eurocurrency transactions. The absence of controls by the Bank of England over non-sterling banking, particularly for non-resident depositing and borrowing, made London a natural focus for the eurobanks that wished to participate in the new markets. From the inception of these new markets, the accepting houses played a leading role. As one commentator has put it 'eurodollars or eurocurrencies – synonymous with . . . the world's freely convertible currencies – were thought up by the London merchant bankers' (Kellett, 1967). The accepting houses had always been principal dealers in the foreign exchange market and their connections with overseas banks made it natural for them to play a major part in the re-cycling of US dollars held outside the United States of America. By 1967 London accounted for over one-third of all eurodollar and eurocurrency business and the accepting houses and foreign banks in London had played and continued to play an important role in the market. The market itself was, as the Bank of England said, 'highly organised, with large amounts dealt in . . . for a variety of maturities and with the minimum of formality' (*Bank of England Quarterly Bulletin,* 1964).

It has been estimated that about 10 per cent of the total eurodollar loans made by London in the mid-1960s went directly to borrowers other than banks, although statistical data are lacking. The Bank of England maintained that the eurodollar market 'helped to stimulate banking competition and reduce interest rates in the main borrowing countries, and has probably added to the total funds available for the finance of international business' (*Bank of England Quarterly Bulletin,* 1964). Much third-country trade was financed in London by eurodollars or other eurocurrencies, mainly because it used to be customary to use London banks (particularly the accepting houses) when sterling was allowed to be used to finance external transactions, and it was found that the London banks concerned could continue to provide an efficient service in currencies other than sterling.

As in the interbank market, all lending in the eurodollar market and other eurocurrency markets which developed in the 1960s was unsecured and was carried out in very large sums of the equivalent of US $1 000 000 or more. Because the individual transactions were very large, the interest rate differentials could be low and still yield a very satisfactory profit. The eurocurrency markets are attractive for both depositors and borrowers because the deposit rates offered are higher and the lending rates lower than the domestic rates in the country of origin. Interest rates in London are geared to the London interbank offered rate (LIBOR) which became institutionalised as the most important interest rate. Statistics regarding the size of the market in London, and of the shares in it held by the participating banks, are difficult to interpret, due largely to an unknown amount of switching between foreign currencies and sterling, and to the inevitable double counting in the reported figures from the presence of a number of intermediaries. However, growth in non-resident foreign currency holdings with British banks and foreign banks in the UK is indicated in Table 6.1. The involvement of each type of bank in this market is indicated in Table 6.6.

The bulk of foreign currency banking is done by overseas banks in the United Kingdom with the accepting houses holding, by the end of the period, only about 3 per cent of the overseas foreign currency deposits with banks in the United Kingdom. Their role as innovators was far more important than their current share of the market suggests.

Banks involved in the eurocurrency markets match maturities to a much greater extent than in domestic banking. This reflects the wholesale nature of the liabilities concerned. A comparison of

TABLE 6.6 *Overseas foreign currency deposits with banks in the UK (£ million)*

End year	*Clearing banks*	*Accepting houses*	*Other British banks*	*Overseas banks*	*Total*
1962	—	195	3	762	960
1970	—	1 027	780	11 514	13 321
1974	2 199	1 460	2 211	36 920	42 790
1975	2 558	1 639	5 607	47 230	57 034
1980	8 639	3 677	13 595	98 213	124 124
1984	21 630	7 425	31 044	276 650	336 749

NOTE A number of banks formerly included as 'overseas' were reclassified to other 'British' in 1975. Certificates of deposit are not included in the data above.

SOURCE *Bank of England Quarterly Bulletins.*

liability and claim maturity for foreign currency banking in the UK is shown in Table 6.7.

In 1963 the United States' authorities imposed an Interest Equlisation Tax, supplemented in 1965 by exchange controls. These measures effectively closed the United States bond market to most foreign borrowers and brought the development of a two to three year market in eurodollars to a halt. Borrowers therefore turned to eurobonds which complement the market in eurocurrency bank finance by making funds available for a longer term. The market offering anonymity as one of its attractions expanded rapidly and

TABLE 6.7 *Bank foreign currency assets and liabilities by maturity (February 1985)*

Maturity	*Liabilities*	*Claims*	*Net position ($bn)*
<8 days	139.4	107.2	−32.2
8 days to <1 month	131.8	105.0	−26.8
1 month to <3 months	171.8	140.4	−31.4
3 months to <6 months	121.0	99.1	−21.9
6 months to <1 year	37.4	40.4	3.0
1 year to <3 years	16.5	45.6	29.0
3 years or over	22.3	110.2	88.0
Total	640.3	647.9	7.6

SOURCE *Bank of England Quarterly Bulletin.*

produced a range of innovative financial instruments. The major eurobond market is dollar denominated, but for a period in 1977, and again since 1982, relatively low sterling long-term interest rates have led to some sterling borrowing. The ease with which United Kingdom organisations could raise funds in the eurobond market was given a stimulus by tax changes in the 1968 and 1969 Finance Acts, which allowed interest paid on foreign loans (whether used at home or abroad) to be deductible for corporation tax purposes, and which abolished loan capital duty on foreign financing. Both nationalised industries and private corporations have used the eurobond market to finance investment either domestically or abroad. The merchant banks not only play a major part with United States brokers in arranging and syndicating the issues, but also make a market in eurobonds. They have raised substantial sums for their own use in the expansion of their international banking services.

6.7 ACCEPTANCES

Although acceptance credit cannot be considered a new market instrument, substantial growth in the volume of acceptance credit occurred during the period. It is sensible to consider this form of finance here because it often formed a substitute for credit intermediated through the traditional banking system.

The value of acceptance credits increased steadily during the 1960s. The use of acceptance credits for the financing of foreign trade was and continued to be the traditional form. Such credits were normally self-liquidating, were drawn to cover a genuine transaction involving the movement or production of goods and were arranged independently, with two 'good names' on the bill, in order to avoid any danger of collusion between the drawer and the acceptor. Bills could be drawn in any currency although a United Kingdom resident could only receive the proceeds in sterling, the foreign currency conversion being carried out by the accepting house. When the total credit being arranged was beyond the resources of a single accepting house, it was syndicated with other banks. The total credit was divided between the banks in the syndicate, and between a number of bills of not more than £100 000 each in order to meet the needs of the discount market when re-discounting the bills. Acceptance credits were normally unsecured because they were self-liquidating, but an accepting house would usually ask the drawer not to pledge its assets with another bank without the accepting house's permission. For the merchant bank, the profit from acceptance credits derived from the discount at which it offered its name to the bill plus the commission (ranging from 1 per cent to 2 per cent) it charged.

During the 1970s the rate of increase in acceptance credits was more striking as many major industrial and commercial groups in the United Kingdom found such credits a welcome additional source of working capital to complement other short-term borrowing arrangements. There was a particular advantage for companies in having access to different borrowing facilities after the Bank of England imposed restrictions on bank deposits through the supplementary special deposit scheme (the 'corset') introduced in 1973. Acceptances provided a source of short-term finance which did not need to be funded by bank deposits since the acceptances were marketable, but had the security of the bank which underwrote them. Thus they were particularly useful when the demand for credit recovered after the depression of the mid-1970s. For many of the large companies in the United Kingdom, acceptance credits were as important a source of short-term finance as clearing bank overdrafts, and could be negotiated on much the same basis. It was normal for a company to negotiate with an accepting house a line of credit which could be made 'available either until "further notice" like an overdraft, or for a certain minimum period, in which case the customer paid a "commitment commission" in order to compensate the (accepting) house for the earmarking of some of its resources to that customer' (Clay and Wheble, 1983). The Inter-Bank Research Organisation also suggested in 1973 that a number of companies were drawing bills of exchange that were immediately discounted in order to provide themselves with funds which could be loaned direct to other companies needing short-term finance (The Inter-Bank Research Organisation, 1973). Although the ending of the corset removed the 'disintermediation' advantage of acceptances, the Bank of England was keen to see as wide a market in commercial bills as possible so as to facilitate overfunding (Chapter 4), and the total has continued to grow rapidly. This expansion was helped because the Bank of England announced, in 1981, that any bank whose bills commanded only a small discount on Treasury bills, would be able to apply for 'eligible' status. The growth of the market is shown in Table 6.8.

A related market in direct intercompany loans started in 1969 when the ceilings on bank lending were having a marked effect on overdraft facilities, although evidence is lacking on its size relative to other

TABLE 6.8 *Acceptances outstanding*

End year	*Acceptances (£ million)*
1960	200
1965	658
1970	963
1975	2 095
1980	5 558
1984	19 053

SOURCE *Bank of England Quarterly Bulletin.*

markets; it is generally believed, however, that the total amounts outstanding are unlikely to have exceeded some £50 million to £100 million.

During the 1950s and 1960s there was a substantial expansion in world trade, particularly in capital goods. In order to assist United Kingdom exporters, the government operated schemes under which the clearing banks provided fixed-rate medium- and long-term credit facilities guaranteed by the Export Credits Guarantee Department; short-term schemes up to two years were included from 1965. These facilities were more advantageous for exporters than the use of acceptance credits, since the rate of interest was fixed for the term of the credit and was lower than the discount rate on commercial bills. The bulk of the business in export credits was undertaken by the clearing banks, the accepting houses acting as middlemen in bringing customers and clearing banks together. For buyer credits, however, the arrangements were more complicated since the exporter negotiated direct with his overseas customer as purchaser who found some 15 per cent to 20 per cent of the total value of the contract from his own resources, often from the eurodollar or eurocurrency markets. The balance of 80 per cent to 85 per cent was provided by a United Kingdom bank or banks and the Export Credits Guarantee Department unconditionally guaranteed both the principal and the interest due from the overseas purchaser over the term of the contract which might be for as long as ten years. The procedure involved extensive documentation at which the accepting houses quickly became expert; they could also provide the foreign currencies required by the buyer to meet his direct share of the contract. The accepting houses were recompensed for the work they carried out by a negotiation fee, an annual management fee plus, of course, the profits earned on the provision of the foreign currencies required.

6.8 SUMMARY

The new markets fell into two categories. The local authority and finance house markets, and to some extent also the acceptance market could be constrained by the ultimate willingness of a borrower outside the banking sector to borrow. In the latter case this constraint has not yet been reached. But the other markets were used primarily as a means of intermediation within the banking system. Under normal circumstances an individual bank could regard deposits in these markets as liquid. But during a general withdrawal of deposits from the banking system such deposits would lose their liquidity. This possibility, and the fact that these markets made liability management easy, encouraged a rapid expansion of the non-clearing banks which culminated in the crisis of 1973–5. Since that crisis these markets have continued to grow rapidly at the expense of the traditional markets. The new system of monetary management has partly, if temporarily, restored the role of the discount market as a buffer, because banks have to achieve an average ratio of discount market deposits to eligible liabilities. This average means that the burden of adjustment does not, when funds are tight, fall entirely on the higher-yielding, very short-term, parallel markets. The result is that, since 1981, parallel market rates have been more stable than they were before. The growth of the parallel markets over the past 20 years has obliged the authorities to move away from a position in which they can regulate both the stock of money and the level of interest rates, to one in which only the level of interest rates is under direct control.

The growth of the eurocurrency market has been of rather less importance as far as domestic banking is concerned. However, it too makes liability management easier at an international level, and thus encourages lending. This has led to a position, described in Chapter 8, which has some parallels with the expansion of the non-clearing banks considered in the next chapter.

7 The Other British Non-Clearing Banks

Until 1975 the British non-clearing banks, other than the accepting houses, comprised a heterogeneous collection of financial institutions, some reporting to the Bank of England and for whom statistical information is therefore available, and some with a degree of banking status (the 'Section 123' banks) which did not furnish returns to the Bank and were therefore excluded from its supervision and control. However, the statistical series provided for these banks are harder to interpret than in other cases because changes in coverage are more frequent. The crisis which overtook the banking sector in 1973–5 affected banks in both categories, although mainly affecting the non-reporting banks. This crisis is discussed in detail by Reid (1982). The reporting ('listed' or 'statistical') banks included some which were close in concept to a merchant bank, usually enjoying membership of the Issuing Houses Association but not of the prestigious Accepting Houses Committee, some which had expanded from a small base in the 1960s, and the subsidiaries of the clearing banks set up in the late 1960s to compete in the new money markets.

TABLE 7.1 *The five largest other non-clearing banks in 1984–5*

	Total assets (£ million)	*Net profit*
Barclays Bank International	51 694	37
Standard Chartered Bank	34 460	100
International Westminster Bank	25 424	56
Lloyds Bank International	18 867	38
Grindlays Bank	5 491	−70

NOTE In September 1984 Grindlays Bank was bought by the Australia and New Zealand Bank, taking it outside this group. In 1985 Barclays Bank International was merged with Barclays.

SOURCE *'The Times 1000'*, 1985–6.

TABLE 7.2 *Other British banks' balance sheet (December)*

		Liabilities (£ million)							
		1966		*1974*		*1975*		*1984*	
Currency		£	*Other*	£	*Other*	£	*Other*	£	*Other*
Current & deposit accounts	UK banks	54	39	3 472	2 111	3 375	2 477	13 933	14 533
	Other UK	152	4	2 107	63	3 451	391	8 642	2 189
	Overseas	48	61	314	2 211	1 009	5 607	5 269	31 044
CDs		—	—	937	199	1 032	763	1 222	4 492
Net non-deposit liabilities		40	−14	890	143	1 924	431	7 052	3 371
Total		294	90	7 720	4 727	10 791	9 669	36 118	55 629

	Assets (£ million)							
	1966		*1974*		*1975*		*1984*	
Currency	£	*Other*	£	*Other*	£	*Other*	£	*Other*
Notes and coin (L) and working deposits with the Bank of England	0.3	—	1	—	26	—	5	—
Balances with UK banks (L)	20	39	1 980	918	2 454	1 994	9 262	8 704
Call money (L)	15	—	436	—	376	—	345	—
CDs (L)	—	—	466	—	647	233	1 194	410
Local authority loans	80	—	436	—	964	—	855	—
Treasury bills (L)	15	—	47	—	441	—	1	—
Other bills (L)	2	—	140	—	334	53	143	90

UK government securities	11	—	42	—	308	—	2 366	2 579
Advances & loans: UK residents	134	3	3 741	543	4 240	1 547	17 546	5 018
Advances & loans: Other	7	44	56	3 046	111	5 462	2 588	38 828
Other assets	10	4	255	220	711	380	1 733	—
Special and cash ratio deposits	—	—	120	—	179	—	80	—
Total	294	90	7 720	4 727	10 791	9 669	36 118	55 629
Acceptances	16		55		237		1 920	
Ratios								
1) Non-bank advances / Non-bank deposits	0.71	0.72	1.57	1.58	0.96	1.17	1.45	1.32
2) Liquid assets / All deposits	0.26		0.35		0.36		0.25	
3) Non-bank advances / All deposits	0.56	0.45	0.56	0.78	0.49	0.76	0.69	0.84

NOTES (L) Liquid asset as defined by the Bank of England before 1971.
Non-deposit liabilities are a balancing item.
A break in the series occurs between 1974 and 1975.
The 1984 figures for UK banks relate to monetary sector institutions.

SOURCE *Bank of England Statistical Abstract* Nos 1 and 2; *Bank of England Quarterly Bulletin*.

In May 1975 substantial changes took place to the statistical classification, which makes it difficult to compare the position before and after that date. Some clearing bank international subsidiaries, such as Barclays Bank International and other banks like Standard Chartered, which had previously been included with 'British Overseas and Commonwealth Banks' were included in this group. These now dominate the statistics.

The five largest British non-clearing banks in 1984 are shown in Table 7.1.

7.1 BALANCE SHEET STRUCTURE

Table 7.2 presents balance sheets for those banks recorded as 'other British' in 1966, 1974, 1975 and 1984. It is clear from the table that there was very rapid growth in this type of banking between 1966 and 1974. The effect of the widening of the statistical net is shown broadly by comparing the 1974 and 1975 figures. Not surprisingly, the international banks brought into the group were much more involved in foreign currency banking than the earlier members had been. Since 1975 the redefined sector has grown at much the same rate as the monetary sector as a whole. The growth between 1975 and 1984 is also subject to some statistical changes, but it is probable that it represents the over-all pattern reasonably well. Although this chapter describes the activities of both types, emphasis is placed on those banks which were included in the pre-1975 classification.

The rapid growth of these non-clearing banks was not, as in the case of the clearers, at all a consequence of starting in 1971 with reserves in excess of the requirements of competition and credit control. The Bank of England, at the time of introduction of competition and credit control, had to make special provision for these banks who started with reserves of only 9.9 per cent of eligible liabilities. But they rapidly acquired reserve assets and after two months satisfied the reserve requirements. The extra requirements of these banks were sufficiently small for them to fall well within the reserve creation capability of competition and credit control. As noted in Chapter 4, this was not really exhausted until the end of 1973. The holdings of reserve assets by the other British banks rose from £140m at the start of competition and credit control to £553m by the end of 1973; this was, as a share of total reserve assets, a rise from 5 per cent to 13.5 per cent. Thus these banks were the most active in taking advantage of the reserve creation which competition and credit control made possible, especially in its early days.

The first striking feature about these balance sheets is the large and growing importance of deposits by, and balances held with, other UK banks. Although the liquidity ratios appear high, at least in the early period much of this liquidity is achieved by taking deposits from (or selling CDs to) banks. The ratio of non-bank advances to non-bank deposits is high and has risen over time. Other measures of liquidity also suggest that liquidity has fallen; to the extent that these banks match the maturity of their assets and liabilities, less attention need be paid to liquidity by them than by a retail bank, although had maturity matching been as widespread as Revell (1973) suggests, the 1973 crisis would not have happened in the way it did. These institutions have always tended to use the interbank market, rather than the discount market, as a repository for their surplus liquidity. While this observation also applied to the accepting houses (Chapter 5), it is far more true of these banks. By 1984 almost half of these banks' sterling deposits were supplied by banks. Equally about half of the sterling funds not advanced were deposited in the banking system through the interbank market. It is further noticeable that the crisis of 1973–5 cannot be said to have halted the trend towards a smaller liquid base. This is despite the fact that a liquidity crisis typically draws attention to the importance of maintaining a base of liquid assets. However, the decline in balance sheet average liquidity ratio need not mean that the least liquid banks' ratios have also declined. The impact of competition and credit control is visible. In 1974 and 1975 the banks' holdings of call money, bills and very short gilts were dictated by the need to hold reserve assets, depending on the size of their sterling eligible liabilities. When this requirement no longer held, the banks ran down stocks of these low-yielding assets and replaced them by high yielding assets of appropriate maturity.

Finally we note that although these banks have become increasingly involved in foreign currency business, their importance has grown less rapidly than the market as a whole. Total foreign currency claims by UK banks on the world economy rose 6.3 times between 1975 and 1984. Those of the banks considered here rose only 5.8-fold The bulk of the growth in this market has been achieved by the overseas banks.

The pattern of advances to UK residents by these banks after 1976 is shown in Table 7.3. Comparing it with the pattern of accepting house lending (Table 5.5), one observes that this group of banks put

TABLE 7.3 *Advances to UK residents by British non-clearing banks apart from accepting houses*

£ million February *Sector*	*1976*	*1979*	*1982*	*1985*
Manufacturing	868	1 676	3 311	3 483
Other production	569	604	901	2 714
Personal sector	724	1 006	3 384	6 488
Services	1 556	2 292	5 436	3 838
Financial sector	1 743	1 693	2 351	6 266
(of which property)	(1 000)	(703)	(669)	(808)
Total	5 460	7 271	15 382	22 789

NOTE The 1985 figures include acceptances and represent a classification different from that of earlier years.
SOURCE *Financial Statistics* and *Bank of England*.

rather more emphasis on personal sector loans than the accepting houses did. This probably reflects the role of the domestic clearing bank subsidiaries in consumer provision. At the start of 1976 advances to the financial sector were less important, as a share, than the comparable figure for the accepting houses, but advances to the property sector were rather more important. More recent lending has been to personal and financial sectors. However, these aggregates conceal considerable heterogeneity within the group. There are good reasons for believing, on the basis of studies of particular banks, that, for some of the pre-1975 members of this group, the major part of their loan portfolio consisted of advances to property companies.

7.2 CLEARING BANK SUBSIDIARIES

Revell (1968), discussing the growth of secondary banking, suggested that it was then adequate to regard the secondary banks in three main groups. Apart from the accepting houses considered in Chapter 5, there were then nine domestic affiliates of deposit banks and about 20 other merchant banks. In addition, there were the overseas and foreign banks not considered further here. The deposit bank affiliates were by far the largest, in balance sheet size, of the banks reporting to the Bank of England. The first subsidiaries were set up in 1966; the clearing banks had looked for means of participating, not only in the new money markets, but also in the other lucrative aspects of secondary banking so as to compete more effectively with the accepting houses. The subsidiary of a clearing bank, provided it engages in activities different from those of the parent bank, is able to economise on both liquidity and capital. For, except in the case of a general flight into cash, it is unlikely that both parent and subsidiary will face simultaneous large-scale deposit withdrawal. Equally, losses are unlikely to be strongly correlated, and thus a less than matching increase in the capital base is adequate to give a risk of insolvency for the group no greater than it had been for the parent alone. At a time when clearing banks had to maintain a 28 per cent liquidity ratio, which did not apply to subsidiaries, the establishment of these subsidiaries provided a profitable means of expansion, avoiding the need to tie up funds in low-yielding liquid assets. These subsidiaries continued to expand as the new money markets grew in size and as the variety of financial services offered in London increased.

Particularly important subsidiaries were Barclays Bank International and Lloyds Bank International, although these were only included as 'other British banks' after 1975. The former, previously Barclays Bank DCO, was bought fully by Barclays in 1970; it was, in 1985, integrated into Barclays Bank losing its independent name. A similar move is planned for Lloyds Bank International. It was the former Bank of London and South America and merged with Lloyds Bank Europe to take its present name, again in 1970.

In 1985 Barclays Bank had four subsidiaries engaged in banking in the UK, Lloyds had three, the Midland five (including a 60 per cent stake in Samuel Montagu), and National Westminster six. Other subsidiaries were set up to cover a range of different activities in domestic and international finance, ranging from the provision of consumer credit and investment management to overseas banking.

The clearing banks have used subsidiaries as a way of gaining access to the opportunities for securities dealing offered by the ending of single capacity on the stock exchange. Samuel Montagu, partly owned by Midland Bank, is taking a half share in a broker (W. Greenwell) while the National Westminster's merchant banking subsidiary, County Bank, has bought Bisgood Bishop, a jobber and Fielding Newson-Smith, a broker. Barclays Merchant Bank has merged with the jobber, Wedd Durlacher Mordaunt and the broker, de Zoete and Bevan to form a new investment bank, Barclays de Zoete Wedd. Lloyds is the last to move, but intends to set up a new merchant bank/securities dealer.

The full size of the clearing bank subsidiaries is best indicated by comparing the deposits at a clearing bank group (see Table 7.4) with those at the clearing bank itself, although these figures include deposits with subsidiaries outside the UK, such as Deutsche Westminster Bank. They also cover deposits with banks brought into the category of 'other British banks' in 1975.

Although the subsidiaries increasingly provided a profitable means for the employment of surplus funds held by the clearers, advances by clearers to their subsidiaries did not become common until recently. The extent of this practice is shown in Table 7.5.

These banks, and other non-clearing banks like Standard Chartered which also pursued the business of a merchant/international bank, were firmly based. But the entry of these subsidiaries into the field provided another stimulus to the interbank market. The development of this market encouraged the growth of the fringe banks, not considered in Revell's classification at all. Although this fringe was

TABLE 7.4 *Deposits with clearing bank groups*

£ million	*1969*		*1975*		*1984*	
	With bank	*With group*	*With bank*	*With group*	*With bank*	*With group*
Barclays	2 952	5 121	6 556	14 494	23 205	63 767
Lloyds	1 935	2 490	4 261	9 085	16 987	40 545
Midland	2 248	3 322	7 139	9 213	27 192	56 598
Nat. West.	3 212	4 899	8 014	13 239	32 289	65 515

SOURCE Clearing Bank Annual Reports.

not large in size, it was here that the banking crisis of 1973–5 began. It had its roots in the property boom, which was financed by banks who borrowed in the interbank market and lent on for property development in a manner quite incompatible with the traditions of prudent banking.

TABLE 7.5 *Advances to subsidiaries by major clearing banks*

£ million	*1969*		*1975*		*1984*	
	Current assets	*Loans to subsidiary*	*Current assets*	*Loans to subsidiary*	*Current assets*	*Loans to subsidiary*
Barclays	3 212	33	7 079	142	25 419	3 399
Lloyds	2 094	1	4 389	510	18 208	1 108
Midland	2 247	10	7 576	405	28 768	1 706
Nat. West.	3 171	7	8 228	233	34 627	8 504

SOURCE Clearing Bank Annual Reports.

7.3 THE PROPERTY BOOM

The Bank of England believed that the introduction of competition and credit control in September 1971 would restore the dominance of the clearing banks and the established merchant banks, and would lead to the elimination of the rapidly growing 'fringe' banks, most of which were not subject to its control and supervision (*Bank of England Quarterly Bulletin,* 1971a). For the reasons given in Chapter 3, this belief proved to be unfounded. The effect of competition and credit control was to provide a stimulus for the interbank market in which banks, particularly those not subject to the reserve assets requirement, could bid for deposits offering rates of interest sufficiently attractive to induce lending by some of the listed banks. The authorities viewed the expansion of the wholesale money markets described in Chapter 6 with apparent unconcern and even the Midland Bank (1973) commented that:

> the banking system does not appear to be taking on any additional risk, since interbank borrowings and lendings must net out and, to the extent that funds are obtained from outside the system against certificates of deposit, the same minimum reserves must be kept as for other forms of deposit.

In fact, the risks were growing fast as money brokers, who could earn higher commissions on borrowing by banks with the poorest liquidity safeguards than on borrowing by the more prudent banks, channelled funds towards the secondary banks (Lester, 1974). The re-cycling of deposits around the banking system, which was so important a feature of the interbank market, was stimulated by the competition and credit control definition of eligible liabilities. It smoothed the balancing of borrowing and lending, making it easy for the demand for credit to be met.

That demand did not arise from manufacturing industry. Throughout 1972 and 1973 manufacturing industry's demand for credit was low, despite rising consumption fuelled by the government's drive for economic growth, and resulting in a substantial increase in imports and a growing balance of payments deficit. The government was reluctant to use interest rate policy to constrain demand, partly because it was still committed to economic expansion and partly because it could not contemplate higher mortgage rates in view of the strength of the building societies' lobby. When a run on sterling developed in 1972, the government decided not to use the conventional instrument of higher interest rates but instead allowed the sterling exchange rate to float in June of that year.

Instead of funds flowing to the industrial sector, the major part of the increase in bank lending was absorbed by the property sector whose borrowings quadrupled between 1971 and 1973 (*Bank of England Statistical Abstract* No. 2, 1975). It has been estimated that the total amount advanced to the property sector as a whole, including the construction industry, probably reached at least £5000 million by the end of 1973, despite repeated requests from the Bank of England to restrain lending for property development (Lester, 1974). This was more than the clearing banks were lending to the whole of manufacturing industry. A high proportion of the funds were loaned to property developers. These assumed that, with rising property values, substantial capital gains could be made by disposing of completed, or semi-completed, projects quickly. Hence, borrowing was made in the confident expectation that, when loans came to be renewed, they could either be repaid from the capital gains from disposal, or be rolled over pending disposal. For this type of borrowing, the interbank market was the obvious one in which banks could obtain the deposits they needed for on-lending to the property companies concerned. Interest charges were of far less importance than access to funds, and many property developers were ready to pay high rates of interest for their borrowing. Moreover, the developments into which money poured were not confined to the United Kingdom. In the euphoria of the property boom, ventures in Paris, Brussels, Australia and other centres absorbed a not inconsiderable proportion of the total sums raised.

The property boom between 1971 and 1973 proved a boon for the non-clearing banks which hovered on the fringe of the banking sector. Not only could they profit from the margins between the cost of the deposits they were able to attract and of the advances they made, but in many cases they took equity stakes in their clients' developments. This had a significant effect on their balance sheets which, as a result of the often arbitrary revaluation of the properties in which they held an equity interest, increased enormously and gave an appearance of respectability to their operations, an essential prerequisite for their borrowing in the money markets. Some of the banks which eventually found themselves in difficulties were also involved in the second mortgage market, which flourished as property values rose.

7.4 THE BANKING CRISIS

The growth in the balance of payments deficit and in the public sector borrowing requirement, coupled with a continuing strong demand for money, resulted in a situation in which the Bank of England felt interest rates should rise. In July 1973 minimum lending rate (which had replaced bank rate) was increased suddenly from 7.5 per cent to 11.5 per cent. Rates in the money market also rose sharply and banks which had become involved with property development companies began to find it difficult to renew their short-term borrowing. If they were able to find lenders, they could only borrow at much higher rates of interest. With the oil crisis in the autumn of 1973, minimum lending rate was increased further to 13 per cent in November. At much the same time, the supplementary credit control scheme (the 'corset') was introduced and the government announced that a development gains tax would be imposed on the capital gains of property speculation. The result of all these measures was a collapse in both property and equity values, a crisis situation for those banks whose viability depended on the continuing prosperity of the property and other companies to whom huge advances had been made on a long-term basis, funded by short-term borrowing in the interbank market or by deposits attracted from the public by every marketing device that human ingenuity could conceive. This led to the rise in interest rates discussed in Chapter 6, and severe shortage of bank deposits.

The first bank to collapse in December 1973 was London and County Securities (L & C), described later. The immediate cause of the collapse was the inability of L & C to renew its deposits from the interbank market following a slump in its share price from 400p to 30p in early December 1973. The effect of the L & C collapse, with its possible repercussions on other financial institutions, alarmed the backers of the bank (including Keyser Ullman, National Westminster Bank and Eagle Star Insurance Company) and the Bank of England was consulted to see what could be done. The Bank decided to attempt to save L & C, and thereby to protect its depositors, by calling on the First National Finance Corporation (FNFC) to lead a £30 million rescue operation. It is now apparent that the Bank of England was completely unaware of the seriousness of the financial crisis that was developing and, even further, had no idea that FNFC itself was heading towards a possible collapse. When the affairs of L & C were investigated, it was found that the situation was very serious: some 36 per cent of its deposits were repayable within one month and 43 per cent within three months, whilst its assets were almost completely illiquid, comprising investments in property and equities or loans to associated companies.

The collapse and exposure of L & C led to a widespread financial crisis affecting all those financial institutions which, it was believed, had financed property development from short-term borrowing. The next financial institution to collapse immediately after L & C was

Moorgate Mercantile, which went into liquidation, to be followed by Cornhill Consolidated, a financial group with £50 million of paper assets but which was completely illiquid. Later in December 1973 Cedar Holdings found that it was losing deposits at the rate of £10 million per week and Barclays Bank announced that it was mounting an £80 million rescue operation to save the group. Meanwhile, National Westminster Bank provided £14 million of assistance to Twentieth Century Banking, a subsidiary of Bovis Limited which that company had acquired from London and County Securities. The financial crisis had now reached panic proportions and threatened a large number of financial institutions, including some of the larger established ones. As a result, on 21 December 1973, the Bank of England announced that it was forming a committee with the clearing banks to provide support to any bank which the committee considered was worthy of rescue and the operation which was named the 'lifeboat' was put under way. The objective of the 'lifeboat' was to re-cycle deposits which had been withdrawn from the non-clearing banks facing liquidation and placed with the clearing banks, back into those non-clearing banks which the committee deemed warranted such support. As well as the clearing banks, other financial institutions (including some leading pension funds and insurance companies) were associated with the rescue operation. The funds re-cycled were charged at a commercial rate of interest, plus a margin of 1.5 per cent or 2 per cent to cover the risks involved but, inevitably in the circumstances, the interest charges had to be rolled over until the financial institutions assisted were able to meet them. The funds were subordinated to other deposits. They therefore had the effect, not only of maintaining the liquidity of the institutions concerned, but also of protecting other depositors against insolvency.

As the Bank of England has described the support operation, there were three distinct phases (*Bank of England Quarterly Bulletin*, 1978). The first lasted from the beginning of December 1973 to March 1974, during which period 21 institutions were assisted at a cost to the members of the 'lifeboat' in terms of amounts at risk of around £400 million. The economic situation further deteriorated in the early part of 1974 with the miners' strike, the three-day week and a tough March budget adding to the difficulties caused by a quadrupling of oil prices at the end of 1973. In April 1974 Triumph Investment Trust and J. H. Vavasseur were added to the list of banks requiring assistance. The Lyon Group of property companies faced a liquidity crisis in May 1974 and in June the Stern Group failed with liabilities of more than £100 million, further adding to the banking crisis, and the 'lifeboat' found that its commitments were increasing sharply. Larger financial institutions, including First National Finance Corporation and United Dominions Trust were unable to renew their short-term borrowing and needed assistance. By August 1974 the total value of the support committed by the clearing banks had reached some £1200 million, equal to about 40 per cent of their combined capital and reserves. At this stage the clearing banks were prepared to go no further since 'this would risk provoking doubts about their own financial soundness' (*Bank of England Quarterly Bulletin,* 1978). Continuing assistance was therefore left to the Bank of England alone which considered that the financial crisis threatened the stability of the entire financial structure and needed to be solved as best it could. 'The Bank's concern was not fanciful [and] was subsequently underlined when the National Westminster Bank found it necessary at the beginning of December 1974 to issue a statement to the effect that current rumours that they were receiving support from the Bank were without foundation'.[1] The Bank of England therefore extended support at its own risk to further companies, including some authorised banks. This second phase lasted until December 1974. The third phase began in January 1975 and included the assumption by the Bank of England of direct responsibility for Slater, Walker Limited, at a cost to the Bank of a £70 million loan and a £40 million guarantee, and the rescue of Edward Bates and Sons Limited by new shareholders from the Arab world. The amount at risk from the support operation gradually declined from its peak, but as late as March 1978 still totalled some £656 million, and in October 1984 £33 million was outstanding. This last sum was all owed by FNFC who expected to repay it during 1985.

Losses incurred by the clearers as a result of the lifeboat operation are estimated by Reid (1982) at £50 million; she also estimates that the Bank of England incurred costs of £100 million, of which two-thirds was lost in Slater, Walker and Edward Bates. But this figure does not include the losses of the Crown Agents. These were of the order of £200 million and were effectively a loss to the taxpayer as shareholder in this public corporation.

It was not only banks mentioned above which found themselves in difficulties during the crisis. Other institutions like United Dominions Trust and Mercantile Credit were also badly affected by the collapse of property values and required assistance. Indeed United Dominions Trust was the largest 'lifeboat' user, with borrowings which reached a maximum of £500 million. They were efficient in the provision of consumer credit, their primary business but, as soon as they tried to emulate their banking competitors, they behaved no more prudently than other Section 123 banks, borrowing heavily in the interbank market in order to finance property development; their problems were only finally resolved in 1981 when they were taken over by the Trustee Savings Bank.

The Bank of England has stated that, in total, 26 companies were assisted, of which 18 continued trading, either in their original form or after reconstruction or absorption into other companies (*Bank of England Quarterly Bulletin,* 1978). Among the 18 companies were William Brandt's and Anthony Gibbs, both accepting houses before the crisis, Slater, Walker, United Dominions Trust, Mercantile Credit, Bowmakers, Keyser Ullman, First National Finance Corporation, Edward Bates, The Hodge Group, Burston and Texas Commercial Bank, the Anglo-Portuguese Bank, Western Credit Holdings and Cripps Warburg. Eight financial institutions were put into liquidation, Cornhill Consolidated, Moorgate Mercantile, Israel-British Bank, London and County Securities, Cannon Street Acceptance, Triumph Investment Trust, First Maryland and Burston Finance (*Financial Times*, 1975). In addition, the Crown Agents, arguably the financial institution with the largest losses of all, were reorganised and assisted by the government.

In its June 1978 article, the Bank of England attributed the United Kingdom banking crisis to three factors. First, the existence of financial intermediaries not subject to its supervision and control. Secondly, the lack of investment by the industrial sector of the economy compared with the marked attraction of property development as a hedge against inflation and as a vehicle for large capital gains. Thirdly, the ready availability of finance for the fringe banks from the money markets in which brokers played an important part. Each of these factors, which are self-evidently true, needs to be examined in turn. The danger to the stability of the banking system from the activities of intermediaries which were able to enjoy a measure of banking status but which neither reported to the Bank of England nor were subject to any control or supervision had been clearly pointed out to the Bank by the Accepting Houses Committee in 1968 and again in 1971. Such banks needed a closer degree of supervision and control than any others yet there is no evidence of any move prior to the crisis by the authorities to bring them into the reporting net. As stated earlier, the Bank of England's belief that the non-listed banks would simply wither away in the competitive aura after competition and credit control proved mistaken. The increasing investment in property development despite the Bank of England's request to the contrary was well enough known to the Bank, but it was certainly not confined to the so-called 'fringe' banks. The clearing banks lent directly some £1300 million to the property sector and their advances to property companies increased by 70 per cent between May 1972 and May 1973 (Lester, 1974). The foreign banks in London also lent heavily to the property sector and one at least (the Italian International Bank) needed a substantial reconstruction to overcome the losses it thereby suffered. By far, however, the most important factor was the ability of financial intermediaries to increase their deposit liabilities by bidding for funds in the unsecured money markets which had been allowed by the Bank of England to grow without any attempt at control. The attractiveness of the interbank, CD and eurocurrency markets, to financial institutions which required deposits in order to on-lend to other intermediaries or to their customers had been apparent for nearly a decade before the crisis, and yet the Bank of England viewed their expansion with an approving, or at least a benevolently neutral, eye. Moreover, if the yields that could be obtained in the parallel money markets, particularly from banks that were prepared to bid up rates in order to acquire deposits, were higher than were available from capital investment, this would lead to the injection of a substantial amount of money into the interbank and CD markets by corporate treasurers. Lester refers to the General Electric Company (GEC) and Courtaulds, each of which placed £200 million in the money markets. The arbitrage possibilities from borrowing on overdraft and lending at a higher rate in the money markets, ('round-tripping' as it was later called) also inflated the level of funds flowing through the interbank and CD markets; in 1972 one company alone borrowed and placed £20 million in order to profit from the interest differential.

The support operation mounted by the Bank of England almost certainly prevented a domino effect from the financial crisis on the whole of London's financial structure; the Bank clearly believed that there was a danger of a major collapse of confidence in London as a financial centre which might have had damaging consequences. As the concern over the National Westminster Bank showed, the risk of contagion was not exaggerated. In retrospect, however, it is surprising that the Bank of England failed to appreciate the dangers that the uncontrolled growth of the parallel money markets and of the non-clearing banks posed to the stability of the banking sector.

Most of the authorised non-clearing banks which reported to the Bank of England survived the crisis in 1973–5 albeit with losses, or, at best, reduced profits. Two banks which required assistance from the Bank of England rescue operation about which it is possible to construct detailed time series of balance sheets are Keyser Ullman and First National Finance Corporation. Reid (1982) provides a more detailed narrative about the history of these and other banks. These banks provide excellent examples of the way in which expansion was made possible by the uncontrolled development of deposit sources on which the non-clearing banks could rely. From comparatively small bases, they built up an astonishing aggregation of assets by taking short-term deposits from wherever they could find them and lending or investing those funds long-term wherever borrowers could be found. As every commentator has pointed out, this has always been the classic recipe for banking failures yet, not only were the two banks allowed to expand in this way without check, but the Bank of England even included them as 'lifeboatmen' in the initial stages of the rescue operation for other banks before they, too, required massive financial assistance.

7.5 SOME NON-CLEARING BANKS

Keyser Ullman was an old-established issuing house which decided, in the 1960s, to develop into a major merchant bank. Indeed, at one stage it could boast that it was as large, in terms of balance sheet totals, as most accepting houses. Its major expansion, and the seeds of its later financial troubles, came from its acquisition of a small 'fringe' bank, Dalton Barton, whose chief executive took over responsibility for the combined banks' operations. It borrowed heavily short-term in the interbank market and, like its competitors who were also confronted with a crisis in 1973–5, loaned substantial funds for property development, principally to the Stern and Lyon groups. The bank also loaned £17 million to Christopher Selmes, a Slater protégé, to acquire Grendon Securities, a property development company. Heavy loans were made to directors of the bank on the most favourable terms and on minimal security, and for the purchase of shares in Peureula Investments, a property company investing in residential property in London. By 1974 some 80 per cent of its lending was in respect of property and, in its 1974–5 accounts, it was forced to make a provision of £82.5 million against bad debts which, with previous provisions, made a grand total of £119 million. It was only kept afloat by a loan of £65 million from the 'lifeboat' consortium and was radically reorganised by a vice-chairman from Barclays Bank.

The balance sheet of Keyser Ullman is shown in Table 7.6, between 1964 and 1980 when it was taken over by Charterhouse Group Ltd. Its banking activities had expanded in the 1960s; the ratio of advances to deposits (gross of interbank items) reached almost 70 per cent in 1969, which is appreciably higher than that typically found for non-clearing banks. The jump in deposits between 1972 and 1973 reflects the acquisition of Dalton Barton, but even before this there was more than a five-fold expansion in banking liabilities between 1964 and 1972. In 1973 the ratio of advances to deposits of 0.66 was not historically high by the standards of this bank and capital assets amounted to over half of advances. Thus the bank did not give the appearance of being about to run into difficulties. Despite having to make substantial debt provisions in 1973–4 it was still able to expand its capital base. However, borrowing and lending expanded more rapidly with a fall in liquidity as the advance/deposit ratio rose to 80 per cent.

The general down-turn in 1975 came with the necessity to make large provisions for loss. Thus the major part of the fall in the book value of advances is explained by loss provision. Although the capital base was able to withstand the losses, a withdrawal of deposits, only partially offset by 'lifeboat' support, ensued. Thus the ratio of deposits to advances was held at 80 per cent despite the writing down of advances. Although the margin of current assets over advances is larger than the £65 million provided by the lifeboat, there can be little doubt that, without lifeboat support, withdrawal of deposits would have continued leaving Keyser Ullman illiquid and forcing it to close its doors.

After this the position gradually stabilised. As it became clear that, despite the losses, the bank was able to continue to trade, deposits returned. But the bank was still left in a relatively illiquid position with advances at over 80 per cent of deposits and over four times the capital base. The development of the bank since then has been aimed at rebuilding a sound position; thus despite growth in the capital base after 1977 advances were allowed to continue to decline leaving the advance/deposit ratio at 72 per cent and the advance/capital ratio at

TABLE 7.6 *Keyser Ullman Holdings Ltd*

	Liabilities (£ million)														
	1964	*1966*	*1968*	*1969*	*1970*	*1971*	*1972*	*1973*	*1974*	*1975*	*1976*	*1977*	*1978*	*1979*	*1980*
Capital & reserves	2 127	2 276	2 422	4 050	4 209	4 346	11 475	92 056	100 344	42 610	36 699	31 513	34 932	40 726	44 181
Current	28 637	39 339	47 143	61 143	68 059	69 230	84 754	245 102	326 969	231 564	191 210	184 605	187 290	202 030	222 107
Other	—	—	—	—	—	—	—	5 911	6 164	5 299	4 331	3 815	3 837	8 941	8 213
Total	30 764	41 615	49 565	65 193	72 268	73 576	96 229	343 069	433 477	279 473	232 240	219 933	226 059	251 697	274 501
Memorandum current & deposit accounts	14 777	21 180	27 416	40 521	44 106	50 507	81 948	243 037	314 805	218 993	180 837	173 735	177 045	186 026	191 873

	Assets (£ million)															
	1964	*1966*	*1968*	*1969*	*1970*	*1971*	*1972*	*1973*	*1974*	*1975*	*1976*	*1977*	*1978*	*1979*	*1980*	Taken over by Charterhouse Group Ltd
Fixed	—	—	—	254	475	533	596	4 117	4 971	5 531	3 457	2 064	2 098	2 171	2 058	
Other	2 792	3 232	5 755	6 274	6 113	2 932	8 905	80 123	14 984	13 030	8 233	8 230	7 630	6 532	4 011	
Current	27 972	38 383	43 810	58 665	65 680	70 111	86 728	258 829	413 522	260 912	220 550	209 639	216 331	242 994	268 432	
Total	30 764	41 615	49 565	65 193	72 268	73 576	96 229	343 069	433 477	279 473	232 240	219 933	226 059	251 697	274 501	
Memorandum advances	9 583	11 413	17 211	27 784	25 255	27 857	42 701	161 159	254 259	175 948	152 733	141 829	129 407	134 351	138 916	

NOTES Before 1973 figures for the banking group only are shown. The total value of assets and liabilities of this group in 1973 was £264 939 000 with current and deposit liabilities of £237 558 000 and advances of £149 924 000. All balance sheet items refer to 31 March.

SOURCE Extel Statistical Sercices, who have kindly given permission to reproduce the figures shown here.

Provision for bad and doubtful debts £'000*	
1974	30 556
1975	63 974
1976	7 250
1977	6 500
1978	−3 500
1979	−1 000
1980	−1 000

*Release of interest carrying costs is offset here.

just over three by March 1980. Keyser Ullman provides a good example of a bank which was threatened with a loss of liquidity but not by insolvency as a result of the banking crisis.

The First National Finance Corporation traces its origins back to the Birmingham Wagon Company in 1960. However, in 1961 it took over Cassel Arenz, a moribund small bank. It was backed by the Phoenix Assurance Company, Hambros Bank, the Electricity Supply Pension Fund and the Crown Agents. Seeking a niche in the City establishment, it expanded into merchant banking, investment banking and property investment and development. An inspection of the bank's balance sheet (Table 7.7), shows that it had traditionally maintained a much higher ratio of advances to deposits plus bank loans than is normal in the banking world. Indeed, in 1969 the ratio was over 100 per cent, and this was coupled with an exposed capital position in which property development advances and properties held for resale were, in 1970, before the property boom had really started, over five times the value of the capital base. Not only was First National Finance Corporation in a rather stretched position but its lending was of a specialist nature which made it very sensitive.

After a period of rapid growth and deteriorating liquidity and solvency margins in the 1960s, the bank made a major coup in 1971. It purchased some 8000 flats from Metropolitan Estates and Property Corporation for £33.5 million, which it then divided between a proportion jointly owned by itself and the Stern Group, and the remainder which it eventually sold at a paper profit of £24 million. But this profit could only accrue to the First National Finance Corporation when the flats were sold individually to the tenants or other purchasers and in the meantime the bank financed the sale of the flats by a loan from funds which it raised in the interbank market. Over 50 per cent of the bank's total capital of £42 million in 1972 was represented by a deferred revenue reserve from the sale of the flats. Growth was not accompanied by any shift towards more prudent banking practice. Advances remained at much the same level as deposits in 1971 and 1972 while the ratio of development advances to capital rose to six in 1972 and seven in 1973. After this, increasing capital losses drove the ratio to ten although the bank was able to retain its deposits at this stage.

The losses continued to mount during 1975, so that by the end of the year the bank had a substantial capital deficit. Seen in balance-sheet terms the bank was insolvent. The withdrawal of deposits thus had rather more rationale to it than in the case of Keyser Ullman. For if a bank is insolvent the implication is that depositors must lose some of their money. But a capital deficiency may not allow adequately for the value of a bank as a going concern. Despite the fact that the First National Finance Corporation showed a capital deficiency, shareholders were prepared to attach a positive price to the shares, in the hope that some bad debts might eventually be recovered and dividends would be resumed.

But while such a prospect may be attractive to an equity holder, it is unlikely that high interest rates alone would induce a depositor to risk his money with a capital deficient bank rather than deposit in a sound bank. Thus the flight of deposits was almost complete. The bank was only able to continue as a going concern because the 'lifeboat' team obliged. Indeed, its current revenue derived mainly from consumer credit operations did continue at a fairly high level, leading to a return to solvency by 1982. But the balance sheet only just shows a solvent position, and lifeboat advances remain at a high level. In 1984 the First National Finance Corporation was the last lifeboat user. A decade after the crisis it still borrowed £33 million from the support group. The auditors noted in successive reports that, 'Accounts have been prepared in accordance with accounting principles applicable to a going concern. Withdrawal of such (support group) facilities would make a going concern basis inapplicable and further substantial unprovided losses may be suffered.'

Clearly the First National Finance Corporation has obviously recovered from the position it reached in 1977, it is only now able to attract deposits on a significant scâle and its position remains rather highly geared. Nevertheless, that puts it in a relatively good position at a time of falling interest rates and it is periodically the suggested target of takeover bids. Its share price at 168p (November 1985) as against a low value of 3p reflects continuing faith in the value of the corporation as a going concern. Comparing this bank with Keyser Ullman shows how lending from an inadequate capital base can lead to capital deficiency but that a capital-deficient bank can continue to trade provided people are prepared, as the support group was, to deposit with it. The support offered by the clearing banks through the lifeboat amounted, in fact, to a willingness by the clearers to bear any further capital loss, and it was for this reason that the Bank of England did not insist on its closure.

If these two banks provide detailed balance sheets on which to study the rapid growth and partial contraction of secondary banks in

TABLE 7.7 *First National Finance Corporation plc (Birmingham Wagon Co. Ltd to 1963)*

	Liabilities (£ million)									
	1963	*1965*	*1967*	*1968*	*1969*	*1970*	*1971*	*1972*	*1973*	*1974*
Capital & reserves	3 463	4 371	5 123	5 721	10 742	13 901	22 824	41 665	49 215	38 651
Current	3 290	14 252	20 281	32 754	56 254	76 793	145 747	266 412	446 323	421 067
Other	118	360	1 120	1 754	3 453	10 423	11 972	44 562	47 740	41 700
Less provision	—	—	—	—	—	—	—	—	—	—
Total	6 871	18 983	26 524	40 231	70 449	101 117	180 543	352 639	543 278	501 418
Memorandum										
Deposits	93	4 178	758	9 336	10 528	56 285	107 239	243 580	413 343	396 762
Bank loans	2 779	9 161	10 696	20 387	40 589	11 061	23 415			
Liabilities to support group	—	—	—	—	—	—	—	—	—	—

	Liabilities (£ million)									
	1975	*1976*	*1977*	*1978*	*1979*	*1980*	*1981*	*1982*	*1983*	*1984*
Capital & reserves	−41 034	−72 375	−76 173	−58 415	−37 975	−29 066	−11 076	4 463	16 575	34 179
Current	372 701	260 472	234 511	207 330	197 696	196 746	200 652	219 440	121 771	168 960
Other	85 711	90 323	95 893	84 440	74 164	75 419	66 064	65 599	175 606	126 736
Less provision	—	—	—	—	—	—	—	—	—	—
Total	417 378	278 420	254 231	233 355	233 885	243 099	255 640	289 502	313 952	329 875
Memorandum										
Deposits	46 776	33 603	13 440	9 072	8 901	7 225	10 450	10 678	18 654	111 599
Liabilities to support group	351 866	286 699	286 322	251 391	226 430	225 531	221 014	244 292	85 774	33 012

Assets (£ million)

	1963	*1965*	*1967*	*1968*	*1969*	*1970*	*1971*	*1972*	*1973*	*1974*
Fixed	1 318	2 512	507	1 068	2 172	3 250	7 598	7 204	13 927	14 044
Inv.	26	—	50	20	—	—	—	8	8	8
Current	5 429	16 367	25 967	39 143	68 277	97 867	171 960	345 427	529 343	487 366
Goodwill	98	104	—	—	—	—	985	—	—	—
Total	6 871	18 983	26 524	40 231	70 449	101 117	180 543	352 639	543 278	501 418

Assets (£ million)

	1975	*1976*	*1977*	*1978*	*1979*	*1980*	*1981*	*1982*	*1983*	*1984*
Fixed	14 306	10 224	9 335	7 476	7 121	5 403	3 838	2 494	1 846	1 676
Inv.	4 463	59	—	—	—	—	—	—	—	—
Current	398 609	268 137	244 896	225 879	226 764	237 696	251 802	287 008	312 106	328 199
Goodwill	—	—	—	—	—	—	—	—	—	—
Total	417 378	278 420	254 231	233 355	233 885	243 099	255 640	289 502	313 952	329 875

NOTE Assets and liabilities shown at 31 December up to 1974 and on 31 October from 1975 onwards.
SOURCE Extel Statistical Services Ltd who have kindly given permission to reproduce the figures here.

Provision for loss[1] was as follows (£'000):

1973	12 774
1974	35 780
1975	110 616
1976	13 754
1977	−2 492
1978	−11 400

1. Release of interest carrying costs is offset here.

the period under study, Slater, Walker Ltd, now renamed as Britannia Arrow Holdings plc, provides a third example of growth, contraction and resurrection of a firm which was only able to continue in operation at all as a result of Bank of England support. Its balance sheet data are, however, not amenable to presentation in the same form as those of the other two banks.

Slater, Walker Limited was originally Ralli Brothers, a small listed bank which Slater, Walker Securities acquired from Sir Isaac Wolfson as part of the deal to purchase Drages in 1968–9. Having acquired Ralli Brothers, and renamed it Slater, Walker Limited, Slater, Walker Securities decided to expand it into a major non-clearing bank and recruited staff from outside the group to strengthen the banking team. The proposed merger with Hill, Samuel in 1973 fell through, reportedly because it proved impossible to reach agreement on who was to control the enlarged bank, but this did not prevent Slater, Walker Limited from expanding fast. A considerable proportion of the bank's profits were derived from the fees and commissions charged to other members of the Slater, Walker Group, whilst the funds required for the bank's operations were borrowed from the interbank market. In 1974 and 1975 rumours circulated in the City that Slater, Walker Limited was facing a financial crisis, rumours strenuously denied by the Bank of England. But the rumours proved to be correct since the balance sheet and profit and loss account were artificially inflated by the internecine dealing within the group: the bank had investments of some £75 million in property in the United Kingdom, of which at least £14 million had to be written off. More than 50 per cent of the bank's loans were unsecured advances within the group, financed by heavy borrowing in the interbank market, and the reporting accountants were highly critical of the way in which Slater, Walker Limited had conducted its banking operations with a small number of very large loans out of all proportion to the bank's resources. By the autumn of 1976, when the accountants reported their findings, it became clear that Slater, Walker Limited:

> had needed a lifeboat all to itself: the Bank of England, it was now revealed, had made a standby available to Slater, Walker . . . which had been formally re-negotiated a month later with a maximum of £70 million, of which £45.2 million had been used by 31st July, 1976. On top of this, the Bank had . . . guaranteed and indemnified Slater, Walker against losses from bad debts on loans

its banking subsidiaries had made up to £40 million over and above Slater, Walker's own provision of £9.6 million. (Raw, 1977)

The consequence of these losses, revealed at a time when the clearing banks were unwilling to put any more money into the lifeboat, was that the Bank of England took over Slater, Walker Ltd at a time when it, like the First National Finance Corporation was capital deficient. The Slater, Walker Group was allowed to survive the failure of its bank and continued to trade as Britannia Arrow. Recently it has shown an impressive recovery. It has expanded as a fund manager, and has now acquired accepting house status by taking over Singer and Friedlander, an accepting house formerly owned by European Ferries. This move is likely to restore the company to an important position in the City.

Information on some of the other non-clearing banks is available from reports by government committees of enquiry or inspectors appointed under the Companies Acts. The following data indicate the very rapid growth of those banks and the sources on which they were able to draw for the sustenance of that growth. Most of the non-listed banks developed late in the 1960s from an earlier beginning as hire purchase companies or stock market dealing companies. They found it highly worthwhile to seek banking status from the Board of Trade because it gave them access to deposits from the public or, even more important, borrowing in the money market to fuel their investment policies. Some enjoyed the support of pension funds and insurance companies whose investment managers were looking for capital gains on their investments rather than an assured but pedestrian income.

The Section 123 bank which attracted most attention, because it was the one whose financial difficulties precipitated the banking crisis in 1973, was *London and County Securities*. This company was originally incorporated in 1968 as a small credit finance company, but in 1969 it acquired a company that had received Section 123 recognition from the Board of Trade in 1967, re-named it London and County Securities Limited, and floated its shares on the Stock Exchange. The company expanded its banking business by soliciting deposits from the public through branches which it opened in 22 departmental stores around the country, and in 1971 it attempted to gain authorised banking status by making an abortive bid for Leopold Joseph, a listed merchant bank. Following this failure, London and County acquired a second mortgage business and moved into investment banking in order to take equity stakes in quoted companies. Under the direction of the chairman and his close associates, a series of incestuous deals within the group were made which attracted the strong criticism of the inspectors appointed by the Department of Trade to investigate the affairs of the group (Department of Trade, 1976). The bank expanded very fast and its current, deposit and other accounts grew from just over £2.5 million in 1969 to nearly £90 million in 1973, whilst its total assets increased from £9 million in 1970 to £129 million in 1973, largely through dealing in the interbank market. It was supported by the Eagle Star Insurance Company and the National Westminster Bank, and was intimately involved in 'window dressing' deals with other secondary banks like Wintrust and Cornhill Consolidated. It borrowed heavily in the money market in order to finance its inter-company share deals and its property acquisitions and, as the inspectors pointed out in their report, it was prepared in 1973 to pay an average rate of interest of 13 per cent on its borrowings in the interbank market whilst earning only 8 per cent on the funds it placed in the market. Its banking strategy was to borrow heavily short-term but to invest its borrowing in property and other long-term assets, a sure recipe for disaster if the property market turned against it. In 1971 the bank maintained in its annual report that its ratio of net borrowing to shareholders' funds was 2:1 but, from the inspectors' report, it is clear that by March 1972 the real ratio was much nearer 10:1. It manipulated its balance sheet to conceal the loss it incurred through the purchase of Drakes, a property company, and never disclosed the extent of its loans to its directors, including an unsecured loan of £1 million to its deputy chairman. Contrary to normal banking practice, it credited its accounts with fees for the banking services it rendered, mainly to other companies within the group, as soon as loan facilities were negotiated, and not when the fees were due to be received. By concealing the true financial situation, the bank was able to bid up its share price from 150p in 1969 to 305p in 1973. When the property market collapsed, doubts regarding the bank's viability began to mount and its share price slumped to 30p in November 1973, and began the banking crisis.

After London and County Securities' collapse, the next and most serious failure was that of *Cedar Holdings* which was another aggressive Section 123 bank seeking deposits wherever it could find them, particularly in the money market, and bidding actively for retail deposits in branches which it opened by offering interest on current accounts and a variety of free gifts to large depositors. Its deposit liabilities increased from £2.5 million in 1969 to £75 million by the end of 1973, of which some 85 per cent or more was obtained through short-term borrowing in the interbank market. It made advances totalling £74 million, of which more than two-thirds was in respect of medium-term second mortgages (*The Banker,* 1974). When the crisis came at the end of 1973, the bank found that it was unable to renew its short-term borrowing in the interbank market and its share price collapsed from 90p to 15p.

Although there is little published information about most of the secondary banks which faced a liquidity crisis, there is one which has been the subject of an official inquiry. This is the *Crown Agents* which was the subject of a report by the Fay Committee (*Report of the Committee of Inquiry into the Crown Agents,* 1977): this provides much-needed evidence of the involvement of a non-clearing 'bank' in the money markets. The following part of this chapter is based on the findings of the Fay Committee which was set up in order to enquire into (a) how the Crown Agents grew into a secondary fringe bank and property developer on its own account in a speculative market, (b) why the agents incurred huge losses and (c) why there was no control over the agents' operations. The Committee found that the amount either written off, or provided for, totalled £212 million, a measure of the size of the revealed deficiency.

As part of their services for overseas governments, the Crown Agents accepted funds which the agents were responsible for placing. They managed three funds – the Joint Consolidated Fund, the Joint Miscellaneous Fund and the Marine Insurance Fund. In the early 1960s the future for the Crown Agents looked uncertain with more and more of their former colonial clients gaining independence and their free reserves down to a level of some £180 000. It was therefore decided to build up their reserves and a number of limited liability companies were set up for this purpose between 1963 and 1967. In March 1966 it was decided that 'funds under the direct control of the Crown Agents . . . should be invested at the discretion of the Crown Agents', and in 1967 own account operations began with the creation of a new vehicle – Finvest. Dealings began in the interbank market in short-term money, which was a significant departure, since before the Crown Agents had only placed money. By 1968 Finvest was borrowing around £50 million from the interbank market with the intention of building 'up a banking operation with the object of making money by it'. Initially, principals' funds (that is, the funds from overseas governments) were kept separate, but by 1968 principals' money was being taken in Finvest as term money and was being used to lend to fringe banks in the interbank market, to property companies and for investment in equities. By the end of 1969 Finvest's balance sheet totalled £127 million, of which £70 million to £80 million was being lent to secondary banks, finance houses and commerce, and invested in property. Substantial stakes had been taken in E.D. Sassoon Banking Company, in property development in Australia and in Sterling Industrial Securities, another fringe bank. By the end of 1970 Finvest, which had started as an own account fund fed by borrowing from the money market, was increasingly using principals' money. By the beginning of 1972, Finvest's balance sheet had grown to over £400 million, of which £300 million represented deposits by principals and £100 million borrowings from the money market. It dealt heavily in the shares of the First National Finance Corporation and the England and Continental Property Company, and made substantial losses on loans to Vehicle and General Insurance Company (£1 million), Mersey Docks and Harbour Board (£1 068 000) both of which failed in 1971 and two USA companies, the Great South West Corporation and the Republic Corporation (£1 399 000).

Following critical press comment on the Crown Agents' dealings in financial markets with huge risks, a Committee of Enquiry was appointed under the chairmanship of Sir Matthew Stevenson. This Committee, in its report published in March 1972, rejected any proposal that the Crown Agents should discontinue its borrowing from the money market. No doubt encouraged by this endorsement of its actions, the Crown Agents plunged deeper into property speculation with a major involvement with the Stern Group to which it made substantial unsecured loans. Towards the end of 1973 the crisis in secondary banking occurred, and the Crown Agents found borrowers in plenty but a scarcity of lenders. Even so, no change in policy was made and, ironically, the Bank of England asked the Crown Agents to join the 'lifeboat' operation! Support was given to the First National Finance Corporation, Triumph Investment Trust, the Burston Group and the Northern Commercial Trust, to a total amount of £26 million. Nemesis was not long delayed, however, and at a meeting at the Treasury in May 1974 it was obvious that the Crown Agents were either 'bust or capable of being bust'. A new chairman was appointed in 1974 (John Cuckney), who found massive deficiencies and a complete restructuring of the Crown Agents' affairs was put in hand.

The importance of the Crown Agents' affair is the light it sheds both on the parallel money markets and on the Bank of England's attitude to secondary banking. As regards the money markets, it seems reasonably clear that the Crown Agents could have had no opportunity to speculate on the scale they did but for the existence of unsecured markets in which they were free to deal without supervision or control. And if this is true for the Crown Agents, it must be equally true of the other non-clearing banks whose dealings closely paralleled those of the Crown Agents. So far as the Bank of England is concerned, it had had plenty of warning about the dangers which were looming for the Crown Agents. As early as April 1970 *The Sunday Times*, in an article entitled 'Crown Agents: who carries the final buck?' had drawn attention to the agents' increasing involvement in the money markets in which they had become an important force, and had criticised the scale of their property dealings. Yet the Bank took no action to restrain the Crown Agents, partly, no doubt, because it regarded the Crown Agents as the business of the Treasury, and it is no wonder that the Fay Committee was driven to comment:

> The Bank of England is the national central bank . . . It possesses the practical skills and contacts enabling it to detect flaws in the financial world and to provide assistance in remedying them . . . we think it would not have been unreasonable for the Bank to have played a greater part in this affair than it did. (para. 42)

Much the same could have been said about the Bank of England's attitude to the development of the parallel markets and to the expansion of non-clearing banks *in toto*.

The 'lifeboat' did not make any advances available to the Crown Agents. It was not clear that their capital deficiency could be recovered from trading profits, and a 'repayable grant' of £175 million was made available by the government to the agents. They have now reverted to the more traditional role of investing funds on behalf of foreign clients and the Crown Agents are now seen as a candidate for denationalisation.

A decade after the secondary banking crisis, in 1984, the fact that regulation is not perfect was demonstrated by the failure of *Johnson Matthey Bankers*. They were a subsidiary of Johnson Matthey, the London bullion dealers. The bank had its origins in bullion and commodity trading, but in 1981 it was decided to expand the non-bullion side of its business. As a consequence non-bullion lending rose from £50 million in 1981 to £500 million in March 1984.

This rapid expansion was achieved by a small number of large loans. As the Bank of England Report on the Johnson Matthey affair (*Bank of England Annual Report,* 1985) makes clear, Johnson Matthey had faced the classic dilemma over these loans. The debtors ran into problems and Johnson Matthey increased its advances in the hope that the money would eventually be recovered. The directors, for reasons which are unclear, did not report the full extent of their exposure to the Bank of England. In June 1984 an advance to a customer, who was not a first-class name, of 38 per cent of capital was reported. In fact the advance amounted to 76 per cent of the capital base. It became clear that very substantial provisions were needed to cover bad debts; these exceeded the bank's available capital.

When the nature of the bank's problems became apparent, the Bank of England attempted to find a purchaser for the bank. Despite considerable effort it was not possible to find any buyer for the bank and eventually Johnson Matthey plc, its owner, agreed to inject £50 million and sell it to the Bank of England for £1. The Bank of England then idemnified the bank for £150 million, half of which was met by a counter-indemnity from private sector banks in the City. The Bank of England argued that the rescue was justified on the grounds that Johnson Matthey's role in the gold market gave it much greater importance than its size alone suggested. Furthermore the uncertainty created by the failure of Continental Illinois earlier in the year, made the banking world nervous, and under these circumstances the cost of allowing failure was likely to be high. But, while the Bank of England was obviously keen to avoid giving the impression that any bank would be rescued, many observers drew precisely this conclusion. Part of public opinion failed clearly to distinguish the fate of shareholders (Johnson Matthey plc) and senior employees, who were penalised, from that of depositors who were not. The political sensitivity of the issue was augmented by the suggestion, in the summer of 1985, that fraud had been involved.

A joint Bank of England/Treasury Committee was set up to consider the regulatory implications of the affair. Its main conclusions (*Report of the Committee to Consider the Question of Banking Supervision*, 1985) were that the confidentiality requirements which prevent co-operation between the banking supervisor and a bank's auditors should be lifted, and that the distinction between banks and licensed deposit takers should be ended. The latter was seen as a source of some confusion to the public. The committee also recommended that the maximum sum covered by deposit insurance should be raised to £20 000.

7.6 SUMMARY

Clearing bank subsidiaries falling into this group dominate it, although this was not the case before 1975, when none of the banks listed in Table 7.1 were in this category. These subsidiaries have been the major vehicle for diversification by the clearing banks. The recent fusing of Barclays with its international subsidiary, and the similar move proposed by Lloyds suggest that banks now see little distinction between domestic and international banking. However at present no similar moves are proposed with regard to other types of subsidiary. The non-clearing banks other than the accepting houses, and excluding these international subsidiaries, grew with astonishing rapidity from the late 1960s, as Table 7.2 illustrates for those banks which reported to the Bank of England. They were able to do so for two main reasons. First, they were able to exploit segments of the market which the other established banks were not prepared to monopolise. Although the clearing banks and the accepting houses made loans to the property sector, they were never prepared to do so on a scale which would have cornered this segment of the market for themselves. Secondly, the weaknesses in the system of credit control implicit in the Bank of England's competition and credit control system from 1971 allowed bank lending to rise without any deterrent action by the authorities. Moreover, the authorities may not have fully appreciated the implications of the growth of the interbank market from which so many banks obtained the funds they required to provide the deposit liability base on which they could structure their lending and investment policies.

The most important fact that emerges from what is known about the growth of the fringe non-clearing banks is that their expansion was only made possible by the existence of money markets in which they were free to borrow without security, and with no central bank supervision or control. Whilst recognising that there was much sharp practice, coupled in some cases with illegality, in the affairs of some non-clearing banks, there can be little doubt that a number of financial institutions saw in the example of the rapid growth of the accepting houses a model for expansion which they also could follow.

And since this expansion was fuelled by heavy borrowing in the interbank market, the question that inevitably arises is – what were the sources of that borrowing? There is no clear answer to this question since the interbank market was an anonymous one in which it was impossible to trace the movement of funds between lender and borrower. Two possibilities have been suggested in discussions with bankers. The first is that, in the light of the substantial sums involved, part at least of the lending to fringe non-clearing banks must have been made by the subsidiaries of the clearing banks. The other is that the foreign banks in London, who were not so closely in touch with financial institutions as were the British banks, were sufficiently influenced by the rates offered by brokers, and by the attractions of property development, to be prepared to lend to the secondary banks concerned. There were compelling reasons why they should have done so. 'The cost of establishing a full London branch has been estimated at approximately $1 million per annum . . . the smaller US banks have increasingly been forced to rely upon money market transactions to cover their overheads' (Channon, 1979). Moreover, Channon points out that the London branches of the American banks were seriously affected by the property collapse in 1973 and by the secondary banking crisis. The Continental Illinois National Bank of Chicago, for example, needed a $15 million capital injection by its parent bank in view of a $12 million possible loss through its involvement with Cornhill Consolidated and the Lyon and Stern property groups. Other US banks in London suffering substantial losses were the First National Bank of Maryland and the Texas Commerce Bank whose joint venture with the Burston Finance Group collapsed. Those which were unsupervised by the Bank of England were able to expand without any constraints at all, because they did not officially count as banks. After 1975, as the Bank took more institutions under its wing, as a preliminary to the statutory controls of the Banking Act, it became easier to form a clearly quantified picture of the activities in which this redefined banking group engage. Unfortunately no similar aggregate picture can be built up of the pattern of lending in the period leading up to the banking crisis.

Appendix: FOREIGN AND COMMONWEALTH BANKS

In addition to the British banks there is a large number of foreign and commonwealth banks operating in Britain. Although they lie primarily outside the scope of this book some indication of their operations must be given. Foreign banks operate in Britain in one of three ways. Many set up branches in London so as to allow themselves to participate in the financial markets of the City. Citicorp, the largest bank in the world falls into this category. Other banks are foreign-owned subsidiaries registered as companies in Britain. Still others are 'consortium banks'. These banks are owned by consortia of British and foreign banks and are again companies registered in Britain. There are no published figures for the size of the individual branch operations of foreign banks in Britain, but the figures in Table 7.8 indicate the size of the banks in the second and third groups.

TABLE 7.8 *Foreign and consortium banks in Britain, 1984–5*

£ million	*Assets*	*Net profit*
Saudi International	3 045	11.6
Scandinavian Bank	2 871	8.8
Moscow Narodny Bank	2 272	5.9
Libra Bank	2 321	16.1
Orion Royal Bank	2 606	8.2

SOURCE *'The Times 1000'*, 1985–6.

These banks compare in size with medium-sized accepting houses; the branch banking operations of foreign banks are probably considerably more important since it is clear that (Introduction, p. 1) the sterling business of the foreign banks is as large as that of the accepting houses and the other British banks taken together. Of this total the American and Japanese banks have the largest shares, although there are banks from a wide range of countries, as the list above shows. Many of them qualify only for 'licensed deposit-taker' status, although they are allowed to use the name under which they trade internationally and thus can call themselves banks.

Foreign banks in Britain regarded themselves as providing a merchant banking service, financing international trade and providing special expertise about their country of origin. But if the eurocurrency market was a creation of the accepting houses, it is the foreign banks in London which have become the major participants. Their balance sheet composition is most similar to that of the other British non-clearing banks, as Table 7.9 shows. The extent of their

TABLE 7.9 *The balance sheet of foreign and commonwealth banks (December)*

Currency		*1960*	*1966*		*1974*		*1975*		*1984*	
			Liabilities (£ million)							
		All	*£*	*Other*	*£*	*Other*	*£*	*Other*	*£*	*Other*
Current & Deposit Accounts	UK banks	—	322	761	3 085	11 648	2 711	14 693	17 529	73 632
	Other UK	372	558	93	2 435	1 629	2 244	1 636	8 655	10 494
	Overseas	1 095	1 073	2 507	1 756	36 920	1 101	47 230	14 926	276 650
CDs		—	—	—	1 588	4 601	1 127	5 148	3 570	73 218
Net non-deposit liabilities		209	355	−9	777	384	1 426	105	10 780	−1 207
Total		1 676	2 308	3 352	9 641	55 182	8 609	68 812	55 460	432 787

Currency	*1960*	*1966*		*1974*		*1975*		*1984*	
		Assets (£ million)							
	All	*£*	*Other*	*£*	*Other*	*£*	*Other*	*£*	*Other*
Notes and coin (L) and working deposits at the Bank of England	1	2	—	6	—	8	—	24	—
Balances with UK banks (L)	187	382	655	2 696	12 786	1 889	15 176	14 603	69 821
Call money (L)	172	151	—	575	—	433	—	1 302	—
CDs (L)	—	—	—	1 185	—	520	1 323	1 827	10 236
Local authority loans	101	261	—	741	—	592	—	1 416	—
Treasury bills (L)	80	32	—	50	—	273	—	83	—
Other bills (L)	81	112	—	220	—	173	206	289	1 265

UK government securities	313	465	—	315	—	124	—	766	—
Advances & Loans: UK residents	229	584	126	3 296	4 458	3 640	4 941	18 018	27 574
Advances & Loans: Other	496	255	2 455	310	36 414	129	46 977	9 295	305 376
Other assets	16	64	116	102	1 524	689	189	7 705	18 515
Special and cash ratio deposits	—	—	—	145	—	139	—	132	
Total	1 676	2 308	3 352	9 641	55 182	8 609	68 812	55 460	432 787
Acceptances	69	323			1 322		732		10 624
Ratios									
Non-bank advances / Non-bank deposits	n.a.	0.51	0.99	0.86	1.06	1.13	1.06	1.16	1.16
Liquid assets / All deposits	0.36	0.25		0.28		0.27		0.21	
Non-bank advances / All deposits	0.49	0.43	0.77	0.41	0.75	0.52	0.76	0.61	0.77

NOTES (L) Liquid asset as defined by the Bank of England before 1971.
Non-deposit liabilities are a balancing item.
A break in the series occurs between 1974 and 1975.
The 1984 figures for UK banks relate to monetary sector institutions.

SOURCES *Bank of England Statistical Abstracts* Nos 1 and 2. *Bank of England Quarterly Bulletin.*

eurocurrency involvement is shown by the magnitude of loans and deposits in foreign currency.

Many banks are already major market-traders in the eurobond market; they have developed links with stockbrokers of major importance so as to become equity traders when regulations permit. The Australia and New Zealand Banking Group has linked with Capel-Cure Myers, Chase Manhattan with Simon & Coates, Citicorp with Vickers da Costa and Scrimgeour Kemp Gee, Credit Suisse with Buckmaster & Moore, Hongkong and Shanghai with James Capel, Security Pacific Bank with Hoare Govett, Shearson Lehmann with L. Messel and the Union Bank of Switzerland with Phillips and Drew. Most of these stakes now amount to the permitted maximum of 29.9 per cent but will rise to 100 per cent when this is authorised in 1986.

As noted elsewhere, foreign banks pose particular regulatory problems. The guidelines adopted in the Basle Concordat in 1975 suggested that the central bank of the host country should be responsible for monitoring the adequacy of liquidity, while that of the parent country should monitor capital adequacy. But this does not always work smoothly. The Bank of England would not want to maintain the liquidity of an insolvent bank, and thus has to devote some attention to capital adequacy. In 1982 the Bank of England stated that lender of last resort facilities would not necessarily be made available to foreign banks in London (*Bank of England Quarterly Bulletin,* 1982c). It thus became clear that the foreign banks would not be treated in the same way as domestic banks. A revision to the Basle Concordat after the Banco Ambrosiano affair (p. 179) made this explicit.

The monetary control arrangements of the 1960s did not apply to the foreign banks. But since 1971 control has not discriminated against the domestic sector. Competition and credit control was intended to treat all banks equally, and thus the reserve requirements, special deposit and supplementary special deposit schemes applied to these banks. In 1971 they were short of reserves but these were obtained without great difficulty. During the period before the introduction of the corset, sterling deposits (excluding interbank items) grew at much the same rate as those with the British non-clearing banks and this roughly parallel expansion has continued.

8 International Problems

There are two rather different types of international comparison which should be made in a study of this type. First, the instability of the 1970s was not restricted to the British economy. In a number of countries a situation in some ways analogous to that in Britain developed. The first part of this chapter, therefore, briefly recounts some crises occurring in other countries. However, the more interesting comparison is made not with other countries, but with the experience of the world as a whole. The international debt crisis, which began in 1982, can be seen as a liquidity crisis on a world scale, although not one arising from the problems of any one bank; the second part therefore attempts to identify similarities between the development of international banking in the period leading up to the debt crisis, and the growth of the UK non-clearing banks before 1973.

8.1 BANKING INSTABILITY

The crisis that hit the United Kingdom banking sector between 1973 and 1975 and which threatened the stability of the entire financial system was not confined to this country. The collapse of banks in the United States, West Germany, Italy, Switzerland and Belgium between 1973 and 1976 imparted an international dimension to the crisis: this strengthened the Bank of England's resolve to limit the damage which the domestic financial distress might cause. As in the United Kingdom, the crises in countries overseas stemmed from speculation (in those countries principally by entrepreneurs and foreign exchange dealers) but they nevertheless reflected a malaise in the financial institutions involved which central banks needed quickly to overcome if the international banking system was not to face collapse. The failure of a number of banks outside the United Kingdom:

> caused a great deal of nervousness in international banking circles and the Bank [of England] were particularly concerned that UK

> banking institutions should not be seen to default on any external obligations. Even though the international financial community had recognised and welcomed the general success of the lifeboat operation and the original fears of major failures had receded, there was still a significant risk that an isolated default by a UK bank, in the highly charged atmosphere of the time, might have triggered a chain reaction. (*Bank of England Quarterly Bulletin*, 1978)[1]

If the Bank of England went out of its way to stress the seriousness of the financial crisis, it must be supposed that the dangers to which the Bank pointed were very real.

In the United States credit was tightened in the early 1970s as a world recession deepened, with the OPEC (Organization of Petroleum Exporting Countries) oil price rise in 1973 adding to the problems of the major industrial countries. Interest rates rose to the financial detriment of corporations which had over-borrowed before the period of economic growth came to an end. As in the United Kingdom, property companies and Real Estate Investment Trusts (REITs) were the first to suffer. The property market fell in the face of forced sales of completed and uncompleted properties. With the collapse of the property market much of the collateral for bank advances vanished and the concomitant fall in the stock market made matters worse. A number of banks in the United States faced the prospect of liquidation, and a hasty rescue operation had to be staged by the Federal Reserve in order to prevent a domino effect throughout the banking system. The story was much the same in West Germany and Italy.

The US bank which attracted most notoriety was the Franklin National Bank of Long Island which incurred substantial losses at the beginning of the 1970s; for example, it reported a loss of $7.2 million in 1971. An entrepreneur, Michele Sindona (subsequently sent to gaol for 25 years for his criminal activities in connection with the Franklin National Bank collapse) acquired control of the bank and attempted to merge it with Talcott National Corporation, a major factoring organisation. Sindona appointed new foreign exchange dealers who, he hoped, would restore the bank's fortunes through foreign exchange speculation. This hope was thwarted by bad luck and by 1973, when the bank was borrowing as much as $1000 million a day from Federal Reserve Funds, Franklin National was in desperate trouble. Sindona attempted to conceal the losses which the bank was incurring through paper deals with a Swiss bank, Amincor, which he controlled. With a deficit of $40 million on foreign exchange dealing alone, this could only postpone for a short time the inevitable collapse which duly occurred in 1974. A consortium of banks took over Franklin National's branches, the Federal Deposit Insurance Corporation provided $2000 million to protect depositors and the Federal Reserve Bank of New York made an emergency loan of $1720 million to maintain the bank in its final hours. The Federal Reserve system must take some part of the blame for the nature of the bank's failure since the Comptroller of the Currency admitted that for several years problems had been identified at the bank but no action was taken.

Other banks in the United States which faced problems in the period after 1970 and 1975 included some of the largest. The United States National Bank of San Diego was placed in receivership by the Comptroller of the Currency and the Federal Deposit Insurance Corporation in 1973, owing National Westminster and Barclays Banks $14 million and $4.5 million respectively; these amounts were subsequently recovered. The Bank of America, then the world's largest bank had potential losses of $175 million in 1975 and First National City Bank and Chase Manhattan Bank had loans at risk of $2600 million and $4000 million respectively. By 1975 the American banks held $3000 million of uncollectable bad debts, and the Federal Deposit Insurance Corporation met the claims of small depositors in 1975 at ten times the average annual rate since its formation. The collapse of the REITs, beginning in 1973 when the Kassuba Development Corporation filed for bankruptcy, threatened the survival of many banks which had imprudently both made loans for property development and also acted as managers for the trusts. The difficulties, and sometimes failures, of large corporate clients, and perhaps even more important of large public utilities like New York City, which had all borrowed heavily from the banking system affected even the largest commercial banks and only action by the Federal Reserve and by the Federal Government succeeded in averting a major financial crisis.

More recently the international debt crisis has led to general concern about US banks. It combined with high interest rates to make 1983 the year with the highest number of banking failures since the Second World War. But the largest banking run to date was not directly a consequence of imprudent speculation or a major boom. The failure of the Penn Square Bank in 1982 has already been mentioned. Continental Illinois had used this bank as a vehicle for loans in the energy exploration business, and faced substantial losses when the fall in oil prices led to the closure of Penn Square. Despite this Continental Illinois seemed to be securely capitalised, although the proportion of non-performing loans in the portfolio may have given rise to some concern.

In May 1984 a run suddenly developed. The bank, like the British non-clearers, relied mainly on wholesale deposits, since US banking regulations prevent the establishment of large retail networks. And it found it was unable to renew deposits as they matured. An initial 'safety net' of $4.66 bn (later raised to $5.3 bn) was offered by a group of banks on 14 May, but this proved inadequate to staunch the run. Three days later the Federal Reserve announced it would meet any abnormal liquidity requirements and would provide $2 bn of subordinated deposits, which were in effect a capital infusion. The run was now over and Continental Illinois announced it was seeking a merger or takeover as a solution to its problems. It is not clear that this run was a consequence of inadequate supervision or actual insolvency, but the problem was finally resolved by measures amounting to nationalisation.

In West Germany, the troubled bank which created most problems internationally was the Bankhaus I.D. Herstatt which in June 1974 was closed by the West German authorities. With current liabilities of DM 2189 million and assets of only DM 984 million, it was hopelessly insolvent, largely as a result of foreign exchange dealing which had neither been reported nor recorded. The subsequent prosecution and conviction of its chairman, for signing a false balance sheet, showed that the bank had actually been insolvent for a while before its collapse. Problems arose through the method used by the West German authorities to close the bank which, due to the time difference between West Germany and the United States, allowed a number of foreign exchange deals to be completed after the bank had been closed. Some major United States banks and Hill, Samuel, the United Kingdom accepting house, all found themselves facing potentially large losses, but after a good deal of wrangling, the problem was eventually solved. As a result of the failure of the Herstatt bank, the West German authorities acted to improve their methods of control and supervision, particularly over currency dealing, whilst the Bundesbank, the state banks and the commercial banks formed a consortium with an initial DM 1 million reserve to assist any bank which in future found itself facing a liquidity crisis.

The United States authorities also introduced new regulations, making it possible to reverse interbank transactions up to one day after funds had been transferred and requiring disclosure of foreign exchange positions over $1 million on a weekly and monthly basis.

Among other banks in West Germany which lost heavily in foreign exchange and/or property dealing were Hessische Landesbank-Gironzentrale and West-deutsche Landesbank-Girozentrale, both of which survived because they were state-owned and were able to draw on interest-free loans from other state-owned organisations. Hessische Landesbank made substantial advances for property development in Frankfurt and Munich which proved to be irrecoverable; the bank had to write off losses of DM 500 million in 1975 and its parent company, Helaba, had total losses for the period 1973 to 1975 of some DM 2200 million. Some of Hessische's difficulties arose from the collapse in Switzerland, in 1974, of the International Credit Bank of Geneva, which had become a haven for funds from Investors Overseas Services, the Cornfeld mutual trust, and criminal sources. In the later 1970s and early 1980s more general losses arose for the West German banks. For they were maturity transformers to a much greater extent than their British counterparts. The period of high interest rates in the early 1980s led to several banks being forced to suspend dividend payments. Moreover, the closure of Schroeder, Muenchmeyer, Hengst and Co. in late 1983 showed that West German banking supervision was by no means adequate. This bank had lent very heavily to a single doubtful customer.

In Italy the Sindona empire collapsed after the Franklin National Bank failure in the United States with the Banca Privata Finanziaria incurring a deficit of $260 million and being put into liquidation. The Banca di Roma guaranteed the payment of Sindona's depositors but some of the major clients of the bank, including the Vatican, lost heavily. A curious echo of the Sindona affair resurfaced in 1982 with the failure of the Banco Ambrosiano. It had lent money to companies owned by the Vatican for the purpose of buying shares in itself. This was designed to maintain the control of the chairman, Roberto Calvi. He was a former associate to Sindona and was found hanged in London in June 1982. The atmosphere of intrigue surrounding the episode, in which $1200 million was lost, is likely to fuel speculation as to the precise circumstances of the failure of the Banco Ambrosiano for many years to come (Cornwell, 1984).

From this brief résumé of the difficulties which affected the banking systems in some other countries, it is reasonably clear that financial systems internationally suffered severe problems after 1970 when a period of instability followed many years of growth, problems which threatened to impair the stability of the banking systems and requiring intervention by central banks in order to stave off an even greater loss of confidence. The reasons are not difficult to find. In the conditions of the 1960s, when the major industrial countries were experiencing a period of consumption-led expansion, there was no particular disincentive (except regulations by the authorities) against banks acting like their entrepreneurial customers by aiming at earning profits through speculation in property, foreign exchange and commodities and neglecting the risks involved. After currencies were allowed to float in 1972, there was considerably increased scope for speculation in foreign exchange in the hope of quick profits. It is true that most banks kept their trading within the limits of prudential banking, but there were bound to be some that were prepared to assume the substantial risks involved in speculation if success led to large increases in profits; furthermore fraud was present in some of the larger failures. But consideration must be given to the possibility that the troubles which have afflicted the world's financial system since 1970 are a natural consequence of the adjustments necessary at the end of the long post-war boom.

8.2 THE INTERNATIONAL DEBT CRISIS

However, before looking at this issue in Chapter 9 it is useful to discuss what is potentially the largest source of world financial instability.[2] The international debt crisis began with a unilateral Mexican moratorium in August 1982, and has continued to occupy the minds of international bankers since then. It has similarities to the crisis which had enveloped the British non-clearing banks nine years earlier. It was able to arise in a banking system which was unregulated for the reasons considered in Chapter 6.

The origins of the crisis go back to the need of the developing countries to import capital in order to expand their economies. But a problem has always been that many of them produce goods for which the world as a whole has a fairly low income elasticity of demand. An expanding developing country may want to spend an increasing fraction of its income on imports. But an expanding developed country tends to have a buoyant demand for imports of manufactures and not for raw materials. Thus, if a developing country tries to grow at the same rate as the developed world it will have an increasing tendency to a balance of trade deficit. If it actually tries to catch up on the developed world this problem will be much aggravated. Both Latin America and Africa grew faster than was compatible with trade balance (Weale, 1984). This rapid growth thus led to trade deficits. As these continued the size of the stock of debt and the fraction of export income needed to service this debt rose (see Table 8.1).

Although favourable movements in prices can lift the constraint for a time, and the commodity price boom of 1973–4 had this effect, such relief will only be temporary. The developing countries have to develop enough to achieve the structural change necessary for them to produce goods which have a high income elasticity of demand in the developed world. At such a point the benefit of the past investment in capital will become visible and they will be able to pay off their debts. Many of the recently settled regions started with very large external debts, built up as they developed their infrastructure in the nineteenth-century, and were able to repay them as the demand for their output rose. Thus, it is not abnormal for countries at an early stage of development to incur debts and this need not in itself be a source of difficulty or financial distress. But just as a favourable movement in prices can afford relief from the process, so an adverse movement in the terms of trade can dramatically heighten the problems of a developing country. Therefore, although, as seen from Table 8.1 substantial debt had been accumulated before the oil crisis of 1973, and indeed arose from an attempt to grow rapidly, many commentators find it useful to locate the roots of the crisis at this time. For those countries which had ambitious development programmes suddenly found that they had to pay a much higher price of oil imports. The impact was cushioned for a time since other raw material prices continued to rise until 1974. But the drain in purchasing power to the OPEC countries with high savings propensities, depressed the world economy, leading to a fall in raw material prices and non-oil producing developing countries found themselves heavily in deficit.

The much-vaunted 'recycling' process was a means of ensuring that they would be able to fund their deficits. For, if every country deflated its economy so as to restore trade balance after a change like the oil price rise, there would be a dramatic contraction in the world economy. By recycling deposits from surplus countries to deficit countries it was possible to maintain a higher level of activity in the world economy.

TABLE 8.1 *External debt and debt service of the less developed countries 1973–82*

Year	*1973*	*1974*	*1975*	*1976*	*1977*	*1978*	*1979*	*1980*	*1981*	*1982*
Debt (US $ billion)	110	135	165	200	250	310	365	430	505	555
Debt Service/Exports	15.3	15.9	17.9	16.8	17.3	22.0	21.9	20.0	23.1	27.7

SOURCE *Federal Reserve Bulletin,* November 1983.

There is obviously a major problem in this approach. If money is lent against a self-liquidating transaction such as the sale of goods already ordered, there is no doubt about the ability of the borrower to repay. This leads to low rates of discount and general marketability of instruments such as bills of exchange which are associated with transactions of this type. Equally a long-term loan to finance an infrastructure project may, provided the project is carefully appraised and successful, not lead to problems because the loan can be funded and serviced out of the extra income generated by the development. Such projects must be part of balanced growth. If export industries are not also developed, a country will find itself lacking the foreign exchange needed to pay interest on its debts. Where borrowing is carried out with no particular project in mind and with the aim of maintaining a high general level of spending, there is a grave risk that a borrowing country will run into problems in servicing its debt.

8.3 INTERNATIONAL LIQUIDITY AND SOLVENCY

The distinction between liquidity and solvency plays an important role in any study of a banking system: as we have seen, both are important. An illiquid bank may be perfectly solvent while an insolvent bank may be trading and remain adequately liquid. But if the distinction between the two can become blurred when applied to a bank, it is even less clearly a relevant issue when applied to a sovereign borrower. Often sovereign risk is treated as an issue rather differently from other types of banking risk (Cooper, 1984, Chapter 4). For while a sovereign borrower can become illiquid, and Mexico and Brazil have at times been on the brink of illiquidity, it is not immediately obvious that a sovereign state can become insolvent. Quinn (1983) points out that the major asset of a country is its people and their managerial skills. But such an asset cannot be liquidated. Unlike a company, which can go bankrupt and disappear, there is always the possibility that a sovereign state may pay its debt. Indeed, until recently, the Inland Revenue, influenced by these considerations, refused to let UK banks write off provision for bad debt on loans to sovereign borrowers against tax. Despite these observations some indicator of ability to pay is important.

Typically attention focuses on the debt service ratio which shows payments of interest and repayments of principle as a fraction of current exports (Table 8.1). While this gives a good indication of the liquidity needs of a country, if seen in conjunction with its import bill, it nevertheless provides a poor indicator of its solvency position, interpreted broadly as the ability to pay off debts in the long run. For high nominal (as opposed to real) rates of interest and early repayment dates affect liquidity but they cannot affect solvency. The permanent burden of debt service on a country with debt the size of its income is not large.[3] Only a small fraction of income has to be paid out each year in order to keep the debt/income ratio stable. Even a moderate rate of growth much reduces the annual debt service needed to maintain stability of this ratio.

If this analysis suggests that countries can incur debts of similar size to GDP without facing a large burden it must be reconciled with the widely-held view that a country needs foreign exchange in order to repay its debts, and a shortage of foreign exchange, arising from a repeated current account deficit, is an indicator of insolvency. Such a view requires the assumption that, at the margin domestic output cannot be exported. The idea that a country will not be able to switch its resources into exporting so as to generate the foreign exchange implies a structural rigidity. Such a rigidity is certainly present in the short term, but there is no reason why it should be in the long term.[4, 5] Nevertheless, reallocation of resources is likely to have costs attached to it, and policies which require a rapid reallocation are likely to lead to more lost output than those allowing a gradual change. An attempt to meet debts as they fall due is, if the debts are short-term, likely to impose an additional unnecessary cost on the debtor nations;[6] on the other hand the debtors need to adopt policies which will, in the long run allow them to prevent their debt/income ratios increasing without limit. Because of the general air of uncertainty about future growth prospects, it is likely that lenders will have a more pessimistic view than borrowers about the ability to switch resources into the export sector, and about the over-all rate of growth of the economy. Thus lenders are keener on rapid adjustment policies than borrowers. Furthermore, banks have a preference for liquidity – they need to maintain their liquidity ratios. Attention continues to focus on the liquidity issue rather than the solvency issue; the banks would not be willing to convert the debt into long-dated bonds with a specified real, rather than nominal, rate of interest.

In the current position the large indebted countries, Brazil, Mexico and Argentina, have debts approaching half of GDP but equal to four or five times export earnings. Thus if the debts could be funded at a 5 per cent pa real interest rate the service cost would be of the order of 2.5 per cent of GDP or about 25 per cent of export earnings whereas, because of high nominal interest rates associated with the end of the inflationary era, the ratio has risen to 50 per cent of export earnings. The current account deficits faced by these countries as a result of their external borrowing arise from much the same reasons as the high budget deficits of the industrial countries. The need for inflation adjustment of budget deficits is often discussed; it extends to current account deficits (Buiter, 1983) although this aspect has hitherto received much less attention. Furthermore, at a time of high real interest rates it may be sensible for the debtor countries to increase their borrowing. This slows down the adjustment which is necessary and is likely to reduce its cost. It is likely that the major debtor countries can service their debts in the long run. They do not have the foreign exchange (liquidity) to pay them back in the short run, and there is always the possibility that they will choose not to repay.[7]

8.4 BANK LENDING TO DEVELOPING COUNTRIES

Before the start of the oil crisis, the non-oil developing countries had tended to rely on a mixture of different types of long-term finance to cover their deficits which were, by the standards of later years, small. But high oil prices led to rapid growth in the deficits which the less developed countries (LDCs) found they could conveniently finance by recourse to credit. At the same time the demand for credit in the industrial countries was weak, and the OPEC funds, deliberately invested by OPEC in liquid bank deposits, were recycled to the LDCs. The LDCs absorbed the higher deficits fairly efficiently, and adjusted, by 1977, to a position in which their real deficits were close to the level of the early 1970s. They continued to borrow in order to improve their reserve position, feeling benefits from increased liquidity. But this success led the lenders to regard sovereign lending as safe, and created a general willingness to lend at fairly narrow margins. Equally, the ease with which the LDCs could borrow and the fact that short-term real dollar interest rates were negative, encouraged further borrowing, associated with expansionary policies. This approach might have been sustainable were it not for the second period of oil price increases which restored the large deficit of the

TABLE 8.2 *Lending by banks to underdeveloped countries (US $ billion)*

		Lending by offshore banks		*Lending by largest 9 US banks*	*Lending by UK banks*	
End year	*Total lending*	*To non-OPEC LDCs*	*To Latin America*	*To non-OPEC LDCs*	*To non-OPEC LDCs*	*To Latin America*
1977	657	92	64	30	16	11
1978	893	121	80	33	20	16
1979	1 110	156	104	40	29	20
1980	1 322	194	130	48	39	27
1981	1 550	230	158	58	49	34
1982	1 689	247	169	64	47	31
1983	1 954	256	176	66	52	33

NOTE 'UK banks' includes all offices in UK and not just companies registered in the United Kingdom. A data discontinuity makes comparable 1984 figures unavailable.

SOURCES *Bank of England Quarterly Bulletins* (various), *Federal Reserve Bulletin* (November 1983).

non-OPEC LDCs. Moreover, although, for the LDCs as a whole, non-banking debt dominated, for the largest borrowers (Argentina, Brazil and Mexico), banking debt, which is almost always of short maturity and variable interest rates, dominated.

At the same time as oil prices rose the developed countries adopted deflationary policies based on high interest rates. These policies directly added to the cost of funding the floating component of foreign debt and, because long-term rates also rose, added to the cost of refinancing the fixed-rate component when it fell due. Secondly, the high oil prices had a deflationary effect, which was compounded by high interest rates leading to a fall in price of, and contraction in, demand for LDC products. Finally the rise in the dollar aggravated the problem for the LDCs since most of their debt was denominated in dollars. This rise is often, perhaps with excessive confidence, seen as a consequence of high interest rates in the United States.

After 1973 the International Monetary Funds (IMF) set up a special facility for lending to countries hit by the oil shock; subsequent moves like the Lomé Convertion, adopted by the EEC, were also designed to help the poorest countries. But as Bird (1983) points out, the banks tended to lend to the countries which were regarded as credit worthy while the IMF lent to those which were not. Thus the IMF had little involvement in the big expansion of lending to the Latin American countries during the 1970s.

The growth in bank lending to underdeveloped countries is shown in Table 8.2.[8] As a footnote to this table it should be recorded that, by the end of 1982, the US banks' claims on the LDCs were 2.2 times their capital base, although this ratio had fallen to 1.7 by the end of 1984. Most of the UK lending to less developed countries is carried out by overseas banks and by the clearing bank subsidiaries. Thus a rough picture of UK exposure can be obtained from Table 8.3, comparing lending by clearing bank groups with the capital and reserves of these groups. However, these figures do not include subordinated loans in capital and reserves.

These figures may be complemented by the statement in the Bank of England Annual Report (1984) that loans by UK-owned banks to the eight largest debtor nations[9] amounted to about 75 per cent of capital and reserves. Since the debts are in US$ while the capital and reserves are broadly still fixed in sterling, the degree of exposure is very sensitive to the exchange rate. In any case there is always the hazard that, despite the ability of the LDCs to pay, they will choose not to. It is perhaps this aspect which has led to pressure for

TABLE 8.3 *Lending to Argentina, Brazil, and Mexico by clearing bank groups*

£ million December 1984	*Lending*	*Capital and reserves (not loan capital)*
Barclays	1 581	2 774
Lloyds	3 122	2 067
Midland	4 300	2 171
National Westminster	1 375	2 688

NOTE The figures for Barclays and National Westminster exclude lending to Argentina.
SOURCES Clearing Bank Annual Reports.

repayment, leading to liquidity problems. These liquidity problems could themselves lead to default.

As Teeters and Terrell (1983) note, much of the lending was of relatively short maturity, and was achieved by syndicated euro-currency credits of relatively short maturity. This allowed small banks to lend by participating in such syndicates. It increased competition in the market and effectively raised the supply elasticity of funds. In the United States the importance of foreign trade measured by the share of GDP exported doubled, with exports reaching 12.5 per cent of GDP in 1982. Banks felt a need to participate in this sector of growing importance. The demand for credit arose as developing countries facing oil deficits wanted to borrow more, and the supply was available from the surpluses of the OPEC countries. It is suggested by Bird (1983) that the banks played an active role in persuading developing countries to borrow. Certainly the idea fits in to the other suggestions that banks thought it was an area of their business they ought to expand. The rapid expansion of the international interbank market added to the level of liquidity, if not the total stock of credit, and made it easier for individual banks to participate in the boom. To this extent also there are similarities with the UK experience of a decade earlier, but, even if each bank assiduously matches maturity, the liquidity of the system is still put at risk because of the illiquidity of the final borrower. And, since the loans are not self-liquidating, the liquidity of the final borrower is only guaranteed provided the credit is renewed.

During the first half of 1982 banks continued to expand their lending at much the same rate as in 1981, although increasing concern was being expressed about the expansion of lending to the LDCs (although the surprising stability in the share of LDC borrowing in reporting to the Bank for International Settlements (BIS) banks' total assets, shown in Table 8.3, should be noted). However, the spread on loans to developing countries (measured as a margin over the London inter-bank offered rate of LIBOR) had started to rise in early 1980. During the mid 1970s lending to LDCs had commanded a premium over lending to OECD countries, but the supply of funds had outstripped the demand and by the late 1970s it was very small. Since then a steady rise took the average rate on loans to LDCs to one point above those to developed countries and one and a half points above the LIBOR. Again this average conceals a wide divergence. Some developing countries had little trouble in borrowing at rates close to those paid by LDCs. On the other hand the yields on some types of LDC debt rose to levels normally associated with institutions on the brink of default, as Figure 8.1 comparing the yields on UK and Mexican Government sterling loans show.

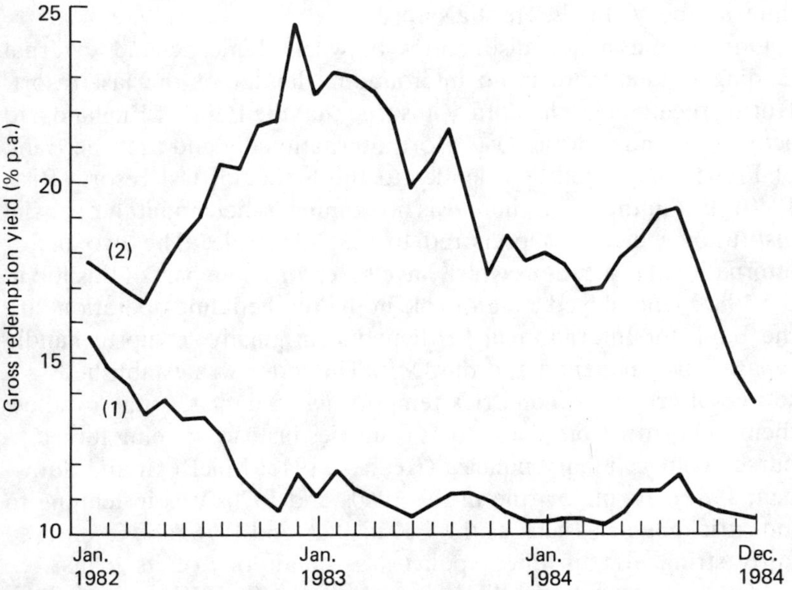

FIGURE 8.1 *Yields on UK and Mexican government stock*

SOURCE *The Financial Times* – Yields on (1) Treasury 13½% 2004–2008 and (2) Mexico 16½% 2008.

Although the figures suggest that the UK banks were not in a very risky position and the US banks were not seriously over-extended in their lending to LDCs, the position does vary from bank to bank. If a bank which has pursued an aggressive lending policy has lent heavily to a country which is particularly heavily in debt, and the two are likely to be found together, then the averages shown in the text are likely to conceal institutions which want to reduce their exposure even though there are no others which would willingly step into the breach. That was the position reached by mid-1982.

8.5 DEBT RESCHEDULING

The problems of the sovereign borrowers came to a head on 20 August 1982 when Mexico announced a 90-day moratorium on repayments to banks of all principal; this must have led to a loss of liquidity for all banks which had carefully pursued a policy of maturity-matching. It came after a period in which the maturity on refinanced borrowing by LDCs had been shortening, at the same time as the yield differentials rose.

One of the major distinctions between domestic and external lending is that there is no international lender of the last resort. During the nineteenth-century it is true that the Bank of England had acted as a lender of the last resort internationally and that the Bank of France had acted as a lender to the lender of last resort (Rist, 1940). But in the 1970s there was no dominant metropolitan financial institution which was prepared to play this role. The two major international institutions which have taken on some part of this job in the 1980s, and played a major role in the rescheduling operation, are the Bank for International Settlements (originally set up to handle reparations payments) and the IMF. The latter was established as a source of credit for countries temporarily in deficit, so as to allow them to borrow from the surplus countries instead of being forced to pursue contractionary policies (Keynes, 1942; MacBean and Snowden, 1981). Its major role in the 1960s and 1970s was in lending to industrial countries such as the UK in 1968 and 1976, and it imposed fairly stringent adjustment policies as conditions of its loans.

In an analogy with the 'lifeboat' operation, the IMF persuaded the commercial banks to extend an additional $5 bn credit so as to make a fund programme involving SDR (Special Drawing Rights) $3.4 bn viable. These events marked the beginning of a major rescheduling exercise. Brazil, Argentina, Chile, Ecuador and Venezuela were also involved. Several Eastern European countries had also borrowed heavily and rescheduled their debt. West German banks had been particularly heavily involved in lending to Eastern Europe under the influence of 'Ostpolitik', although they were probably less connected with South America than the American banks.

The BIS traditionally liked to keep a low profile; early in the debt crisis it tended to offer bridging finance provided by the central monetary authorities of the industrial countries, to cover an immediate loss of liquidity while other arrangements were being negotiated. Hungary was thus offered an emergency credit in the first quarter of 1982 by the BIS. It then received an IMF credit and was able to renegotiate matters with the commercial banks. In August 1982 the BIS joined the US monetary authorities in offering a bridging credit to Mexico, and this was followed by bridging credits to Brazil and Argentina. Yugoslavia, too, was a beneficiary.

Such loans seemed vital to maintaining the stability of the banking system; without them default would have appeared a more likely response to the inability of the debtors to repay on time. Even moratoria on the Mexican pattern might have led banking supervisors in the developed countries to doubt the solvency of their domestic banks; however more recently interest arrears have proved an alternative means of short-term finance (Cline, 1984). This has not been disastrous for the banks concerned. The IMF has been making credit available to the countries facing a shortage of liquidity, on condition that they adopt IMF measures designed to ensure that the external position of the debtor nation is transformed. Such measures are widely discussed (Killick *et al.*, 1983) and, as in the case of Brazil, often the subject of much negotiation by the debtor country. There is no doubt that very great importance is attached to an IMF programme by banks and the supervisory authorities.

Liquidity crises are crises of confidence and the acceptance of an IMF scheme is enough to stabilise or restore confidence. But although this requires an increased role for the IMF, and IMF resources were increased, in 1982, to an extent which allowed this, the position of the IMF is much closer to that of the Bank of England during the 1973–5 crisis than to any classic lender of last resort, which lends freely to sound but illiquid borrowers. For the IMF's major role is in persuading the commercial banks to maintain the liquidity of the developing countries. In exactly the same way most of the Bank of England 'lifeboat' consisted of mainly commercial bank funds which were recycled; only a fairly small proportion of the resources involved came from the Bank of England. Bird (1983) does draw attention to the risk that, if the IMF is committing its resources to 'lifeboat' loans, this will deprive the poorest countries of fund finance. But while the main role of the IMF is in restoring confidence, it may not need to commit large sums. If the crisis is a pure liquidity crisis there is no reason for an international authority to re-discount debts, while there are other ways of restoring confidence; discussions which focus on a question of reallocating the debt burden away from the debtors to some other body are unhelpful; the debtors do not face an insupportable long-run burden.

The rescheduling which took place had the effect of postponing debts of over $40 billion, due between 1981 and 1984, to fall due mainly between 1987 and 1990, but in most cases the rescheduling has not resulted in delays in interest payments. Although rescheduling of this magnitude is very considerable from the point of view of the banks, the question must arise of whether it is in fact adequate. The same shortage of liquidity may occur in the future if the debt falls due at a rate faster than the natural ability of the debtor countries to pay.

There are perhaps two main reasons for short-term rescheduling, despite the likelihood of future problems. First, because the banks attach importance to their liquidity ratios they may not want to lose fully the cosmetic liquidity of these loans, although by rescheduling they are recognising the actual illiquidity (*Bank of England Quarterly Bulletin,* 1983d). Secondly, they may feel that the probable need to renegotiate again is likely to impose a greater discipline on the debtors than if the debt were fully funded. Recent evidence suggests that bankers are now taking a longer-term view of the problem. However, while real interest rates remain high, there is an understandable reluctance to fund the debt by the issue of fixed rate loan stock; while much of the debt is at floating rates one must look to a marked decline in interest rates so as to lead to a fall in the debt-burden. A recovery of the world economy leading to higher demand for, and higher prices for, the exports of the less developed countries is likely to provide sustained relief.

It is too early to write a postscript to the debt crisis. In 1984 Argentina attempted to organise a debtor's 'cartel' and seemed very reluctant to negotiate with the IMF. Overall, however, the position of the indebted countries appeared to be improving. Lower interest rates and rescheduling created a fall in the debt-service ratio of about 2 percentage points between 1982 and 1984, with a much larger fall in the debt-service ratios of the Latin American countries (IMF Annual Report, 1985). However a feature of 1984 was rapid growth in the US economy; this was the major factor behind 8 per cent growth in the volume of exports from the developing countries. Sustained export growth at this rate would have removed debt-financing problems.

In 1985 the growth rate of the US economy seemed to have slowed very markedly, and it was clear that export growth would not provide an immediate solution to the debt problem. The re-emergence of liquidity problems late in 1985 led to renewed concern. The United States proposed international co-operation between banks, the World Bank and the IMF in ensuring that the liquidity needs of the developing countries continued to be met. It is not clear how this proposal will develop, or whether some other solution will be found to the difficulties which seemed to be re-appearing.

8.6 CONCLUSION

Banking problems have become more common in the 1970s and 1980s than in the earlier post-war period. But the major failures outside Britain were more closely associated with fraud than was the case in Britain in 1973–5. Greater similarity is found between the British banking crisis and the current debt crisis. The discussion as to the causes of the crisis is as old as the crisis itself. On one side there are the arguments that it is the fault of the debtor nations who did not ensure that their foreign currency borrowing was used to fund investment which would generate the exchange needed to repay the debt. If there are cases where the burden of debt is so large that it could not possibly be repaid under any circumstances, then a careful assessment needs to be made of reasons for protecting the shareholders in the lending bank from bearing the loss. Certainly it is hard to see why the monetary authorities of the developed countries should seek to safeguard shareholders. On the other hand they clearly have a duty to maintain the operation of the banking system. This may imply that, to some extent, it might be necessary to redistribute the losses.

If the bankers actively encouraged borrowing, the debtors may have misunderstood the availability of refinancing when debts of short maturity fell due. In any case neither the bankers nor the debtors may have foreseen the rigour with which deflationary policies would be pursued by the developed world. The sustained high interest rates and contraction in demand arising from these policies will have made otherwise profitable projects unprofitable. However, a reasonable rate of growth in the industrial world (Cline, 1984, suggests 2½ to 3 per cent per annum) will ensure long-run decline in debt–income ratios. Encouraging signs are to be found in that the debt–service ratio (corrected for the effects of rescheduling) has stopped rising and that the current account deficits of the debtor countries have been much reduced. If one accepts the hypothesis that the problem is one of liquidity rather than solvency then the solution to the crisis might be the widely floated idea of recycling credit in the short term and funding the debt in the long term.

One particular aspect of the crisis has been that it has focused attention on the capital base of the banking system, and has led to pressure from supervisory authorities for improvements in capital ratios (Lascelles, 1984). Thus, after many years of decline capital is growing relative to deposits in both Britain and the USA. Supervisory authorities are now co-ordinated to some extent, and are able to assess banking groups in their entirety. This removes much scope for 'window-dressing'. However, while the possibility for unsupervised banking exists in some centres, there is always the risk of inadequately capitalised banks emerging. One could not rule out the possibility of problems occurring again at some time in the future.

Study of the international debt crisis illustrates clearly the way in which a crisis can arise from the prospect of default created as much by short-term illiquidity as by insolvency. It demonstrates that maturity-matching, while of undoubted importance, is not always sufficient to protect banks. The prospect of slightly higher yields on sovereign lending led to neglect of the risks involved, in much the same way as had happened with lending to property companies in the UK. In the UK there was uncertainty as to whether the Bank of England would support the secondary banks. In the initial stages of the debt crisis there existed similar doubt about the extent to which bridging finance would be available to maintain the liquidity of the debtor nations.

9 Conclusions

9.1 THE EVOLUTION OF THE BANKING SYSTEM

By 1960 most controls which had remained after the Second World War had been relaxed or abolished. But, after a brief period of freedom between 1958 and 1960, controls on the clearing banks were tightened during the 1960s. The traditional system of monetary management relied on the requirement that clearing banks held as cash or deposits with the Bank of England 8 per cent of their deposit liabilities, and that they held another 22 per cent of their deposits as specified liquid assets. Administered interest rates were rigidly linked to the bank rate, and under such a system the Bank of England was able to impose both desired administered rates and a target stock of money on the economy (Keynes, 1931).[1]

But such a system required a freely-floating gilt market to be effective. For if there was any attempt by the Bank of England to peg the price of gilts, the banks would be able to counteract any attempt by the Bank of England to restrain their holdings of deposits at the Bank, by selling it gilt-edged stock. And until 1968 the Bank of England regarded a stable gilt-edged market as a necessary condition for the orderly funding of the national debt. It also sought to keep up gilts' prices in order to reduce the interest burden of the debt.

A second condition needed for the traditional system to work was that it should be the sole banking system. Development of parallel credit markets would allow borrowing needs to be met, at least to some extent, independently of the ability of the banks to take in extra deposits. As in the acceptance trading, such markets may well rely on the role of banks as guarantors and intermediaries.

During the 1960s neither of these conditions held. The Bank attempted to replace the first condition by the imposition of quantitive controls on the clearing banks. But the development of the new money markets and the non-clearing banks was allowed to proceed rapidly. Had all the non-clearing banks been brought into the same regulatory framework as the clearing banks, it might have been possible to regain control over the system. In fact the Bank of England made no obvious attempt to exercise any control over the new money markets and, apart from an aborted proposal in 1967–8 to introduce a cash deposits scheme for listed non-clearing banks, allowed the uninhibited expansion of the non-clearers to proceed.

There was probably a variety of reasons for the Bank's apparent inaction. Encouraged by the Inter-Bank Research Organisation, and by the financial community itself, it probably wished to see London develop and maintain a position as the leading financial centre in Europe. It was wedded to an informal system of control and supervision which worked reasonably well when the financial sector was dominated by the clearing banks and the discount market; the number of chairmen whom the Bank of England could summon for discussion was limited, and all were within a stone's throw of the Bank. When the banking sector widened to include 200 or 300 banks, the informality that was so much prized by the Bank needed strengthening by a corpus of banking law. In any case, doubts have been expressed whether the officials at the Bank of England were sufficiently aware of the implications of the rapid development of the non-clearing banks and of the money markets on which those banks increasingly relied, to be able to take remedial action.

The non-clearing banks expanded rapidly for a variety of motives. The accepting houses saw an opportunity to increase the size of their respective balance sheets and of their resultant profits by utilising the money markets, for whose development they were initially responsible. Each accepting house was anxious neither to allow its competitors to exceed its own rate of growth nor to fail to provide additional services which would maintain its own standing in the market. Other non-clearing banks saw in the ready availability of funds from the money markets the opportunity to finance acquisitions, investments in property and equities and what was hoped would be profitable lending to companies and individuals closely associated with those banks. Foreign banks developed sterling business at much the same rate as the British non-clearing banks. The opportunities were there both for the more prudent banks and for the wheelers and dealers. It is hardly surprising that they were taken.

Competition and credit control marked an attempt to extend control over the whole of the banking system. In principle, such an attempt might have been successful. But the end of the clearing bank cartel implied that regulation of both the money stock (or the supply of bank credit) and interest rates was no longer possible. At the same time a variety of factors combined to lead to a major credit inflation. The government was keen to see the economy expand; a property boom was developing and the floating exchange rate seemed to lift external constraints.

The Bank of England, having justified the introduction of competition and credit control on the argument that credit could be controlled by price, could not follow its own argument to its logical conclusion in the face of other competing targets; these included the stimulation of the economy and appeasement of the house-owning lobby. This demanded a ceiling on interest rates lower than the demand for credit would have justified. Slow administrative response by the clearing banks allowed arbitrage opportunities to develop which further inflated the stock of credit. The consequence of competition and credit control was that the liability structures of many small banks became stretched to danger point, and the whole financial structure became unstable. The collapse of one non-clearing bank in December 1973 precipitated a financial crisis that was overcome by the Bank of England's 'lifeboat' operation. There is no doubt that the rescue operation was mounted effectively; the Bank of England acted in its traditional role, first formally recognised in 1873, to contain a banking panic.

The imposition of the corset succeeded in restraining credit, and a second attempt at decontrol in 1980 focused solely on giving the Bank of England the ability to regulate short-term interest rates precisely. It was recognised that a price can be imposed on a market much more easily than any quantitative restriction. Such a move paved the way for the integration of the traditional and parallel markets, a change which has broadly happened by now. Any reversion to the traditional system would now probably prove impossible because the clearing bank cartel, which underpinned the independence of the money stock and the deposit and lending rates, has now broken down. Technical change makes it much harder for any quantity rationing system to be introduced. As a result, it is now much more difficult to predict the precise consequences of a change in interest rates on any particular monetary aggregate (Goodhart, 1984, Chapter 5).

9.2 PRUDENTIAL REGULATION AND THE BANKING CRISIS

Associated with this transition in the banking system has been a change in the nature of prudential regulation. Under the traditional system it was assumed that the clearing and old-established merchant banks did their own prudential regulation. But with the increasing importance of the non-clearing banks such an approach became unsatisfactory. For some, especially the newer, non-clearing banks, were less than prudent in their behaviour. And the new money markets enabled them to find the resources needed for speculation.

The consequences of lack of either voluntary or enforced prudence became apparent in the crisis of 1973–5. The 1979 Banking Act, which followed as a direct consequence of the crisis, obliges any deposit-taking institution to hold Bank of England approval. This enables the Bank to supervise liquidity, solvency and foreign currency exposure in a manner which was not done earlier. Such regulation should avoid the need for future rescues on the scale of the 'lifeboat', although of course there is always the risk that fraudulent behaviour will create problems specific to individual institutions. And the failure of Johnson Matthey Bankers shows that the regulation is not perfect.

A question which requires to be considered is whether the crisis in 1973–5 could have been averted or whether it was an inevitable consequence of a period of economic growth which came to an end with growing inflation and unemployment coupled with the OPEC oil price rise in late 1973 and industrial disruption. It is tempting to argue that the Bank of England could have forestalled a financial crisis if only it had taken the appropriate measures to control the rapid growth of the interbank and CD markets and to bring all financial institutions enjoying banking status effectively under its supervision. It might also be necessary to contend that the crises in other countries since 1970, and indeed the international debt crisis itself could have been prevented by more effective central bank action.

Whilst, therefore, there is an hypothesis that the banking crisis in 1973–5 resulted from failure by the Bank of England to appreciate the dangers from the uncontrolled expansion of the non-clearing banks and of the parallel money markets, there is another argument that the crisis was as inevitable as other crises had been in the past. The long list of banking crises in the United Kingdom in the nineteenth-century, particularly the Overend Gurney crash in 1866 and the Barings crisis in 1890, the history of bank failures in the United States, and the development of central banks with regulatory powers to forestall such crises all lend some argument. Minsky has developed most fully the theory that financial crises are endemic to a mature capitalist economy because decisions must be taken in conditions of uncertainty, leading during a period of sustained economic growth to changes in liability and asset structures which are inherently destabilising (Minsky, 1982). His analysis follows from the work of Keynes (1936) and Marx (1894). Keynes argued that, 'during a boom popular estimation of the magnitude of . . . these risks, both borrower's risk and lender's risk, is apt to become imprudently low' (Keynes, 1936, p. 145).

It was observations like this which led Minsky to argue that the characteristic of a capitalist economy is speculation about the value of assets, and that the relevant paradigm for its analysis is one in which asset holdings are financed by debt. Financial intermediaries occupy a key position in advanced capitalist societies because they alone are capable of providing the funds for increasing the debt-financing of investment. During periods of economic expansion, confidence increases, and the owners of an inherited stock of assets find themselves with an unused margin of borrowing power. This enables such owners to increase their liability structures in the hope that the cost of borrowing can always be met from increased cash flows. As Goodhart has summarised Minsky:

> systematic shifts in the financial structure of companies have been, and still may yet prove to be, a significant factor contributing to major trade cycles. During booms growing confidence tempts companies to adopt a riskier financial structure with a top-heavy debt ratio and a shortening debt-maturing structure whose service requires a steady cash flow. (Goodhart, 1975, p. 101)

When demand falters, some companies are pushed to the brink of bankruptcy, if not over.

During a period of economic growth, Minsky argues, everyone becomes a speculator of sorts. Consumers, who have assumed debt liabilities, speculate that they will earn sufficient income to meet their interest payments and to repay the principal. Manufacturers assume uninterrupted growth in sales and profits which will be sufficient to meet their debt costs and to leave a satisfactory margin for their shareholders. Speculators take it for granted that prices will go on rising whilst banks, who finance the credit expansion, assume that economic growth will continue. But all such speculation is precarious because many factors can bring the period of economic expansion to an end: these factors may be an excess accumulation of stocks, the over-production of capital goods, a reduction in consumer demand, a squeeze on profits or the inability of the banking system to continue to expand credit. When deceleration in the growth rate occurs, the fact that debt has been layered on debt results in a domino effect as debtors scramble to collect funds to repay their creditors. A liquidity crisis leads to a contraction of trade.

Set against Minsky's argument is the fact that crises are not an endemic feature of modern capitalism. The American credit contractions in 1966 and 1974 to which Minsky refers cannot be compared with those of 1929–31 or earlier. It is argued that many capitalist countries have developed institutions which prevent such crises occurring. To these points can be added the argument that, while layering of credit may be a feature of speculation, it is also present in situations which are not preludes to financial crises. The interbank market has continued to expand despite the fact that there has been no obvious successor to the property speculation of the early 1970s. But while these arguments are clearly more than substantive criticisms of any claim to have developed a general theory of capitalist development, they do not detract from an analysis of those developments leading up to a crisis which did occur. Minsky does provide a useful framework in which to interpret the development of the banking system before 1974. Flemming (1982) is right in arguing that Minsky's model depends on a failure 'to distinguish a run of good luck from a favourable shift in their environment'. But this was to a large extent what happened in the property boom, and in the expansion of lending to the less developed countries. Kindleberger (1981) would regard it as being a characteristic of the prelude to those financial crises which do occur. For thus he justifies his reference to manias.

The observation by the Committee of Economic Information (Stamp Committee) (1932) that the frequency of crises had reduced, because it was known that the Bank of England would intervene, merits some discussion in the context of the events of 1973–5. Certainly the secure knowledge of intervention might be thought to encourage the speculation which would make such intervention necessary. But if the Bank is known to lend freely to sound but illiquid banks, and at a penal rate, liquidity crises will be less likely to occur while the frequency of solvency crises would be unaffected. The knowledge that the Bank would take steps to ensure orderly liquidation of insolvent institutions would help reduce the risk of contagion, and thus prevent the failure of one institution leading to a general liquidity crisis. Seen in this context the 1973–5 crisis becomes easier to understand. It occurred in a market where there was no history of Bank of England support, and it affected those institutions in which the Bank of England had hitherto taken little interest. It can perhaps be seen as support for the Stamp Committee's observation, or at least as the exception which proves the rule.

If one is to try to pin down the causes of the crisis, it does seem that the idea that a crisis is a natural consequence of every boom has to be rejected. Obviously there are periodic disturbances to the financial system, and these are perhaps more likely to occur when opportunities for profitable fixed investment have diminished. But Hirsch's (1977) comment, 'many analysts . . . had assumed this class of problem [banking crisis] to have been left behind with the Kredit-anstalt in 1931', seems more appropriate than the idea of inevitability. Thus it does seem more sensible to distinguish banking failure such as affected the Herstatt Bank from the general panic which affected a significant part of the UK banking sector, and to come down on the side of those who would argue that the UK crisis was a consequence of the lack of supervision. In the same way the international debt crisis is better seen as a consequence of the lack of security for sovereign lending and inadequacy or impossibility of full international supervision than as the natural phenomenon Minsky would have us expect.

9.3 THE CHANGING FINANCIAL SYSTEM

The financial system is again in a state of rapid transition. The 'financial supermarket', which the Hill, Samuel/Slater, Walker merger would have provided, seems once again to be emerging. The extent to which all types of bank are seeking to develop a role as market-makers on the stock exchange has already been discussed. And the prominence of Britannia Arrow, taking over Singer and Friedlander, again points to the development of a new financial conglomerate. It is not clear how such conglomerates, which are only partly banks, should be supervised, since it is much harder to assess the risks involved in their business than is the case for a straightforward bank.

Associated with these changes is the technical progress which has blurred much of the distinction between banks and building societies, for example. Reduced costs to account keeping mean it is possible to offer interest on cheque accounts. Building societies have gone further down this road than banks, which hope to maintain the endowment factor of current deposits for as long as possible. The increasing use of credit cards, facilitated by these changes, makes the notion of monetary control much harder to comprehend. Although it is to be hoped that the Bank of England's supervisory net is now cast sufficiently widely to prevent another crisis, the net is not designed to regulate any particular aggregate. It is virtually certain that, given the incentives, institutions will continue to adapt to provide deposit taking and credit facilities for which there is a demand.

The clearing banks were increasingly criticised before 1971 for their assumed lack of competition, regarding themselves too much as public utilities:

> The banks, for their part, tended to see themselves in the main as public servants . . . In the early 1970s two major changes occurred which should have gone some way both to halt the widespread criticism of the banks, and to arrest the decline in their business. In February, 1970 the clearing banks published their true profits for the first time . . . In September, 1971 the Bank of England introduced a new system of credit control which put an end to the banks' cartel. (MacRae and Cairncross, 1973)

As we now appreciate only too well, the fostering of uncontrolled competition resulted in the banking crisis which, according to the Bank of England, might have led to a widespread collapse of financial intermediaries.

There are reasonable arguments that competition to improve the quality of service offered to the customers of banks is desirable since the banking sub-sector of the economy in the United Kingdom operates as a competitive market. But competition to secure deposits wherever they can be found and then, by liability management, to deploy them to earn the maximum profit regardless of risk cannot be justified, particularly when it is necessary to control the flow of credit to secure macroeconomic objectives. The primary duty of any bank is to its depositors and this the Bank of England has recognised in its proposals for depositor protection. No financial system can operate efficiently without the confidence of the public which uses it, and trust in financial institutions should be the crux of such an efficient and secure system. The vast majority of the depositors in the banking system are not risk-takers but people who seek a safe repository for their surplus funds and an efficient money transmission service. If the provision of such services demands that the banks should operate a service industry essentially no different in kind from a communications or a transport service, that is no valid criticism. Moreover, the privileges attached to the right to operate as a clearing bank too can be argued to carry a parallel duty to act in the public interest. The Midland Bank (1976) recognised this, stating 'Banks have long since recognised not only that their economic power must be exercised in the national interest but also that governments have the right and duty to seek to ensure this'.

Whilst the clearing banks have been expanding the range of services they provide, the other banks have also extended their services to cover most of those provided by the clearing banks with the obvious exception of full retail deposit facilities. But even here merchant banks are beginning to offer high interest cheque accounts, and the clearing system is likely to expand. All the British banks face the competition from the foreign banks in London, numbering over 300, and from consortium banks as well as from building societies. As a consequence, employment in the United Kingdom in banking and bill discounting has increased from 178 000 in 1959 to 324 000 in 1984, despite the increased use of computers, cash dispensers and other labour-saving aids. The result is that there is now considerable competition between banks of all types.

9.4 SUMMARY

Finally, the conclusions can be summarised briefly as follows:

(1) After a stable period in the first half of the century the British banking system has changed radically. Constraints on the growth of the clearing banks encouraged the development of non-clearing banks, and led to a gradual decline in the relative importance of the traditional sector. The discount market suffered particularly from this. Although competition and credit control freed the clearing banks from these constraints, it also encouraged the growth of the new money markets. These made it easier for non-clearing banks to obtain deposits, some of which were used to finance property speculation. Statistical changes make it difficult to compare the pre- and post-1975 positions, but it seems that since 1975 the two systems have grown at the much same rate. Technical progress and competi-

tion have encouraged the clearing banks to offer a much wider range of services in recent years than earlier in the period. They have also developed subsidiaries to allow them to compete fully with the British and foreign other non-clearing banks.

(2) The expansion of the new money markets, for which the major merchant banks were initially responsible, made it possible for other non-clearing banks to obtain the funds they required for speculation in shares and property. It was the unrestricted access to deposits which eventually led to the banking crisis commencing at the end of 1973.

(3) Despite the measures which the Bank of England is taking under the Banking Act, 1979, to ensure that banks act prudently, there is still a major area of instability. The growth of the eurocurrency markets has imparted an international dimension to the risks which face all banks in their extension of credit. The eurocurrency markets have undoubtedly assisted in making available to less developed countries funds which they are presumed to require for their economic development. But the developing countries borrowed on the assumption that debts could be rolled over. This has led to a liquidity crisis and the need for rescheduling.

(4) The number of independent merchant banks is declining and is likely to decline further. But the ability of the major accepting houses to survive has been demonstrated in the past and there is no reason to believe that they will not survive in the future. In theory, the clearing banks which have developed merchant banking subsidiaries should be able to provide all the services which their customers require and it might be expected that the role for independent merchant banks would shrink. But it is equally probable that clearing bank customers welcome the personal and independent advice they can obtain from the established merchant banks.

(5) There is always the possibility that the resumption of economic growth will lead to circumstances which are again favourable to speculation. The rapid rate of financial innovation which is observed increases the possibility that some new form of speculative finance may be found outside the ambit of Bank of England supervision. Such developments are unlikely to lead to another banking panic provided the speculative fringe is clearly a small fringe and does not interact with the rest of the system to any significant extent. The possibility of contagion, which was a

major concern during the 1973–5 crisis, is thereby avoided, and the fringe is not of sufficient size to require stabilisation in its own right. As new types of financial institution develop, new supervisory problems are created. However, it is likely that the Bank of England is far more aware of the dangers than it was in the 1960s and will act rapidly to extend the supervisory net.

Notes and References

INTRODUCTION

1. Goodhart (1984, p. 188) criticises the simple approach of some texts.
2. The work of Barnett (1980) has recently attempted to quantify this notion of a liquidity indicator.

1 AN OVERVIEW OF THE ECONOMY, 1960–85

1. The initial effect of the devaluation on the trade balance was perverse. Import values rose, but it was a while before export values increased. Thus in 1968, for the first time, Britain had to seek credit from the International Monetary Fund.
2. Although this growth rate is close to the average for the 1960s, it takes place in a background of high unemployment and is slow for a period of economic recovery.
3. Money is principally a product of the banking system. Apart from the relatively small amount of banknotes in circulation, money consists of deposits with banks. Interbank deposits are netted out and the simple identity

   Private sector sterling
   bank deposits = Bank lending to private sector +
   Bank lending to public sector +
   Bank lending overseas –
   Overseas, public and foreign currency private deposits –
   Net non-deposit liabilities

   holds. After 1981 'banks' include all the monetary sector.

   Bank lending includes not only overdrafts and advances but also purchases of securities such as gilt-edged stock. Non-deposit liabilities include debentures and share capital of the bank, less assets such as fixed capital; they are normally a relatively small item.
4. Although there have been occasions in which large changes in the money stock have been associated with changes in lending overseas (for example, 1977), normally changes in domestic lending dominate.
5. The contribution made by the public sector to monetary expansion can easily be overstated. See, for example, Cooper (1984, Chapter 6).
6. The IMF agreements of both 1968 and 1976 required control of domestic credit expansion. This is equal to the change in the money stock, less the deficit in the current account of the balance of payments.

7. £M3 represents holdings of sterling notes and coins, and sight and time deposits in the hands of the public, while M3 includes holdings of foreign currency as well.
8. Nominal GDP is the volume of output multiplied by the price level; if long-run forces generate a tendency to full employment, the volume of output is given, and thus control of nominal GDP ensures control of the price level.
9. The minimum lending rate was 'formula related' to the average yield on Treasury bills during the three preceding weeks, whereas the Bank Rate had been fixed administratively. But the minimum lending rate was in fact fixed administratively on occasions and the formula approach was abandoned in April 1978.
10. An early casualty was the Scottish Co-operative Wholesale Society's Banking Department which had undertaken to lend at prefixed rates and faced losses of £29m as interest rates rose in 1973. More recently Clive Discount lost half their shareholders' funds in 1979 with the jump in the minimum lending rate. Smith St Aubyn earned a reputation for playing the gilts market, rather than restricting themselves to the normal business of a discount house. They lost all their equity base in 1981, mainly as a result of losses on a large holding of 15 per cent Treasury Stock, 1985, whose price showed unusual volatility. Nevertheless, they were able to float a rights issue in order to rebuild their capital base.

2 RISK AND FINANCIAL INSTITUTIONS

1. A recent analysis of the behaviour of unit trusts (Corner and Matatko, 1984), suggests that the average unit trust has done worse than the market as a whole (although investors may not know this). But it is not clear in their analysis what allowance has been made for management charges, which are probably lower than those which a small investor managing his own portfolio would face. In any case, maturity-matching institutions have attractions apart from investment skills. Hills (1984) draws attention to the tax efficiency of different types of investment and suggests that the tax treatment may be very important.
2. This was true even before the statistical change of 1975 (see Chapter 7).
3. A secondary bank is one which relies mainly on other banks as a source of deposits.
4. This policy is now embodied in the liquidity and solvency requirements which the Bank of England can impose under the 1979 Banking Act (Chapter 3).
5. Galbraith (1955) cites land speculation as a precursor of the Wall Street boom and crash.

3 BANK OF ENGLAND CONTROL AND SUPERVISION

1. Cooper (1984) offers a discussion which emphasises the first topic. Artis

and Lewis (1981) and Bain (1979) discuss monetary control; Moran (1984) looks at the interaction of political and monetary developments since 1971, and its implications for monetary control.

2. Perhaps the best explanation of this is that the fund is meant to protect the small investor who may be misled, but not the large investor who is in a position to inform himself about the status of a deposit-taker. But, as noted above, banks do not make much information available about the customers to whom they lend, and so it is difficult to come to an informed view.
3. Keynes was referring to administered interest rates and not to the return on market instruments such as Treasury bills or gilt-edged securities. The Treasury bill rate was, in any case, bounded above by the bank rate and below by the minimum call money rate (Chapter 4).
4. Under the Bank of England Act, 1946, the Bank was empowered to give directions to any bank, after consultation with the Treasury. This power has never been used: instead 'moral suasion' has been applied by the Bank of England whose requests have usually been met in the letter if not in the spirit.
5. Moran (1984, Chapter 6) suggests it was concerned not only about the economic implications of this, but also over the risk that it could lose influence if the position of the clearing banks continued to decline.
6. Although the Committee of London Clearing Bankers (1977) argued that, because the authorities were in close touch with the markets, this was not a practical obstacle to monetary control. If this were the case it is not clear why the supplementary special deposits scheme (p. 58) would have been necessary.

4 THE TRADITIONAL BANKING SYSTEM

1. More recently, the Bank of England has retained this power to determine short-term rates through its holding of commercial bills. As the bills it holds mature, it is necessary for the resulting shortage of cash in the discount market to be met. This can be done either by loans from the Bank of England, or by its discounting of bills to replace those maturing. In either case it is able to impose an interest rate on the market.
2. The reason was that certificates of deposit, unlike commercial bills, were not self-liquidating instruments (Chapter 6).
3. Money GDP divided by the money stock.

5 THE ACCEPTING HOUSES

1. Hill, Samuel stated in discussion that it is only comparatively recently that investment management services have shown a worthwhile profit.
2. Report by the Takeover Panel on the Leasco affair in 1969 quoted by Spiegelberg (1973).

6 THE NEW MONEY MARKETS

1. This double-counting did not affect estimates of the money stock. These net out transactions within the banking system.
2. Lester (1974) has given an interesting description of the role that the money brokers played in the market, and of the attraction to the brokers of the high fees they could earn from the more risky borrowers.
3. I am grateful to Robin Matthews for drawing this to my attention.

7 THE OTHER BRITISH NON-CLEARING BANKS

1. *Bank of England Quarterly Bulletin* (June, 1978) p. 235. The National Westminster Bank, as a result of its historical development, had all but two of the troubled non-clearing banks on its books. There were persistent and widespread rumours in the City that the National Westminster was itself facing financial difficulties. Whether this was so or not will never be known, although it is very likely that the 'lifeboat' operation saved the clearing bank from more severe losses.

8 INTERNATIONAL PROBLEMS

1. The collapse of the Kreditanstalt in Vienna in 1931 is often seen as a major factor in aggravating the depression then. People were concerned that the collapse of a bank in 1974 might again act as a trigger for a down-turn.
2. Cline (1984) offers an excellent general survey of the problem.
3. If we assume that the real rate of interest is r, the country has a growth rate of g and it is prepared to devote fraction λ of its national income to debt interest, then one can calculate the steady state debt income ratio.

   With Y = income, D = debt

   $Y = gY$ $\qquad$ $D = rD - \lambda Y$ since debt grows by the interest due less that paid.

   Further $\frac{\dot{D}}{D} = r - \frac{\lambda Y}{D} = g$ $\qquad$ since, in the steady state, debt and income grow at the same rate.

   Thus $\frac{D}{Y} = \frac{\lambda}{r - g}$

   If g = 3% pa which is not unreasonable, and r = 5% pa which would incorporate a considerable risk premium, then a country with debt equal to its income ($D/Y = 1$) would have to devote 2% of its income to debt service. This is less than one year's growth and is hardly an insupportable burden.

4. This debate on the generation of the foreign exchange needed to pay a transfer was much considered after the reparations settlements of 1871 and 1919 (Keynes (1929) and Ohlin (1929)).
5. The Council of Economic Advisers (1984) analyse the problem in a manner which reconciles, to some extent, the need to service debts out of foreign exchange with the idea that the long-term burden of debt is best analysed by looking at the debt/income ratio. They look at the ratio of the current account deficit to debt and point out that provided this is less than the growth rate of net exports, the debts can be serviced in the long run. The debt/income analysis assumes that growth in net exports is in the end constrained by income growth. In any case the deficit/debt ratio for Argentina, Brazil and Mexico was, in 1983, 2.8 per cent and it is hard to believe that the nominal value of net exports cannot grow at a faster rate than this.
6. If the marginal propensity to import is m, the short-term social cost of foreign exchange is the amount of income foregone in order to release one unit of foreign exchange. Income has to fall by $1/m$ in order to do this. Thus if $m = 0.5$ the social cost of short-term adjustment is twice that of long-term adjustment.
7. For the developing countries actually to reduce their debts would cast them as capital exporters. Such a state of affairs is almost certainly without historical precedent. Normally, developed countries export capital to underdeveloped countries.
8. Historical accounts of the development of bank lending are provided by *Bank of England Quarterly Bulletins* (1982b, 1983a, 1984a) and *Bank for International Settlements Annual Report* (1984 and 1985).
9. Argentina, Brazil, Chile, Mexico, Philippines, Poland, Venezuela and Yugoslavia.

9 CONCLUSIONS

1. In fact emphasis focused on bank lending and there were no monetary targets.

Glossary

Acceptance
A bill of exchange guaranteed by a bank

Accepting House
A bank for whom an important part of business consists of the accepting of bills of exchange. A member of the Accepting Houses' Committee

Bank Rate
The rate at which the Bank of England was prepared to lend to discount houses. It was renamed minimum lending rate in October 1972

Base Rate
An interest rate set by each commercial bank to which its lending and deposit rates are linked

Bill of Exchange
An instrument issued against an agreed transaction by a commercial company. It allows the company to receive the proceeds of the transaction in advance. Also known as commercial bills

Call Money
Money deposited by banks in the discount market available without notice

Capital and Reserves
Issued equity capital plus cumulated undistributed profits

Certificate of Deposit
A negotiable instrument representing a term deposit of specified interest rate

Clearing Bank
A bank which settles cheques directly with other clearing banks, not needing an intermediary

Discount House
A financial institution whose main business consists of discounting Treasury bills and bills of exchange

Eligible Bill
A bill of exchange eligible for discount by the Bank of England. It must have been accepted by an approved bank

Eurocurrency
A deposit with a bank not denominated in the currency of the country where the bank is based

Finance House
An institution which takes deposits to provide industrial and consumer credit. These were classified outside the banking sector. In 1981 the large houses were reclassified in the monetary sector.

Hidden Reserves
Reserves kept by a bank which are not identified in its accounts

Licensed Deposit Taker
An institution not a bank authorised by the Bank of England to take deposits

Liquidity Ratio
The ratio of easily realised (liquid) assets to total deposits with a bank

Minimum Lending Rate
The Bank Rate was renamed minimum lending rate in October 1972. It was suspended in August 1981

Monetary Sector
This includes

(a) all recognised banks and licensed deposit-takers
(b) National Girobank
(c) certain institutions in the Channel Islands and Isle of Man
(d) Trustee Savings Banks
(e) the Banking Department of the Bank of England.

The old banking sector excluded some banks and licensed deposit-takers and all Trustee Savings Banks

Nostro Account
An account held by a home bank with an overseas bank denominated in foreign currency

Reserve Asset
One of a range of assets, specified by the Bank of England, which banks were, between October 1971 and August 1981, required to hold to a minimum proportion of deposits with them derived from outside the banking system (eligible liabilities)

Retail Bank
A bank with an extensive branch network

Secondary Bank
A bank which derives most of its deposits from other banks

Special Deposits
Interest-bearing deposits which banks are periodically required to make with the Bank of England

Subordinated Loan
A loan to a bank which is, in the case of liquidation, only paid out after the claims of depositors have been met in full

Supplementary Special Deposit
A non-interest-bearing deposit which banks were, at times between December 1973 and August 1980, required to make with the Bank of England. The scheme was also known as 'the corset'

Treasury Bill
A bill issued by the Treasury against future tax receipts

Bibliography

Artis, M. J. (1978) 'Monetary Policy – Part II' in *British Economic Policy 1960–74,* ed. F. T. Blackaby, Cambridge University Press, pp. 298–9.

—— and Lewis, M. K. (1981) *Monetary Control in the United Kingdom,* Philip Allen.

Bagehot, W. (1873) 'Lombard Street', in *The Collected Works of Walter Bagehot,* published by *The Economist,* 1978.

Bain, A. D. (1979) *The Control of the Money Supply,* Penguin.

—— (1982) *'Bank Lending, Monetary Control and Funding Policy',* Bank of England Academic Panel, no. 19.

Ball, J. and Matthews, R. C. O. (1973) 'Opportunity for Economic Growth', letter to *The Times,* 14 May.

Bank of England Act (1946) HMSO.

Bank of England Annual Report and Accounts (1980).

—— (1984).

—— (1985).

Bank of England Quarterly Bulletin (1963) 'Speech by the Governor of the Bank of England', vol. 3, no. 4, pp. 295–7.

—— (1964) 'UK Banks' External Liabilities and Claims in Foreign Currencies', vol. 4, no. 2, pp. 100–8.

—— (1968a) 'Control of Bank Lending: the Cash Deposits Scheme', vol. 8, no. 2, pp. 166–70.

—— (1968b) 'Commentary', vol. 8, no. 4, p. 347.

—— (1971a) 'Competition and Credit Control', vol. 11, no. 2, pp. 189–93.

—— (1971b) 'Key Issues in Monetary Policy', vol. 11, no. 2, pp. 195–8.

—— (1973) 'Sterling Certificates of Deposit and the Interbank Market', vol. 13, no. 3, p. 308.

—— (1974) 'Credit Control: a Supplementary Scheme', vol. 14, no. 1, pp 37–9.

—— (1976) 'Controlling the Euromarkets', vol. 16, no. 1, pp. 74–7.

—— (1978) 'The Secondary Banking Crisis and the Bank of England's Support Operations', vol. 18, no. 2, pp. 230–9.

—— (1980) 'The Measurement of Capital', vol. 20, no. 3, p. 324.

—— (1981a) 'The Liquidity of Banks', vol. 21, no. 1, p. 40.

—— (1981b) 'Foreign Currency Exposure', vol. 21, no. 2, pp. 235–7.

—— (1981c) 'Monetary Control Provisions', vol. 21, no. 3, pp. 347–9.

—— (1982a) 'The Supplementary Special Deposits Scheme', vol. 22, no. 1, pp. 74–86.

—— (1982b) 'The International Banking Markets in 1980–1981', vol. 22, no. 4, pp. 42–55.

—— (1982c) 'The Role of the Banking Supervisor', vol. 22, no. 4, pp. 547–52.

—— (1983a) 'The International Banking Markets in 1982', vol. 23, no. 1, pp. 43–60.

—— (1983b) 'Monetary Control Arrangements', vol. 23, no. 3, p. 346.

—— (1983c) 'Regulation in Financial Markets', vol. 23, no. 4, pp. 499–501.

—— (1983d) 'International Debt: a Central Banker's View', vol. 23, no. 4, pp. 541–5.

—— (1984a) 'The International Banking Markets in 1984', vol. 24, no. 1, pp. 54–67.

—— (1984b) 'The Future of the Securities Market', vol. 24, no. 2, pp. 189–94.

—— (1984c) 'The Gilt-edged Market—Draft Proposals', vol. 24, no. 4, pp. 513–40.

Bank of International Settlements Annual Report, 1983–4 (1984).

—— *1984–5* (1985).

Banking Act (1979) HMSO.

Banker The, January 1974, July 1980 and January 1985.

Barnett, W. A. (1980) 'Economic Monetary Aggregates', *Journal of Econometrics,* vol. 14, no. 1, pp. 11–48.

Barro, R. (1974) 'Are Government Bonds Net Wealth', *Journal of Political Economy,* vol. 82, no. 6, pp. 1095–117.

Bills of Exchange Act (1882) HMSO.

Bird, G. (1983) 'The Banks and the IMF—Division of Labour', *Lloyds Bank Review*, no. 150, pp. 19–33.

Brealey, R. (1983) *An Introduction to Risk and Return from Common Stocks,* Basil Blackwell, 2nd edn.

British Bankers' Association (1975) *Prudential Regulation of Banks in the EEC.*

Brown, A. J. (1982) 'Accelerating Inflation and the Growth of Productivity', in *Slower Growth in the Western World,* ed. R. C. O. Matthews, Heinemann, pp. 45–59.

—— (1983) '*Monetary Trends in the United Kingdom',* Bank of England Academic Panel Paper No. 22.

Brown, B. (1978) *Money Hard and Soft on the International Currency Markets*. Macmillan, pp. 39–41.

Buiter, W. H. (1983) 'Measurement of the Public Sector Deficit and its Implications for Policy Evaluation and Design', *International Monetary Fund Staff Papers,* vol. 30, no. 2, pp. 306–49.

—— and Miller, M. (1981) 'The Thatcher Experiment: The First Two Years, *Brookings Papers in Economic Activity,* no. 2, pp. 315–79.

—— and Miller, M. (1983) 'Changing the Rules: the Economic Consequences of the Thatcher Regime', *Brookings Papers in Economic Activity,* no. 2, pp. 305–79.

Cairncross, F. and MacRae, H. (1975) *The Second Great Crash: How the Oil Crisis Could Destroy the World Economy,* Methuen.

Channon, D. F. (1979) *British Banking Strategy and the International Challenge*. Macmillan, p. 14.

Clay, C. and Wheble, B. (1983) *Modern Merchant Banking,* Woodhead-Faulkner, 2nd edn.
Cline, W. R. (1984) *International Debt: Systemic Analysis and Policy Response,* International Institute in Economics.
Coleby, A. (1982) 'The Bank of England's Operational Procedures for Meeting Monetary Objectives', in *Central Bank Views on Monetary Targetting,* ed. Meek, B. pp. 60–7.
Committee of Economic Information (1932) *Survey of the Economic Situation, July 1932.* HMSO.
Committee of London Clearing Bankers (1977) *Evidence to 'Committee to Review the Functioning of Financial Institutions'.*
Companies Act (1948) HMSO.
—— (1967) HMSO.
Cooper, J. (1984) *The Management and Regulation of Banks,* Macmillan.
Corner, D. and Matatko, J. (1984) 'A Measure of Returns against the Average', *Financial Times,* 28 January.
Cornwell, R. (1984) *God's Banker,* Unwin.
Cosh, A., Hughes, A. and Singh, A. (1980) 'The Causes and Effects of Takeovers in the United Kingdom. An Empirical Investigation for the late 1960s at the Microeconomic Level', in *The Determinants and Effects of Mergers,* ed. Mueller, Oegelschlager, Gunn & Hain, Inc.
Council of Economic Advisers (1984). *Report to the President.*
Crouch, R. L. (1964) 'The Inadequacy of "New-orthodox" Methods of Monetary Control', *Economic Journal,* vol. 74, no. 4, pp. 916–32.
Department of Trade (1976) *London and County Securities Group Ltd: Investigation under Section 165(6) of the Companies Act, 1948,* HMSO.
Dufey, G. and Giddy, I. A. (1978) *The International Money Market,* Prentice-Hall, pp. 112–13.
Economist, The, 28 May 1960, 13 October 1962, 5 April 1975.
Exchange Control Act (1947) HMSO.
Feavearyear, A. (1963) *The Pound Sterling,* Clarendon Press, 2nd edn,.
Finance Act (1968) HMSO.
—— (1969) HMSO.
—— (1973) HMSO.
—— (1981) HMSO.
—— (1982) HMSO.
Flemming, J. S. (1982) Comment on a Paper by H. P. Minsky in *Financial Crises,* ed. Kindleberger, C. P. and J. P. Laffargue, Cambridge University Press.
Fletcher, G. A. (1976) *The Discount Houses in London,* Macmillan.
Friedman, M. (1980) 'Memorandum to Treasury and Civil Service Select Committee', Treasury and Civil Service Committee, *Memoranda on Monetary Policy,* HMSO, pp. 55–61.
—— and Schwartz, A. J. (1982) *Monetary Trends in the United States and United Kingdom,* NBER.
Galbraith, J. K. (1955) *The Great Crash,* Hamish Hamilton.
Goodhart, C. A. E. (1975) *Money, Information and Uncertainty,* Macmillan.
—— (1984) *Monetary Theory and Practice,* Macmillan.

Goudie, A. W. (1984) 'Tax Exhaustion: Estimates from a Disaggregate Model of Corporate Tax Liabilities', *Applied Economics,* vol. 99, pp. 205–24.

Gower, L. C. B. (1984) *Review of Investor Protection,* HMSO.

Gowland, D. (1978) *Monetary Policy and Credit Control,* Croom Helm.

Griffiths, B. (1973) 'The Development of Restrictive Practices in the UK Monetary System', *Manchester School,* vol. 41, no. 1, pp. 3–18.

Hendry, D. and Ericsson, N. (1983) *Assertion without Empirical Basis,* Bank of England Academic Panel Paper, no. 23, 1983.

Hicks, J. R. (1939) *Value and Capital,* Clarendon Press.

Hills, J. (1984) *Savings and Fiscal Privilege,* Institute of Fiscal Studies.

Hirsch, F. (1977) 'The Bagehot Problem', *Manchester School,* vol. 45, no. 3, pp. 241–57.

HM Treasury (1984) *Building Societies: A New Framework,* Cmnd 9316, HMSO.

Hogan, W. P. and Pearce, I. F. (1983) *The Incredible Eurodollar.* Unwin.

Income and Corporation Taxes Act (1970) HMSO.

Interbank Organisation (1973). *The Future of London as an International Financial Centre.* HMSO.

International Monetary Fund Annual Report (1985), Chapter 1. IMF.

Johnson, C. (1977) *Anatomy of UK Finance, 1970–75.* Longman.

Kaldor, N. (1981) *Origins of the New Monetarism,* University College of Cardiff Press.

Kellett, R. (1967) *The Merchant Banking Arena.* Macmillan, p. 68.

Keynes, J. M. (1929) 'The German Transfer Problem'; 'The Reparation Problem: A Discussion: II A Rejoinder'; and 'Views on the Transfer Problem: III A Reply', *Economic Journal,* vol. 25, nos 1, 2, and 3, pp. 1–7, 179–82 and 404–8.

—— (1931) *A Treatise on Money, Volume II,* Macmillan.

—— (1936) *The General Theory of Employment, Interest and Money.* Harcourt, Brace.

—— (1942) 'Proposals for an International Clearing Union', in *Collected Works of J. M. Keynes,* vol. 26, Macmillan, 1980, also Cmnd 6437, HMSO.

Killick, A., Bird, G. Sharpley, J. and Sutton, M. (1983) *The Quest for Economic Stabilisation: The IMF and the Third World,* Heinemann.

Kindleberger, C. P. (1981) *Manias, Panics and Crashes,* Macmillan.

Lascelles, D. (1984) 'Why the Banks have built up their Reserves', *Financial Times,* 2 April.

Lester, T. (1974) 'The Secondary Scandal', *Management Today,* pp. 62–9 and 142–6.

MacBean, A. I. and Snowden, P. N. (1981) *International Institutions in Trade and Finance,* George Allen & Unwin.

MacRae, H. M. and Cairncross, F. (1973) *Capital City: London as a Financial Centre,* Methuen, 2nd edn, 1984.

Marx, (1894) *Capital,* vol. III (esp. pp. 512–16), ed. F. Engels, 1894.

Matthews, R. C. O. (1963) 'Expenditure Plans and the Uncertainty Motive for Holding Money', *Journal of Political Economy,* vol. 71, no. 3, pp. 201–18.

—— (1968) 'Why has Britain had Full Employment since the War?', *Economic Journal,* vol. 78, no. 3, pp. 555–69.

McCallum, B. T. (1984) 'Are Bond-financed Deficits Inflationary? A Ricardian Analysis', *Journal of Political Economy,* vol. 92, no. 2, pp. 123–35.

Meeks, G. (1977) *Disappointing Marriage,* Cambridge University Press.

Mendelsohn, M. S. (1980) *Money on the Move,* McGraw-Hill.

Midland Bank Review (1973) 'The Inter-Bank Markets in Sterling', pp. 3–10.

—— (1976) 'Public Control of Bank Lending', pp. 12–21.

Mill, J. S. (1848) *Principles of Political Economy,* 1848, Book IV, Ch. 4.5, vol. III of *Collected Works of J. S. Mill,* University of Toronto Press, 1965, p. 741.

Minford, A. P. L. (1980) 'Memorandum to Treasury and Civil Service Select Committee', Treasury and Civil Service Committee, *Memoranda on Monetary Policy,* HMSO, pp. 131–43.

Minsky, H. P. (1971) 'Keynesian Theory and the Current Crisis in Economic Policy', mimeo.

—— (1982) 'The Financial Instability Hypothesis: Capitalist Processes and the Behaviour of the Economy' in C. P. Kindleberger and J. P. Laffargue (eds), *Financial Crises: Theory, History and Policy,* Cambridge University Press, pp. 13–39.

Monetary Control (1980) Cmnd 7858 HMSO.

Money Lenders Acts (1900–27) HMSO.

Monopolies Commission. (1968) *Barclays Bank Ltd, Lloyds Bank Ltd, and Martins Bank Ltd: a Report on the Proposed Merger,* HMSO.

Moran, M. (1984) *The Politics of Banking,* Macmillan.

Morgan, E. V. (1963) Chapter XII in *The Pound Sterling* by A. Feaveryear, 2nd edn, Clarendon Press.

Murphy, B. M. (1973) *A History of the British Economy,* Longman.

National Board for Prices and Incomes (1967) *Bank Charges,* Report No. 34, Cmnd 3292, HMSO.

Ohlin, B. (1929) 'The Reparation Problem: A Discussion: I. Transfer Difficulties, Real and Imagined' and 'Mr Keynes' Views on the Transfer Problem: II. A Rejoinder', *Economic Journal,* vol. 20, nos 2 and 3, pp. 172–8 and 400–3

Protection of Depositors Act (1963) HMSO.

Raw, C. (1977), *Slater Walker,* Andre Deutsch, pp. 344–7.

Reid, M. (1982) *The Secondary Banking Crisis, 1973–75,* Macmillan.

Report of the Advisory Committee on the Crown Agents (1972) HMSO (Stevenson Committee).

Report from the Committee on Finance and Industry (1931) HMSO Cmnd 3897 (Macmillan Committee).

Report of the Committee on the Working of the Monetary System (1959) Cmnd 827, HMSO (Radcliffe Committee).

Report of the Committee of Inquiry into the Crown Agents (1977) HMSO (Fay Committee).

Report of the Committee on the Functioning of Financial Institutions. (1980) Cmnd 7397, HMSO (Wilson Committee).

Report of the Committee set up to Consider the Question of Banking Supervision (1985) Cmnd 9550, HMSO.
Restrictive Practices Act (1956) HMSO.
Revell, J. S. (1968) *Changes in British Banking,* Hill, Samuel & Co.
—— (1973) *The British Financial System,* Macmillan.
Ricardo, D. (1809) 'Letter to the Editor', *Morning Chronicle,* 20 September, reprinted in *Collected Works of D. Ricardo,* Cambridge University Press, 1951, vol. III, p. 21.
Rist, C. (1940) *Theories of Money and Credit from John Law to the Present Day,* George Allen & Unwin.
Rowan, D. C. (1973) 'The Monetary System in the Fifties and Sixties' *Manchester School,* vol. 41, no. 1, pp. 19–43.
Rowthorn, R. (1977) 'Conflict, Inflation and Money', *Cambridge Journal of Economics,* vol. 1, no. 2, pp. 215–40.
Rybczynski, T. (1973) 'The Merchant Banks', *Manchester School,* vol. 41, no. 1, pp. 107–22.
Sargan, D. (1964) 'Wages and Prices in the United Kingdom: a Study in Econometric Methodology', in *Econometric Analysis for National Planning,* ed. Hart, P. E. *et al.,* Butterworth.
Sayers, R. S. (1960) *Modern Banking,* Oxford University Press.
Shaw, E. R. (1981) *The London Money Markets,* Heinemann, p. 176.
Spencer, P. D. (1982) 'Bank Regulation, Credit Rationing and the Determination of Money Market Interest Rates', *Manchester School* vol. 50, no. 1, pp. 41–60.
—— (1985) *Financial Innovation, Efficiency and Disequilibrium: Problems of Monetary Management in the UK, 1971–1981,* Oxford University Press.
Spiegelberg R. (1973) *The City,* Blond & Briggs, pp. 16–17.
Sunday Times, The, 19 April, 1970, p. 51.
Teeters, N. H. and Terrell, H. S. (1983) 'The Role of Banks in the International Financial System', *Federal Reserve Bulletin,* pp. 663–71.
Tew, J. H. B. (1978) 'Monetary Policy, Part I' in *British Economic policy, 1960–1974,* ed. F. H. Blackaby, Cambridge University Press, p. 240.
Tirole, J. (1982) 'On the Possibility of Speculation under Rational Expectations', *Econometrica,* vol. 50, no. 5, pp. 1163–82.
Tobin, J. (1958) 'Liquidity Preference as Behaviour towards Risk', *Review of Economic Studies,* vol. 25, pp. 65–86.
—— (1963) 'Commercial Banks as Creators of Money', in *Banking and Monetary Studies,* ed. D. Carson, Richard D. Irwin.
Treasury and Civil Service Committee (1980) *Memoranda on Monetary Policy,* HMSO.
Weale, M. R. (1984) 'Quantity and Price Effects in an Analysis of World Trade Based on an Accounting Matrix', *Review of Income and Wealth,* series 32, no. 1, pp. 85–117.
Young, G. K. (1971) *Merchant Banking,* Weidenfeld & Nicolson, p. 19.

Many of the articles listed above from the *Bank of England Quarterly Bulletin* also appears in:

Bank of England (1984) *The Development and Operation of Monetary Policy, 1960–1983,* Oxford University Press.

STATISTICAL SOURCES

Bank of England Statistical Abstract No. 1 (1970) Bank of England.
Bank of England Statistical Abstract No. 2 (1975) Bank of England.
Bank of England Quarterly Bulletin (1960–85) Bank of England.
Barclays Bank plc Annual Report and Accounts (1970–84) Barclays Bank plc.
Brown Shipley & Co. plc Annual Report and Accounts (1970–84) Brown Shipley plc.
Economic Trends (1985) Central Statistical Office, no. 381.
Economic Trends Annual Supplement 1984, Central Statistical Office.
Federal Reserve Bulletin (1983) vol. 69, no. 9. Federal Reserve Board.
Financial Statistics (1962–85) Central Statistical Office.
Hambros plc Annual Report and Accounts (1970–84) Hambros plc.
Hill Samuel Group plc Annual Report and Accounts (1970–84). Hill Samuel Group plc.
Kleinwort Benson, Lonsdale plc Annual Report and Accounts (1970–84) Kleinwort Benson, Lonsdale plc.
Lloyds Bank plc Report and Accounts (1970–84) Lloyds Bank plc.
Midland Bank Group Report and Accounts (1970–84) Midland Bank Group plc.
National Westminster Bank Annual Report and Accounts (1970–84) National Westminster Bank plc.
Pension Funds and their Advisors (1984) A. P. Publications Ltd.
Post Office Report and Accounts (1981–85) HMSO.
Revell, J. S. (1967) *The Wealth of the Nation,* Cambridge University Press.
Schroder Bros Annual Report and Accounts (1970–84) Schroder Bros.
The Financial Times (various).
The Times 1000, 1985–6. (1985) Times Books.

Index